M 2
472-2542

The Homosexuals

Macmillan Publishing Co., Inc.

NEW YORK

The Homosexuals

by A L A N   E B E R T

Macmillan Publishing Co., Inc.
866 Third Avenue, New York, N.Y. 10022
Collier Macmillan Canada, Ltd.

Library of Congress Cataloging in Publication Data

Ebert, Alan.
    The homosexuals.
      1. Homosexuals, Male—United States—Interviews.
I. Title.
HQ76.2.U5E23   301.41'57'0973   76-30579
ISBN 0-02-534770-5

FIRST PRINTING 1977

Printed in the United States of America

Note: The names in this book are fictitious;
also, birthdates and some other nonessential
specific information have been changed to
preserve the anonymity of the subjects.

To the men I love—
my father, Mark and Nick—
and to the women—
Dee, Nancy, Arline, and
Marcia Ann Gillespie,
to whom I am personally
and professionally indebted.

Contents

Introduction

ORIGINALLY, the introduction to *The Homosexuals* was to be written by a Margaret Mead or a Gore Vidal, someone of recognized accomplishment and stature. That it is not reflects but some of the changes the author experienced during the interviewing and writing of this book. Somewhere toward the completion of chapter ten, the idea of using a respected and revered "name" to introduce the men who speak here became unacceptable. It more than angered me—infuriated comes closer. As I said to my editor, Michael Denneny, who was quick to agree upon reading the interviews, these men need *no one* to justify their existence. These men, their thoughts and feelings, are enough in themselves.

In stating this, I am defeating what was one of the aims of the book: to present men who are homosexual without the blemish of bias. From the beginning, the goal of *The Homosexuals* was to create a space where men who love men could discuss freely, without fear of analysis and interpretation, all aspects of their lives. This space had previously not existed. The past has found psychiatrists, psychologists, clergymen and other "names" writing on homosexuality and coloring it with their particular prejudices. A few equally respected men courageously vacated their closets to write of their lives, but these men seemed far removed from the average homosexual. For this book the average was sought and he was assured anonymity in exchange for his truth. It was a trade that more than favored both interviewer and reader. The name of the person is unimportant in comparison to his thoughts, feelings and self. To obtain the true self of the interviewee, the question and answer format, as opposed to the profile, was selected in the hope that it would allow a minimum of interviewer bias.

Because I wanted to present these men in their entirety, the language they used has not been laundered. If beauty is in the eye of the beholder, so is obscenity. As each man speaks of his hopes, fears, loves, hates, frustrations, joys and sexuality, he uses whatever words are at his particular command. Some of these may be rough-hewn but they nonetheless do the job.

A logical question the reader might ask is, Why these particular men? Because they seemed representative and were willing to speak of their lives. *The Homosexuals* is not a scientific study. There is no claim here that the seventeen men interviewed in this book are a scientific sampling. Yet, they may certainly be representative. Although most are residents, but not natives, of New York City, it is my belief that the feelings they express, if not the exact experiences, would match those of most homosexual men in the United States. Only two of the seventeen subjects were known to me prior to interviewing. For several years, I had grunted and groaned with them at a local gymnasium. Yet I knew nothing of their lives other than what they did for a living and that they were homosexual. At most gyms I have frequented, both these facts become known rather quickly. These men then referred me to others who then referred me to still others, and so on. Only three men who were asked to be contributors to this book refused. Two dozen others were emphatic in their willingness to participate. Eighteen interviews were conducted but only seventeen appear in this book. The man-that-got-away after one session—in which he confronted his marriage, his parenthood and his homosexuality, all for the *first* time—was ironically that mythical masculine symbol, the construction worker. Broad shoulders alone proved not strong enough to carry the weight of his own life.

Another question certain to be asked is why no women were included. Upon consideration, it seemed to be mixing apples and oranges. The life-styles of the female and the male homosexual are very dissimilar. In my opinion, a book about women who love women is a separate endeavor.

About the title of this book: the author hates it! Yet, there is no other that seems to say it all and as quickly. What I particularly dislike is the label. Calling the book *The Homosexuals* categorizes people by their sexual preference or compulsion. I am vehemently opposed to this. That a person is homosexual or heterosexual, bi or asexual should not be his initial identification.

In the opening paragraph of this introduction I spoke of changes that I experienced in the course of doing this book. These changes are still in progress. Initially, I came to my interviews "armed" with Freudian and other prejudices that were deeply personal. I have never understood such homosexual phenomena as the baths, the back-room sex bars and the meat racks. Or perhaps I have understood but nonetheless thought them distasteful and destructive. I still find them that. But now I see those places and events as the tip of the iceberg and not indicative of the majority of the homosexual population or of its true nature. Regarding that visible and vocal minority who take their "pleasures" whenever and wherever, I cannot lightly say, "It's your thing; do what you want to do." Although I would defend each person's right to do just that, I remain doubtful that this particular behavior is productive for the person, to those to whom he relates in such fashion, and to the homosexual community in general.

I would suggest to those readers who do not wish to be influenced further by the author's newfound bias to move directly to chapter one. Here I want to speak of the seventeen men in this book who day after day, week after week, appeared and reappeared for their interviews, always struggling, often with great pain, to find their own truths. To a man, they were courageous, daring to reveal themselves as I am sure few others could or would. I often wondered, had the roles been reversed, could I have been so honest. Frankly, as one who finds privacy an inalienable right, I doubt it. I applaud these men. They did not "exhibit" themselves as exhibitionists but as men who time and again expressed the hope that their experiences might help another man who was homosexual to find his own way.

To say these men reached me says very little. Often, in reacting to their pain and their joy, I was touched in a way that I have seldom experienced—too seldom. Often, I wanted to touch back in friendship, support, comfort and even love. But some half-assed thing known as "interviewer's objectivity" restrained me. I regret that. To all the men in this book I can only express my gratitude, admiration and affection for your courage and trust. I am proud to be with you in this, our book.

AUTHOR'S NOTE

All names of all persons appearing in this book are fictitious. All birthdates, birthplaces, and current and past resi-
dences have also been changed to protect identities. Other
nonessential specific information has also been altered,
such as names of family members, their number and their
sex, again to preserve privacy. Other than for the seventeen subjects in this book, all occupations and relevant
details attributed to those persons mentioned have been
significantly changed.

At no time have the feelings, thoughts, attitudes, and
actions expressed by the subjects in this book been altered
or modified.

The Homosexuals

Dr. Gabriel Anthony

H<small>IS SURGICAL GREENS</small> match the institutional green of the hospital cafeteria walls. Exhausted, a usual state for a physician completing his residency program, Dr. Gabriel Anthony * gulps his orange juice—his third—as he is paged by the hospital calling system. Wearily, he walks to a nearby phone unaware that many eyes are following him. He presents quite a figure. His is more the body of the athlete than the doctor. He carries it proudly. He is darkly handsome, this Dr. Anthony, his Italian heritage obvious in his Mediterranean coloring.

At his gentle-but-firm insistence, all interviews with Dr. Anthony took place outside the one-bedroom apartment in a "glassy" Manhattan high-rise he shares with Luis, his lover of three years. As he explained, the couple's home is reserved for intimates and friends. It is his "retreat" from the city life, to which Dr. Anthony has never quite adjusted. Whenever he has consecutive days off, the doctor flies to the Maine backwoods where he was raised. His summertime retreat, shared with Luis, is weekending at Fire Island. Space—that which is real and imagined—is important to Dr. Gabriel Anthony.

Had you always wanted to be a doctor?

No! I wanted to be the fire chief and sometimes I think I still do. I also wanted to be a veterinarian as animals were, and are, a major part of my life. They were often my playmates as a kid, as our backyard was the woods.

Where was this?

In a little city in northern Maine. My father was the town lawyer and we had a big barn of a house, which was filled with my two brothers, two sisters, me and just about every animal my mother would allow us to adopt.

What made you switch from an animal to a people doctor?

I ask myself that a lot now that I'm working one hundred hours per

* See Author's Note, page xii.

week. If I find out, I'll phone you. Well, it beats being a musician, which is what I thought I'd be when I attended Yale. That goal lasted until I read somewhere that seven out of ten clarinetists live on poppy-seeds and welfare.

When did medicine as a career enter your mind?

Not until my senior year. I was looking for work that would be people-oriented and challenging. I particularly liked the complexities of sur-gery, which is the field I am in today. Reconstructive surgery, it is called. It's about correcting and/or repairing trauma from accidents and birth defects. It's important work and I like it for that reason. It's not far removed from what I had thought to do with animals—heal their pain. Each winter, after the hunting season, dozens of the poor things would be left injured and maimed. God how I hated those hunters! I still do. They gave me a rotten view of humanity, one which I still tend to hold. People on a one-to-one basis are just fine but as a species, we're disgusting.

It is interesting, considering your feelings about man as a species, that you have nonetheless chosen to be in a helping profession.

It's more for me than for anyone else. I enjoy it. I like helping people, but I do not picture myself as a pillar of society or as any of the bull-shit doctors love to perpetuate about themselves. I leave that to Marcus Welby. My work is challenging and beneficial. But I do not kid myself, as most doctors do, that I am a savior of mankind or some kind of humanitarian. The doctors with mealymouths are the ones who usually own mansions, yachts and tax-shelters.

You're not opposed to money, are you?

Shit, no! I'm opposed to *not* having it. Fifteen thousand a year for a one-hundred-hour week, fifty weeks a year, is not exactly just recom-pense. I'm all for big money. I'm just against doctors who deny money as a motivation for doing their work and then charge the patient be-yond anything the patient can comfortably afford. Money is fine, but when it becomes more important than the patient's mental and physical well-being, then I say the system is fucked up.

Speaking of the system, is it difficult being a homosexual in the medical profession?

I have recently discovered it is difficult being a homosexual in *any* profession. I always had an inkling that being a homosexual was not among the Top Ten choices in life, but it is only since I came out three years ago that I have realized how deep the hatred toward homosexuals is in the hearts and minds of society. I was raised somewhat differently. My parents did not allow us kids to make judgments about other people's behavior. Labels of any kind to describe others were discouraged. Mother found them ugly. The medical profession is very "ugly" in its attitudes toward homosexuals.

Do your fellow doctors know of your homosexuality?

If they don't, it is because they choose not to. Although I have never declared it, I have also never denied it.

Meaning?

Whenever there is a professional but social function, my "date" is my lover. And the reaction of staff is very curious. Most prefer to see us as close friends. Since Luis is South American, very macho incidentally, they tend to think I am showing him America. And I'm dead serious. The majority truly think I'm his tour director. Since we've been together three years, it has been the longest tour on record. But people—particularly men—cannot deal with the possibility of two masculine men being homosexuals.

If I'm following your chronology, you must have met Luis shortly after "coming out."

Exactly two months afterwards. He is my first lover and with all my heart I hope he is my last. He is the single most important aspect of my life. I am dedicated to him and our relationship—not to medicine. That runs a poor third.

What's second?

My family. I remain very close to all of them. I'm one of those rare birds—a guy who had this super terrific childhood. I always felt loved by both my parents and I still do. They're very special people. Certainly they have the best marriage I have ever seen. And the best attitudes, too. As Catholics, all us kids would get the usual crap from the nuns at our Saturday classes, but my mother would say, "Pay no attention. They only say those things about sex because they *are* nuns."

Was sex openly discussed in your home?

There wasn't any need. Everything we kids needed to know we learned by watching the animals. Sex always seemed very natural.

Periodically, both my parents would ask if there was anything I wanted to know, but there wasn't because I knew it all. And the vibes they gave off about sex were terrific. Lots of overt affection. Even today, they kind of chase each around the house.

I do remember my mother saying that sex, when there is love, is beautiful. Both would stress how normal and healthy it was, and how it was the nicest way two people who loved one another could communicate that love. Like when the rest of the town criticized an unmarried couple for living together, my parents never did. Their criterion was "If there is love, it is good."

What do you think their attitude would be on your homosexuality?

I think my father would be upset by it. He is very much into male roles, thinking them God-and-nature given. My mother would probably be more understanding. Actually, I think they already know. They've met Luis and have asked some thinly veiled questions. My mother has gone so far as to say, "I don't know how I feel about the closeness between you boys." My father went even further. He hemmed and hawed and finally asked, "What is the *nature* of your relationship with Luis?" I replied: "What do you mean?" He sort of turned green and said, "Well, as long as there is nothing abnormal about it." Which allowed me to say what I believe: "No dad, I don't believe there is anything abnormal about it." That's where the conversation ended. I see no point in discussing it any further unless they want to. But I would like to, however, and will, should they ever be ready.

Did you experience homosexual fantasies as a child?

None at all. I masturbated like a little sex fiend as a kid but I recall no fantasies whatsoever. The only homosexual encounter I can recall was at twelve, when a bunch of us boys got into a circle jerk. It didn't impress me.

Did you have peer relationships as a boy?

Many in public school and many more in high school where I became this big jock. I was on the wrestling team and the gymnastic squad. High school was a very positive experience. Previously, whatever attention I gained was through academic excellence, but that can be both a plus and a minus for a kid. You know how some guys resent a kid with the smarts. But no one ever resents the school athlete. Everyone looks up and admires him. I had that position. And I liked it.

I still like attention. I think most people do if they're honest enough to admit it. The difference being, some go after it while others don't. I went after mine.

How good were you athletically?

I took a few statewide championship medals in wrestling.

Did you find wrestling a sexual experience?

Shit, no! Lots of people like to think wrestling is very sexual—two guys rubbing and rolling around together. But I swear, it isn't that at all. I never felt aroused. Those guys were so sweaty, mean and ugly, who could think sex? All I thought about was getting on and off the mat alive.

Did sex play any role in your adolescence?

Oh sure. When I stopped jerking off long enough, I noticed girls. I began dating at fifteen. By seventeen I was into the heavy petting number. At nineteen I went "all the way." And oh God was it beautiful. I mean it totally surpassed my wildest fantasies. She was my college sweetheart and we both gave up our virginity in what had to be the most abandoned lovemaking any two virgins ever experienced.

And still, at nineteen, no homosexual leanings?

None that I was aware of. In fact, just before graduating high school, I took part in a "torture" that will show you how far removed I was from any recognition of homosexuality in myself. One of the kids in the junior class came on with one of the guys on the wrestling team. He spread it around the school and by the next day everyone was taunting the poor guy, calling him "fairy" and "queer." I was one of the taunters. I didn't stop until one of the jocks came forward and told everyone to shut their mouths, that it was the kid's thing and what skin was it off their backs? Do you know, that really stopped us all and it started me into thinking—real thinking. Then and there I learned I'd never get caught up in group reaction ever again. Like today, I'm neither a Republican nor a Democrat. I'm an Independent.

I'm a lot like my father in that I am today a very rational man. But unlike him, it does not come to me naturally. He is analytical by nature and seldom does anything overtly emotional—that's more my mother's style. I have to decide to be his kind of rational, and when I do, I have his logic and his finely honed mind. By the way, my father is not steel. He has a great deal of warmth.

But in truth, I'm more like my mother—ruled by emotions, and I prefer to be. I read once that it is the rational mind that separates man from the animal. Well, since I find much more honesty and nobility in the animal world than I do in ours, I'm glad I'm ruled by something more than just a rational mind. I'm a visceral type and that often allows me lots of different kinds of relationships. My mind has little to do with whether I'm going to like you or not. Most often, that's a gut feeling.

Speaking of "gut feelings," when did you reach yours toward men?

At first, it was purely a head trip. Yale was very into experimentation. People were dropping LSD and their pants all over the place. The Gay Pride people were on campus doing their thing, but I was kind of oblivious to all of it until I joined the Yale Drama Club. There many people were into bisexual experiences. Not me, however. I still had my girl, was passionately in love and planning marriage and a family. But within the confines of the drama group, where there was a helluva lot of cross-pollination, I became curious. I realize now in looking back that I was always curious, that there were always buddies in high school whose bodies I was interested in, only I wouldn't . . . couldn't admit it. At Yale I would allow myself to think about what men might do together in bed, but just as quickly as I thought about it, I would dismiss it from consciousness. I just couldn't see it as something for me. And then, one day, I could and I decided to try it.

Just like that? You made the decision rather than be actively seduced?

Right! But listen how I made the decision. There were a lot of great guys to choose from in that drama group—guys I liked as friends, attractive guys. So who did I choose? A guy I couldn't stand.

Do you know why?

I do now. I was setting it up so I could hate the experience and that is exactly what happened. I had to get sloppy drunk to crawl into the sack with the guy and then we beat each other off. And that's boring as hell after you've been copulating in all forms of expression with your girl. As you can see, I used every protective device known to a closet case *not* to enjoy the experience or to feel how much I might enjoy it. That held true throughout med school, by the way. Except for one difference: I was aware—*painfully* aware—that I had these "feelings." I'd look at certain guys—usually the ones with great bodies —and get bothered. But I could never accept what I was bothered by, so I dismissed it as some phase I was going through.

When did that begin to change?

Gradually. When I came to New York for my internship and residency programs, I looked up a few of the guys I had liked at Yale. Most were actively gay, living with lovers. I became very friendly with most, telling my "independent" and "liberal" self that their sexual proclivities had no effect on our relationship. I could not face the fact that I was friendly with these men because I needed to be. Despite the confusion, it was a good time. I learned. I saw homosexuals as real people and not stereotypes. None were frightened, lonely, disturbed "unfortunates." Most were active, vital men. Several did have problems—severe ones—but the fact that they dug men was not one of them. In fact, I'll never forget my amazement when one guy who was having a particularly hard time getting his shit together in New York said: "But it isn't about being gay. I'm a happy homosexual and if given the choice, I'd be a homosexual every time!" I couldn't understand that then. How could you choose to be something society treated as the lowest of the low? It was a time of lots of thoughts but no actions. I had broken up with my college sweetheart—we discovered that other than sex we had little in common—and although I was dating a few girls, I wasn't very interested. More and more I was allowing myself sexual fantasies with men. But never just me with a man. Always a foursome or an orgy. It took several months before I could fantasize about just me and another guy.

Were you threatened by your fantasies?

No, I enjoyed them. But I was then twenty-four and therefore much too old to become gay. Life ended at thirty, didn't it?

When did you begin playing out your fantasies?

If you mean when did I have sex with a man, that happened about a year after I first came to New York. Playing out my fantasies came later. Oh boy, but do I owe that poor guy an apology! He was a beauty—a Bruce Jenner type who picked me up in the Village. I was so nervous, and I guess excited, that as soon as our bodies touched, I shot off. That done, I then shot off from his apartment as though my life was in danger. Running down the street, trying to put as much distance as possible between me and the experience, I kept wondering why I had done it and vowing that it never would happen again.

Did you go back in the closet?

Yes, but I left the door open.

Did anyone come in?

No, but I would crawl out to visit my friends on Fire Island. They would warn me in advance, worry that I might be offended or shocked and then marvel at how I took all the public on-the-beach-and-off sex in stride. It didn't bother me, I kept saying. Nor does it really interest me, I told myself. Only I forgot to listen.

One weekend after my first visit I returned to the island and within an hour of arrival took a walk down to the Meat Rack—that's where guys let it all hang out and have sex individually or collectively on the beach—picked out a great-looking guy and proceeded to have terrific sex with him.

With no trepidations?

Nope. I remember thinking as I walked to where the action was, "Well, this is it. You're going to do it. Whatever happens, happens." And what happened was terrific. Just like my first experience with a girl, I knew instinctively what to do. We had oral sex and it was right . . . graceful . . . enjoyable. I remember thinking immediately afterwards, "What's so bad after all?" and a voice responding, "Bad? It's not bad. It's terrific!" And I ran back to where I was staying feeling ten feet taller and ten pounds lighter.

I have not experienced one moment of difficulty with my homosexuality since. I feel now that I was always a homosexual, that the urge was always there but denied. In fact, when I came out, I was enraged at society for having influenced me so strongly and negatively about homosexuality. I could have been so much happier so much earlier. I had been struggling to come out for such a long time. I kept denying it because of what I feared would be the price society would make me pay. You see, unless you are deaf, dumb and blind, you hear the fag jokes from the time you're old enough to turn on the TV and hear some witless comedian make limp-wrist jokes. Then in locker rooms you hear fag jokes. At straight parties, too. Everybody makes fag jokes but no one really finds homosexuality amusing. The jokes are ugly as is the attitude. Just think about the words "faggot" and "queer"—how they sound. Ugly. Then think about all the times you heard people speculate about whether some guy was a "faggot" or not. Ugly. And what's the worst thing one man can call another . . . a cock-sucker. So that kind of shit gets to you, makes you pull in even when every part of you is crying to come out.

I always felt, and I believe with just cause, that if you were gay, society would do everything it could to penalize you. And it's true. People get booted out of the military for homosexual activity. A guy who is admittedly gay can't be the fire chief or a policeman. The shit goes on. And when you're a kid, a young adult even, it permeates your thinking even before you're aware of it. I used to think, because I was *made* to think, that gay people were selfish and irresponsible people. Why? Because they lived solely for themselves and did not raise families. What a crock of shit! Some of the least responsible people I know are straight, married and turning out one kid after another even though they can barely take care of themselves.

Homosexuals are as responsible or as irresponsible as heterosexuals. And I now see the true responsibility as being to yourself—to making your own self happy . . . fulfilled. Maybe if you can do that, you can then make someone else happy.

A question about "responsibility." Do you see the "meat racks"—those places where sex takes place in public—and the people who play at them, as responsible or irresponsible?

That depends on your point of view. A lot of people are uptight about public sex. I myself have ambivalent feelings. Like I would hate to think the only place two men—or three or four—can have sex is indoors. Yet, I can see how traumatic it could be for a child to stumble upon *any* two people having sex. Children often mistake sex for something violent. So from that standpoint, it is irresponsible. But I do not think sex outdoors is irresponsible nor do I find the concept of meat racks irresponsible.

I think they are bizarre but fun. They are pure fantasy trips. You can make whoever you meet into whoever you want him to be. Sex at a meat rack is about the moment. It is about pure pleasure—your own. There are no conditions or formalities. And . . . there is no harm done.

Because of the impersonality of it, isn't it dehumanizing?

That's exactly what I like about it. The meat rack brings people to an animal level and I see that as good, not bad. Animals don't require formal relating to fuck. Fucking for them is as natural as eating and sleeping. Why shouldn't it be for us? When I'm at the meat rack, I'm there solely for my sexual enjoyment. I don't expect anyone there to want to *relate* to the *real* me. And I'm not there to be related to. I'm there for a total sexual experience and if viewed and treated as such, it is harmless fun. Now, if I went to the meat rack looking to meet a lover, I'd be looking for a kick in the head. The meat rack is a place to leave your clothes and your personhood hanging on the nearest tree branch. If that idea, concept, bothers you, then the meat rack should never be your thing. You see, many people, straight and gay, try to deny that animal part of themselves. I don't. I enjoy it. Fulfilling it—now mainly with Luis—is a very particular kind of happy experience. And I don't think that the kind of animalism I'm talking about is solely a gay phenomenon. And if it is, then I'm sorry for straights.

Are you exclusively homosexual today?

Yes, but not because I'm turned off women. If an attractive gal came on with me, and if Luis was away, I might be tempted. But I am much more into the homosexual experience. From that moment I came out I liked everything about making love with a man. Sex was always good with women but it never—other than for my first experience—had the depth, the passion, that sense of fulfillment I feel with a man. Emotionally, a man satisfies me beyond orgasm. And no one, but no one, satisfies me as Luis does.

When and how did you meet Luis?

Two months after I came out—at the Meat Rack. This is going to sound like a load of shit but from the moment we made skin contact . . . touched, I knew I would love and be loved by this man. We both knew. The goddamn earth moved! I swear it did. And despite the fact that there was this sex going on all about us, we felt alone . . . as though everything in the world had stopped and there was just us. Two months later, we took an apartment together.

Could you describe your attraction to this man?

Besides being physically beautiful, he *is* beautiful. He sees through the artist's eyes. And what he sees is reflected in his paintings and sculptures. He is a very bright man . . . sensitive, too sensitive as it leaves him very vulnerable. He's just a little older than I but sometimes his vulnerability makes me feel he's my kid brother. He is also somewhat of a Latin lunatic. Lots of temperament to match a nutty sense of humor. We laugh a lot together but one of the main joys is that we teach one another a lot. Like he has learned to share my love of music and I am developing an interest in art. He also loves the outdoors and . . . his family. I went with him to South America last summer to meet them. A nerve-wracking experience until his sister leered at me, shook her head and said, "Too bad. Luis was always the lucky one in the family." Then everybody laughed and it was cool.

Did it go as well with your family?

My parents were polite but distant. My brothers and sisters have been terrific. The boys know because they've visited with us, have seen the one bedroom with the one double bed, and since they're both over twenty-one, figured it out. It didn't hassle them. They're very comfortable with Luis. In fact—and both are straight as arrows—they flirt with him outrageously and he goofs with them in the same way. It's really a kick.

You seem very pleased.

I am. When Luis and I began living together I vowed I would never hide our relationship from anyone, that when my brothers came to New York I would not pretend that Luis, or I, slept on the fold-out couch. I knew if I denied Luis as my lover I would resent my brothers' visits. And I knew if I felt resentment, they would pick it up, feel strange and eventually stop visiting. No way did I want that to happen. I wanted them to feel free to come and go, but I also wanted Luis and me to live as freely as we do. And that is what has happened. It pleases me more than I can say. You see, I like my brothers. Most important, I love them. And it's just great being able to welcome them to my home without embarrassment and without lies.

Do you think your brothers' reaction to the situation is unusual?

I don't know. But I think they reacted to Luis and me in the same way his family did. They *feel* the love between us. It kind of is there, like a beacon. Even after three years, we're always touching. Like my schedule at the hospital is so frenetic that often we have little time to enjoy one another. But whatever time does exist, we spend in bed. No, not for sex but to just *be* together—touching. I'm serious. We'll eat dinner in bed, read or watch TV there, talk, anything actually where we can share that physical intimacy.

Is yours a monogamous relationship?

Almost. When we're together, which is just about always, there is
no one else. But when we're separated—like if Luis is off somewhere
on assignment—there is this agreement that if one needs it, one can
get it. But on the other hand, being separated is not viewed by either
of us as license to fuck.

How did you arrive at this arrangement?

Through trial and error. At one time Luis and I did threesomes and
foursomes. They were very animal, very exciting and very destructive
to what we had together. Suddenly, we were sex objects rather than
lovers. So we gave up that kind of sex to maintain the lovemaking—
which is exactly what we do in bed, make love—that has continued
to work for better than three years. The only difference in our relationship now is we only make love four or five times a week rather
than the ten and twelve we used to. Thank God! I was never getting
my studies completed. But, although the quantity is less, the quality
is so much more . . . so much richer. We share a feeling of oneness,
of unity.

*Considering the intensity of your feelings, is it difficult "sharing"
your lover on those occasions when you are separated?*

Yes, sometimes it is difficult, but I think the arrangement is still
better than if we felt honor-bound to one another. I think that leads
to resentment. But I do experience feelings of jealousy, particularly
when Luis tells me about some hot number he has been with. Why
does he tell me, or I tell him? Again, we discovered the discussion is
better than the non-discussion. That way, in hearing about what took
place, I can put all my fears out on the table.

Fears?

Yeah. Like . . . was he better . . . more skilled. Was he able to go
at it for longer periods of time. Did you *really* like him. All that shit.
The only question I don't ask is about cock size 'cause Luis isn't into
that. Nor am I. Good thing as we're both among the average fellahs.
Anyway, in voicing my insecurities—and I've got them—it's nice to
be reassured, to hear "No" when you ask if the other guy had any
meaning. I need to be told that I matter—that *we* matter—beyond
all else. We both need that. And lest you get the wrong impression,
these infrequent side excursions are generally treated much the way

one enjoys a piece of chocolate fudge cake: at the moment and then forgotten.

Is this the marriage you always wanted?

Yes. Only it is different. It is a marriage of equals, in and out of bed. We share everything—a true give-and-take relationship, from the fucking to the cooking and the cleaning, although the fucking is much more likely to get done than the cleaning. But there are no roles. Both of us are very strong men with weaknesses. We have had to learn how to live together. Two dominant men in one household can make for trouble unless both are unafraid to share the dominance and be passive when necessary. That learning process has been very satisfying. One of the things I truly like about the homosexual life-style is the homosexual marriage. I'm not expected to be the sole supporter—of money and strength. I have yet to see a heterosexual relationship that has the shoulder-to-shoulder sharing that Luis and I have. We take care of ourselves and one another. I find much more equality in a homosexual relationship.

Are there no difficulties?

Of course there are. As I said, two men must learn to live together— to give up certain society-implanted ideas on what's masculine and what's feminine. Then, too, the outside pressures from family and business can kill the relationship. It's amazing how you have to fight for what should be your inalienable right to love whomever you choose to love.

Then, too—although this is not a difficulty for us 'cause we don't give a shit—the neighbors do stare. Luis and I often will walk hand in hand or arm in arm. It blows people away. They could handle it better if we looked effeminate, but the fact that we are both manly looking confuses and irritates them. Their attitude can make me nuts. Why shouldn't I hold my lover's hand? Why shouldn't Luis and I get the same acceptance as a straight couple?

It just makes me so damn angry that society continues to view homosexuals as (1) swishy queens, (2) bearded men in leather and (3) undesirable perverts. Straights have no real knowledge of who we are. They can't conceive that there is a silent gay majority that live lives very similar to their own. Some of us even adopt children. Some of us make very good parents; some don't. And that's no different in the straight world, is it?

Are you aware that you look very angry?

It just pisses the hell out of me that I, or any homosexual, has to justify his existence. In fact, let's end this discussion. Why should I justify me to anyone? Fuck those people who would reject me because I am gay. They wouldn't be of interest to me as people anyway. If my job didn't depend on my staying in the closet, I'd come out publicly and tell people what I think about "straight" attitudes. I feel no shame. I have no hang-ups about my sexuality. But I can't come out . . . not yet, or I'd lose my residency and the chance of another job.

Are you saying the medical profession is less than understanding where homosexuality is concerned?

The medical profession is among the most biased, bigoted and prejudiced. You would think that in a so-called "helping profession," there would be some understanding, but no. They think of homosexuality as an illness—worse, as plague! Strangely, surgeons seem to be particularly vindictive. They make the worst references to gays, tell the coarsest jokes, make the most denigrating remarks. They simply do not treat the gay patient as they would a straight. They may treat his rectal abscess or his colon rip, but behind his back they'll talk about the "queer" who has really done it to himself by taking it up the ass. And that, by the way, is one of the more charming attitudes of doctors: that gay patients, whatever their illness, have brought it on themselves.

Yours is a very harsh indictment.

And I'm not finished yet. Most doctors see homosexuality as an incurable illness which threatens the world by contagion. They will not look at the possibility that homosexuality might be a perfectly valid form of expression—sexual and otherwise—but prefer to cast the first stone and then advocate the extermination of all "queers." The medical profession largely believes the homosexual has forfeited all his rights as a human being. There are doctors who, once they ascertain that the gay patient is not dying, refuse to treat him and send him to a colleague. They don't deem the gay as being worthy of their precious time.

If what you say is true, how do you explain it?

Many of the doctors I work with are closet cases. They have deep homosexual tendencies which terrify them. Rather than work out their own sexuality, they torment those who threaten them. Let me tell you something. Any man who is really straight—and I have some buddies who fit this description—just doesn't give a shit whether you are gay or not. They accept it because they've looked at it within themselves and know it is not their thing.

What do you mean "looked at it within themselves"?

I think everybody has an attraction to members of the same sex. If one is able to acknowledge this, then one is free to either act on that attraction or not. Most straight guys I know who are together can appreciate another man's body—dig it—but not want to do anything more than appreciate it. They're not threatened by the other man's beauty or their reaction to it.

Is the attitude any different among the younger doctors?

In number, there are fewer young doctors mindful of homosexuality than there are older ones. However, even among my peers I see the same terrible prejudices—the same ugly attitudes. Like a lot of these guys will look at my body and want to know where I work out. As soon as I say the Y, they'll say, "How can you go there when it's filled with fags?" I'll ask them, "So what? What's that to do with you?" And they'll say, " 'Cause they're always making passes at me." Which has to be the biggest bunch of crap ever because most of these guys have let themselves go past the point where any self-respecting gay would want them. But I answer: "All you gotta do is say no." And then they really let it hang out. "Well I just don't like those guys. In fact, I hate being around them." That's the kind of shit you hear from the "saviors of mankind." It can kill you—if you let it.

How do you deal with it? How do you work within an atmosphere that you describe as so oppressive?

Sometimes I have to restrain myself from not kicking asses into the East River. But I've adopted an attitude that has helped. I never allow anyone to talk that shit about gays in my presence. I stop them cold. There is not one doctor—no matter what his position at the hospital—who will make a crack about gays when I'm around.

Then you are "out"?

No, not officially. In fact, within my hospital there is no declared homosexual doctor. To declare yourself means possible expulsion. Of course most of my peers suspect I'm gay, but they can't deal with the fact that I play ball, that I don't swish. To them, all gays are pansies. I don't fit. So, although they know, they don't believe what they know.

Of course there are some doctors who not only know but don't give a damn. They are the minority, but they do exist. Their only concern is how well do I do my job. Which is how it should be. But as a near recognized homosexual, I can't allow myself to be just good. Oh no. I've got to be the best . . . beyond reproach. And I am.

Are the nurses' attitudes similar to or different from the doctors?

Much different. Nurses are generally highly intelligent professionals who wish to be treated as such. They resent the macho medical man who comes on to them. I don't do that. I don't extend the promise without later fulfilling it. I am solely professional with them. I don't pretend an interest so that they'll think I'm straight. I'm willing to wager that most, if not all, the nurses know I'm gay and not one of them has ever been anything but courteous and kind.

Considering the attitudes you have attributed to doctors, does the homosexual patient receive adequate medical care?

He will receive treatment but not preferential. Except, of course, for the treatment he receives behind his back—which he will never hear —such as the lewd and disgusting cracks a doctor or a surgeon will make about a rip in the rectum.

Do you see that often?

Lately, we are seeing it too often. Lately, we are getting many rectal abcesses and infections in the intestines.

What are the possible medical ramifications?

Damage to the wall of the intestine can lead to peritonitis, which can be a life-and-death situation, as can a ripped colon. We're seeing a lot of that now too.

What causes these illnesses?

An ungentle lover who uses his cock like a weapon. Foreign objects like cucumbers, bananas and vibrators shoved into the rectum. And the most dangerous, fist-fucking. I have yet to see anything *but* trouble come from that. And I have difficulty understanding it as a sexual act. Fucking, I can understand. It's great—the most intimate act of sharing, of giving and receiving. But taking a fist or an arm up your ass—even though it could be argued as the ultimate sharing—

can have terrible consequences. And a person who is skilled at the receiving has already damaged his sphincter muscle.

What does that damage entail?

Possible anal incompetence . . . dribbling, leaking of stool. And that's the least of the ills. At its worst, fist-fucking leads to rips in the intestines and colon and I've already explained where that can end.

Is this solely a homosexual phenomenon?

Yes and no. Fist-fucking seems to be, but anal intercourse is not. Many women come in with rips in the rectum. Some come in with vibrators lost or stuck in their orifices. But these women aren't judged by their doctors as gay patients are. A woman can come in—as one did—damaged by a Coke bottle insertion, but no one calls her "a fucking queer."

Are there physiological reasons why anal intercourse is pleasurable to the passive partner?

I am not certain, but since the nerves that supply the head of the penis and the anus—S_2—are the same, it would seem logical that stimulation of either should be equally stimulating. Then, too, the nerves in the penis's shaft and nerves around the anus—S_1—are also the same. So obviously there is some kind of intimate association in the pleasure centers. But the exact reasons I'm unsure of as it is not something they teach in medical school.

What do they teach about homosexuality in medical school?

Just some psychoanalytic theory, most of which is written by heterosexuals who try to explain why we are deviant. I dismissed most of it then, and now, as pure conjecture. I also dismiss it because "cause," as such, is unimportant. If less was written on cause and more on acceptance, what a better world it would be.

Do you see yourself making it "a better world" in the future?

In ten years, when I am firmly established as a leading surgeon in this city, I'll come out, declare my homosexuality, and take up the fight for gay rights. The best teacher is example. I can point to both me and my life with pride. Perhaps who and what I am will help to change some attitudes.

Could you be penalized for declaring yourself?

Yes, but sooner or later, those of us who appreciate who and what we are *must* take that risk. We can no longer in good conscience deny ourselves—not if we wish to effect change. Sure there may be a loss of a patient or two once I come out, maybe even the occasional loss of operating room privileges, although if I'm successful as a surgeon that's not very likely, as nothing talks so well in medicine as success as defined by money. But whatever losses I might suffer will be negligible in comparison to the gains. When you can stand up for yourself in this world without shame, when you can perhaps *begin* to change existing attitudes, then your life has a meaning and you've made a rather large contribution.

Suppose you lost your standing within the medical profession?
I'd be angered . . . upset but not devastated. The only loss that would truly matter to me is my relationship with Luis. He is the number one priority in my life. Before him, I think I was always lonely. Now I no longer am. I suppose I've already said this without stating it but . . . I love this man, love him very deeply, more than anything or anyone I have ever known and hopefully *will* ever know. In other words, our mutual hope is . . . till death do us part. What I have with him gives meaning to my existence. I look at my "marriage" and see in it the same things that made my parents' marriage so special—communication, caring, loving. I'm very grateful to them for having shown me what a marriage can be. Actually, I'm very grateful to them for many things—like allowing me to grow, to become my own person—wanting that for me. They loved me, and in their loving, I learned both to give and to receive love.

I am truly a very fortunate man.

Dr. Gabriel Anthony did not look like a "fortunate man" when he paid an unexpected visit the following week on the pretext of wanting to discuss certain medical issues vital to the health of the homosexual community. Still dressed in his surgical greens following a typical Monday of hospital hysteria, he looked more than tired. He looked pained. Even as he spoke of his concern for the dissemination of medical information throughout the gay community, his mind seemed elsewhere. "There's a near epidemic of syphilis and gonorrhea —in the throat. Do you known most men are totally unaware these infections are not confined to the penis and the anus?" Asked about preventives, he spoke of antiseptic gargles after oral sex and urination after anal intercourse. "Immediate cleansing of the genitals and the rectum will also help," he added. Then, suddenly, he said nothing more but made no move to leave. Instead, the look of pain which had never left his face deepened. After a few minutes of silence, he spoke.

I spent this past weekend in Maine. I wasn't there an hour when my mother asked if Luis and I were homosexuals.

What did you reply?

That we were.

What was her response?

There wasn't any. Not immediately. Then, kind of quietly, she said she needed time . . . time to digest and think it out. She was upset. I could see how upset just by looking at her face.

And this upset you?

Badly. I'm not sure why. She didn't damn me or do the Where-Did-I-Go-Wrong number. She just . . . well, was upset.

Where was your father during this exchange?

There. And that was the damnedest thing. The old guy just said, "Well, if that's the way it is, then that's the way it is." But he was upset, too. But in a different way than my mother. He said: "I don't want anyone to ever hurt you. People can be mighty ugly about some things." I told him I knew just how ugly some people can be. He looked at me and then looked away, saying: "I just hope they won't hurt you in medicine." And I couldn't assure him that they wouldn't.

Gabriel, why do you look so hurt?

Because I don't know if my mother understood. She kept asking things like . . . was I sure and had I given women a fair enough chance. She was disappointed. They both were. I could feel that. And I don't want to be a disappointment to them. I never have been.

Do you feel that you are?

That's the damnedest thing. Yes, I do.

Why?

Because I'm not fulfilling their hopes for me. I'm not marrying and raising a family. I tell myself it is *my* life and that my first sense of obligation is to me but when you love others . . . particularly those others who have always been there for you, you just don't want to hurt them. I don't want to let them down. Yes, I have my own hopes and expectations but I can't just divorce myself from those my parents hold for me.

What is it you want?

Dammit! I want their total and complete approval. I've had it all my life and now the child in me is upset because it is being withheld from me.

But is it?

I don't know. I'm so confused. My mother asked just one other question this weekend. She wanted to know why Luis and I couldn't just be friends.

And what did you say?

I told her how much I loved Luis . . . how happy he made me . . . how what I feel for this man is what she feels for her husband and that my love had to be translated as hers had to be—in a way that was closer than friendship.

And what did your mother say to that?

Nothing. Absolutely nothing. She sat there looking above me, below me and finally straight at me. And then suddenly she said, "No matter what I think, I love you. That never changes. It never will."

Frits Sonnegaard

H<small>E WAS ALWAYS AFFABLE</small>, often charming, but the eagerness Frits Sonnegaard * displayed at the beginning of his interviews diminished with each passing session. Initially, he was always punctual. Toward the middle of his participation, he began arriving late. A few time he canceled at the last moment. Although never uncooperative, Frits did become moody. Yet, he never asked to be released from his commitment. Nor did he ask that any area of his life not be discussed.

As a major executive with a multi-national corporation, Frits requested anonymity, mainly because he believes the world will condemn rather than understand. A highly articulate, soft-spoken man, Frits was Jekyll-and-Hyde in dress. When coming from his office, he wore tailored, even conservative, suits. In the evenings, however, his other attire was mainly of leather and denim with assorted keys and colored handkerchiefs used as accessories. With his trimmed beard, close-cropped hair and muscular body, he achieved the tough S&M look which is currently so popular in the gay community.

Frits drank gin martinis at our meetings. Many gin martinis. He never showed the effects.

How long have you been homosexually oriented?

I've never been straight. Whatever sex I've had has been solely with men. I have no sexual feelings toward women—never have, which leads me to think I have always been homosexual.

Do you think you were born homosexual?

I think it is possible. I'm not convinced homosexuality has to be a neurotic disorder. I cannot remember ever having had a sexual feeling toward a girl. Yet, as a child, I played with them, preferred their company even. I always felt more comfortable with women when I was very young.

* See Author's Note, page xii.

If, as you say, you never had a sexual feeling toward a girl as a child, did you then have sexual feelings toward boys or men?

No. When I was eleven I started having fantasies about men but they weren't sexual.

What were they?

They were about love—my being loved. Always that, but sex never entered into it.

Did these fantasies involve masturbation?

Not initially. I didn't know what masturbation was. I didn't know what sex was. In my part-Jewish/part-Protestant and totally Brooklyn middle-class background, sex was never discussed. Sometimes, it was whispered about. Sex was dirty. Little girls could be gotten into trouble. That I remember hearing! Although I didn't know what it meant—which I know is inconceivable when examined under today's light, when kids of eight and nine are doing it—it scared me off girls.

When did you begin masturbating?

When I was eleven and that was by accident. I ejaculated in a twilight sleep. I didn't understand what had happened but it felt so good I tried to make it happen again. But when it did, I was terrified. I thought that white stuff coming out of my penis meant I was sick. I went around thinking I had some awful infection until I heard some boys at school talking about "come" and how good it felt when they did.

Did you receive sex education from anyone in your family?

No. Not ever, but then no one ever spoke to me about a lot of things. Strike that! It sounds so damn self-pitying. I hate that. But it was true. Nobody did. I was an old child. I was more like my mother's friend and confidant than like her kid. I was always around women, gossiping with them and loving it. My identity was much more female than male as a boy. I'm absolutely certain that I was the kind of boy people looked at and knew was in trouble.

What kind of trouble?

That I would become homosexual. All the signs were there. I liked flowers and books and pretty things. Although everyone in the family wanted to prevent my being a "sissy"—as it was called then—nobody wanted to get involved. My stepfather never played baseball with me, never took me to a game. No. He would just drop me on the streets, and later in the Boy Scouts, and hope for a miracle. My parents wanted an All-American boy and Christ, how I wanted to be that. I always felt different. I was overly sensitive. I cried easily. And I was possessive. If I had a friend, I wouldn't allow him to be anyone else's friend. He had to like me and only me.

How would you describe yourself as a child?

As a wretch! A miserable kid from age six through fourteen. I embarrass myself thinking of how unattractive—how sniveling, scared and weak—I was at that age. If I met that kid today, I'd shun him.

You specifically say that between the ages of six and fourteen you were a wretch. Why not before and why not after?

At six, my mother married. I had been an illegitimate child, born in The Netherlands but raised here from the time I was an infant. Actually, I lived with my aunt and her daughter.

Why not with your mother?

I'm not certain. I recall she worked as a manicurist and visited me each weekend. My raising was left to my aunt.

Was she a widow?

Who?

Your aunt.

No, my uncle was alive.

But you say your raising was left to your aunt.

My uncle lived with us but, like all the men in my family, he was a very remote figure. I liked him, I think, but I don't know if he liked me. I was afraid of him. That I do know. Dutch men tended to be very stern and not very loving with their children. He certainly was never loving or tender with me.

Did you know your natural father?

No. He was never discussed. Supposedly, months before I was born . . .

Which was when?

. . . forty-eight years ago . . . he vanished. I don't know anything about him. I never asked and I was never told.

What about your stepfather?

He was a very cold man. I doubt if he could feel love. He certainly never showed it. I think he would have thought it very unmasculine for him to have kissed or held me. And he never did. Actually, from the time my mother married him, my life changed. I became that wretch of a child. My early years with my aunt I recall warmly. Although I idolized my mother, I was happy living with my aunt. I respected her, which, strangely, is not something I can say about my mother. When my mother married, I moved with her and her husband to a new area of Brooklyn and it seems to me my entire personality changed with that change. It's all very complicated even today, but how could I call a man I disliked "father"? Then, too, I felt more loved by my aunt than I did by my mother. I think I was very jealous of this new man in her life, and although years ago I didn't think my mother was bright enough to understand the problem her marriage created for me, I think now she did understand but just didn't know what to do.

What should she have done?

Thrown him out! What else? Actually, there was nothing she could do. I wanted her to choose between him and me and she couldn't.

How do you feel about your stepfather?

Then, I viewed him as some stranger who came to live with us. As I said, he was cold, remote. I don't think, however, that I felt anything about him or anything for him. I just wished he would go away. And when they would have a fight, I would think, "Ah, now he will go!" But he never did. He never mattered to me at all.

Are you sure?

Positive! He never mattered to me. My uncle neither.

Did you feel you mattered to either of them?

Not at all. I was in the way, an embarrassment.

Did you want to matter to them?

If I did, I don't remember it. I can't recall any yearning for a "father's love." Honestly. I only wanted for my stepfather to go away. I never cared that he didn't love me. I had substitutes for his love.

What kind of substitutes?

Movie stars. From the age of five, I had crushes on Janet Gaynor and Fredric March. By the time I was nine or ten, I was "in love" with more dashing types—like Tyrone Power and Errol Flynn. But the idea of sex was not there. These men satisfied something in me. I think they kept me from feeling lonely.

Was there no shared experience with your stepfather that was enjoyable?

The best thing I can think of to say about my stepfather is that he didn't hit me. He would never have spanked me, as he would have done anything to avoid physical contact with me. Actually, he would have done anything to avoid physical contact with anyone.

Is he alive today?

Yes, but I don't see him.

By whose choice?

Mine. I have absolutely no desire to maintain any ties with him.

What are your feelings for him today?

I don't have any. None whatsoever. I think he believes to this moment that he was a good father and by his definition he was. He provided. He put food on the table and a roof over our heads and that was what was expected by his culture. But I disliked him as a child. He was alien, a stranger, to me. And is still alien, a stranger to me. But the difference today is that I don't care!

Then you did care as a child?

Maybe. Maybe I did. I guess I must have . . . I never thought for a second that he would or could make me happy. I never looked for anything positive from him because I knew he couldn't give it. The only affection I ever knew came from my mother. Even after her marriage she continued to love me in a very physical demonstrative fashion. But it was never enough. I didn't want to share her love. I became a very divisive child. I can remember trying to make trouble between her and my father. Actually, I was always trying to separate the people I cared about from one another. I always wanted people solely for myself. I always wanted the undying love of one person.

Did you ever get it?

No. But there was always that one friend in my life and I was never lonely. Not really. But I did feel I was missing something—that I was on the outside looking in—that everyone else had something that I didn't have, but I wasn't sure what. I always felt a kind of exclusion. Particularly at home.

Despite the fact that your mother was, as you say, very affectionate with you?

Yes, affection isn't love.

Did you feel loved by your mother?

I don't know. Truly. I really don't know if my mother loved me. Maybe she did.

Did you feel that she did?

Feel? What do feelings mean? No, I didn't *feel* she loved me but . . . that could be wrong. My feeling could be removed from the reality. That's part of being a neurotic, isn't it—feeling one way when the truth is something quite different?

But how do you know the truth is different?

I don't. But then I don't know where most things are at with me and my mother. She has been dead now for many years and yet I still dream of her at night, wake up after an argument that is so very real. Still . . . yet. All these years of my thinking I have resolved that relationship—have worked it out to where it no longer matters—and then the dreams that say otherwise.

What are your fights with your mother about in your dreams?

It's never quite clear. I'm only aware we are fighting and that I am not winning—that she cannot or will not see the logic in what I am saying. And I am desperately trying to open her eyes. Well, what the hell, I was never able to make it work with her when she was alive, so what makes me think I can do it now that she's dead. My mother and I as I grew older were always fighting. I punished her. I knew my love as an adult, her only child, was important, but I denied it to her. I wouldn't send her a birthday card or visit her on Mother's Day. I could never give up the feeling that she had betrayed me in some way—that she didn't give me something I needed, but what . . . that I don't know.

Yet you said you were like your mother's confidant as a child— her friend.

Yes, but I don't think I wanted to be her friend. I really don't know what I wanted. I just withdrew as a child—from family, from peers. I lived in my own little world and mainly that was of movie stars and imaginings.

Were you a difficult child?

No, not in the sense you are referring to. Quite the opposite. I was a "good" child. I never caused problems at school. I was well behaved and always maintained good grades. That didn't change until my teens, when suddenly I became quite bad. I started cutting classes. I don't know why, and other than going to movies, I don't know what I did with my time. But a strange thing happened. The more I acted out, the more popular I became. Suddenly, at fourteen, I began dressing, talking and acting like other teenagers—even doing things with them. I just stopped being on the outside and was finally in. I became the all-American boy at last. My parents were thrilled.

Were you really the all-American boy?

Of course not. But I pretended I was. I played the part. By then, I knew what I was although it was still non-sexual. I began knowing without knowing by realizing I was lulling myself to sleep at night by thinking, fantasizing, about love affairs with the men I saw on the screen. I would fantasize about a glamorous life with these men, lived in fabulous penthouses overlooking Central Park or in seaside houses in Malibu. Not that I knew what Malibu looked like, but I read about it in a fan magazine.

What else do you remember about these fantasies?

That I, too, was an actor. That was my earliest youthful dream and that I lived with a fellow star and we loved each other enormously. He was very dashing, of course, and made lots of money. I guess I thought of myself as married to these men. I would lie there masturbating, thinking about our relationship as we lived from one party to another in both Hollywood and New York. But sex never entered into it.

How did these fantasies make you feel?

That's what was strange. They felt good as they were happening and bad afterwards. I'd be left feeling very alone and isolated. They didn't frighten me, but they did make me feel different. I knew the other boys my age were not falling asleep dreaming about Gary Cooper and Clark Gable. I think I would have been miserable through most of my teenage years if my cousin hadn't told me about Oscar Wilde—how he was a homosexual and "did it" with men. Although I didn't know what "did it" entailed, I knew from what she explained that I was a homosexual. Finally, I knew what I was. You see, I always knew there was something different about me, but I didn't know what. And when I discovered I wasn't the only one—that there was Oscar Wilde and God knows who else—I felt so much better. It really was like a thunderbolt in my life. I was no longer afraid. From that moment, it was just a matter of finding my way home. I stopped thinking I had to be like "them"—my aunt and uncle, my mother and stepfather, all those motionless, near-dead people living out their dead lives. I could now be this new thing. That's when I settled in and became me, became popular at school. I became this whole other person, one whose identity slowly switched from female to male.

Could you explain that last sentence?

Finding out that there were men who loved men made me feel like a man and not like a woman trapped inside a boy's body. I was a man who liked men—who wanted to be loved by and to love a man. It changed everything for me. I felt free for the first time in my life. Even my parents stopped being a problem. And I never stopped believing that I would find my own man to love.

Did you?

Not right away. I was very slow sexually. I was a virgin until stationed in Iran in 1942.

'42? How old were you then? You said you were born in 1928.

I lied. I was born in '24. I am fifty-two years old—over the hill in gay life.

Despite the fact that you look years younger?

I damn well should. I work out every goddamn day. I live solely to preserve my body. I live to maintain my pecs and my lats and my biceps so that I can look good enough to keep making out. And that's sad. At my age to still be devoted to one cause: making out. I keep thinking it shouldn't matter to me at this point—that I shouldn't need to prop myself up that way any more—that I should know who

I am as a person and use that rather than depend on physical attractiveness.

Isn't it usually a combination of both that attracts?

No. The who-you-are is not valued in the bars, on the streets, in the baths. I don't even value it in myself. It's who you look like and what you represent that matters. It's all fantasy-time and I play along with it—willingly. I'm getting old in the same way most movie stars I admired grew old—hardly at all. One day, I'll either just rot on the pillow or die. But right now, I'm like Lana or Loretta—a walking miracle. I've even stopped aging mentally. In fact, I think I'm becoming retarded. There were times, in the past, when I would lunch with friends or go to a museum but no more. Nothing interferes with my lunchtime workouts at the gym. I've given up anything and everything that might conflict with working on the preservation of my body. And for what? To be attractive! To be a male Marlene Dietrich.

If you resent the amount of time you give to your body, why do you do it?

Because it is the only way I can attract someone. At least, that's how I feel.

What about you, the person? Aren't you attractive?

In gay life, very few look for the person. I even hide my so-called person. Firstly, I mistrust my inner self and I certainly mistrust that anyone would be interested in those qualities that make me, me.

Which qualities?

The softness, the gentleness. My sensitivity. I have all these things. But I'm no longer naïve. I know these qualities are not wanted by others. They're not even wanted by me. So I try to be what my body is . . . tough . . . hard.

What were you, the person, like when you came out?

Soft, romantic, foolish and Victorian. I remember how horrified I was at the goings on in the balcony of a West Side movie theater where I worked as an usher prior to the war. It was 1940 and I was sixteen and in love with love. I knew what the men were doing in the back rows but it didn't interest me. My fantasies were about romance and not about sex. I certainly wasn't frigid or uptight about sex. That's not the reason I refrained from accepting the open invitations. Hardly. No, I was . . . are you ready? . . . saving myself for the man I would love and marry. I was brought up that way. Sex was good only when in love and married. And that's the way it was in the movies. And that's the way it was with me—then. I've come a long way, baby. Maybe too long. Strike that! It also sounds like a line Susan Hayward or Lauren Bacall might say.

When did you have your first sexual experience?

In the Army with my sergeant. He was older and although I didn't really dig him, he dug me. He pursued me and *that* was romantic. He did everything but buy me flowers. But I didn't love him. I wound up in bed with him on a weekend pass and I think he blew me— I'm not sure. I know he wanted me to reciprocate and I couldn't. The thought of it upset me. It was a pretty awful experience, because he felt rejected and I felt guilty. Not for having sex but for not coming across. I also felt very upset by the entire scene. It wasn't romantic. It wasn't clean. It was ugly. There was no love in it at all. I guess it must have really traumatized me, as I didn't have sex for another two years and that was after my discharge.

Where was this?

In New York. Right after the Army, I moved into a tiny apartment in the Village, dyed my hair red because I had always wanted to be a redhead and had a lot of fun. I really did. I was in love with life. I was constantly excited by its possibilities and constantly thinking that love was just around the corner.

Was it?

Well, around the corner was a gay bar. There were a lot of contacts but very little love. My first encounters with sex were not any better than my disaster with the sergeant. I always seemed to go home with older men who wanted me, but I really didn't dig them. Most of the time, I would get away without having to respond. They didn't require it. They seemed to be getting what they wanted.

And you?

It's funny. Up until this second I would have said I got nothing from it. But I think now I must have. In some way I must have wanted those men to want me—give me pleasure but get nothing from me in return. I really must have liked something about that as it happened too many times for it to have been coincidental. You know, that pattern still exists today. I will go with guys who ball me and if I can get away without getting involved, that's all right. Sometimes, my only involvement is to get my cock hard and keep it hard.

Why do you think that is?

I don't know. Maybe it's because of the image I present. Most men want me to be a masculine symbol that they can service. Maybe it is also the image I have of myself. I don't know. When I was a kid, my one-sidedness was often a matter of selfishness. I cared only about my own pleasure and didn't much care about the other person. Actually, if I did care, I had no trouble responding. I'm really getting confused.

Why?

Because ideally I want to be with someone I can respond to. But I realize there is some kind of pleasure, almost a perverse one, in just lying there and letting some guy do it all to and for me. Making him work to please me. Just saying that . . . admitting it, shakes me up. Let's leave this for a while.

Okay. Were attitudes toward the gay community very different then?

Not in the Village. I don't even remember police harassment, although the bars got raided periodically. But I never thought that was about gays as much as it was about the Mafia and payoffs. The Village has always seemed very accepting to me and very safe. My life then was a series of little jobs, all of which meant nothing, but which allowed me to pay the rent and go out nights to the bars. The clubs then were certainly different than they are now. There was no dancing —no touching of any kind at all allowed. An atmosphere of fear usually hung over the place. You simply stood around with your bottle of beer and either made eyes at the guy you dug or conversation with a friend until you could find someone to cruise. It was very different. Today there are the sex bars with people sucking and fucking, but I'm not sure those changes are for the better. Frankly, I can't see what is so wonderful about gays coming out of the closet and screaming their heads off about being gay. It's nobody's goddamn business. Firstly I don't believe for one second that heterosexuals are any more or any less accepting of homosexuality today than they were in 1940 when I came out. I think they are still rocked by it. So I maintain it's nobody's business what I do in bed. And I don't understand why anybody should care what I do. I don't ask heteros about the strange . . .

Strange?

Yes, *strange* things they do in bed. I don't see why anyone's sexual preference should be of interest to another. What you do, and what I do, belong in the privacy of our respective bedrooms. I don't hold with the gay militants who are marching and parading their sexual preferences. I just want to be alone. Call me aggressively passive. For Chrissake! What is so great about being gay—about saying it loud and being proud when gays are fucking and sucking in public bars or falling down stoned on public walks on Fire Island with their cocks shoved in or up one another. Fucking in public isn't freedom and it sure isn't being proud of oneself. That scene at the Anvil—just like most of Fire Island—is about self-hatred.

What is the Anvil?

A sex bar where they put on sex shows. There's one slob who runs a five-foot chain up his ass. Cute? Right? Then there are several who climb onstage to get fist-fucked.

You mean a fist is used instead of a cock?

Right. Only sometimes its more than the fist. It's the entire arm—up to the elbow. That's right. You heard me. Up to the elbow. And on an average night a couple of hundred guys watch this spectacle, while a few dozen others carry on below the stage or in the back room. That's not freedom. That's not gay power. That is self-hatred. That is self-destruction. Although most gays think it's sex. I hate that most about homosexuals. Their self-hatred. Funny 'cause on the other side of the coin is their bravery. They "smile through"—party, even when their hearts are breaking. Strictly a Bette Davis number but it is preferable to moaning and groaning through life as most straights do.

Is that what you feel straights do?

Absolutely. Straights make a lifetime out of feeling bad. When I was a kid I viewed heterosexual life around me as death while alive. I sure wouldn't want that for me. My parents, my uncles and aunts— their lives were joyless. Really unattractive. The men didn't talk to the women and the women complained about the men to the other women. Nothing was shared. Nothing exciting ever happened. Just day-to-day drudgery. Every one of them was old and dead by forty.

They never went anywhere—never read anything. They were out of it. But . . . they had an acceptance because they were doing the accepted thing—raising a family and living like a pack of drones. The fact that they were all miserable meant nothing. I have absolutely no regrets about being homosexual, not that I had any choice in the matter, 'cause I didn't. But in retrospect—and, baby, at fifty-two, it is retrospect—there isn't anything I would trade in my life with any heterosexual. People like to believe homosexuals are more unhappy than straights. I don't believe that. What *is* true is that homosexuals are like Pagliacci. They have a wonderful compensatory mechanism that allows them to act "up" even when they feel down. The word "gay" says it all. The saddest, most unhappy gay learns to put on a gay face. It is almost a religion among gays to be "up." To live! I think straights and gays are equally happy and equally unhappy but the difference between them is what they tend to do with their unhappiness. Gays decide continuously to have a good time in spite of anything that might be happening in their lives or in their heads: whereas straights drown in their nothingness. And it usually is nothingness rather than sorrow or sadness because they stop feeling. They become zombies.

> *You speak of the heterosexual community as though you were as much a part of it as the gay. Is that true?*

No . . . it isn't. My life is almost entirely spent, other than for my work, within a homosexual environment. But I remember vividly my childhood and the life my parents and their friends lived. I also hear the men and women at the office discussing the dreariness of their straight existence. There is always a hopelessness in their attitudes. I only socialize with these people when office politics dictate that I must. Otherwise I stay where I am most comfortable and I don't believe for one minute that living solely within the gay community is bad.

> *But could it be limiting?*

From what? The heterosexual experience? I've seen that. I've also heard the heterosexual points of view. Largely, they are boring. Most trends in art—all forms of the arts—are started by gays.

> *At the office, are you a declared homosexual?*

That's ridiculous. If I were straight you wouldn't ask me if I were a declared heterosexual. No, I'm not. It's nobody's business. And I'm not a closet case hiding my sexual preference. I don't hide anything but I don't flaunt anything either. I don't pretend to date women and I don't talk baseball with the boys. Actually, I never discuss anything personal with anyone in the office.

When you have had lovers, have you included them in your business life?

If you mean do I bring the boss home to meet the "little lover" the answer is no. Never. I do not mix the two. As I said, I don't believe the heterosexual world is all that tolerant. I think as soon as your back is turned there are the snide remarks. Look at what has happened in New York—supposedly our most sophisticated city—with the gay rights bill. Defeated. So for all our 1976 sophistication, it ain't happened yet. And if gays continue to get publicity about the Anvil-type places, it isn't going to happen.

Have you been to the Anvil?

Yes. Yes, I've been. To the Anvil. To the trucks. To the baths. Yes, I've been to all those places.

You say it so wearily?

Wearily? Perhaps. I wish I didn't go. But I do. Desperation gets me there. Desperation is what gets most of us there. Like the baths. That's the one place, except for an orgy, where you can reach out and touch just about anyone you see and not worry about rejection. Everyone is there for similar reasons. Fuck-time. The same is true pretty much at the Anvil. Sure there are the sight-seers and the thrill-seekers, but mainly it's guys looking for an uncomplicated fuck or several uncomplicated fucks. The trucks are a place to hang out your cock and get it sucked or rammed into by anyone, everyone. And . . . you can do your thing. You can make that person who's doing whatever he's doing to you into any one you want. It's pitch-black—like a movie theater—and you can write your own script and cast it with whomever you want.

How do you feel about your own involvement in places like the Anvil or the trucks?

At this point in my life nothing bothers me. I don't judge my behavior. If some guy wants to crawl on a stage and have a bunch of strangers shove their arms up his ass that has nothing to do with me. I mean it just doesn't rub off on me.

You are not affected then by what seems to be a growing sado/ masochism trend?

Not really. I frequent mainly leather bars, but because a guy dresses in leather—as I do—doesn't mean he's into S&M. Most guys in the leather and denim bars dress that way because they are attracted to the butch, the masculine man. But actual S&M . . . there's not all that many that are into it.

What about you?

I've done a few things to people that would qualify as S&M but only at their request. Lots of times I'll meet guys who'll want a scene that really doesn't interest me but I'll go along with it unless it is repellent. Like the guy who wanted me to put needles through his nipples. I walked away from that. If you want the real S&M story, I'll set you up with a couple guys.

Needles through one's nipples is a far cry from the great romance.

For me, yes. For some others, not at all. Quite the contrary. You're showing your own prejudices when you make that remark. Actually, regarding the great romance, even my first love affair was a far cry from what I had fantasized love as being. I was twenty-two and he, the "older man" I so much wanted. He must have been thirty, which seemed very old then. He was very masculine and very much the gentleman. A Tyrone Power type if ever there was one. But I didn't love him. I tried to convince myself that I did . . . it was the idea of being in love with a man who looked and acted as he did that held me. Besides, he couldn't be Tyrone Power twenty-four hours a day.

What do you mean?

He wasn't always strong. He had his weaknesses and they showed. I have trouble with that. I am interested in masculine men. I even wished myself into one because of my need to have one of my own. Feminine things don't interest me. I don't understand guys who dress up in drag. As a child I felt female, but today I feel male, fiercely so.

Fiercely—what makes you choose that word?

I don't know. I hate weak men. Truly. I completely dominate a weak man sexually. Weakness in a man turns me off—it even disgusts me. Ferocity is a manly quality, I guess. I think of male sex as ferocious— animal-like. I seek out that kind of man. Yet, when I find him, I always look for and find the chinks in his armor, the flaws, or . . .

in a word, the weaknesses. I need to find these things but I don't understand why. Why I must reduce what I elevate is beyond me. And on those rare, so very rare, occasions when I find this super-strong masculine male, it never works because a man without feelings, without softness, turns me off.

Then have you ever found the combined qualities you search for in a man?

I think so . . . a few times. But I'm not certain, as the relationships disintegrated as soon as I revealed my real self.

Could you explain that?

As soon as I was me . . . as soon as I showed my softness or my weakness, my fears, insecurities, the other person lost interest. I was no longer what he wanted, no longer his super-strong masculine male.

How do you deal with this?

Today, when I'm out there cruising, I leave that part of me home. Only one person knows what I feel and that's me. I learned long ago to keep to myself those things that make me happy and those things that make me sad. I have been with a lover for twenty-two years and even he cannot be with me on my wavelength. I know that and accept it. It doesn't even make me sad. No more. I have learned to keep my emotions separate from others. Besides, most people don't give a damn. They want the façade—not the person.

Are you sure?

I am now. When I was young, I gave of myself. I was what you would call "open." But over a period of years, a period of one-night stands and gang-bangs, I learned to shut up. I don't expose myself any more, except sexually. That's the only exposure most people want or can handle. The real you is wanted by very few people. Do you know what that does to a person?

Do you?

Yes, you lose your dreams and your illusions. You smarten up. That's the price of promiscuity. You lose your innocence. But you also gain. You become realistic about what life is all about. You don't get as hurt. When I was young, I was wrecked half the time because people were dealing one way—with their dicks in their hands—while I was dealing with me in my hands. But no more. I no longer expect anything from anybody, which is good, because ninety-nine out of one hundred can't give you anything but their bodies. Sucking and fucking is possible. Warmth and interest seldom is.

How do you feel about that?

I'm one of the lucky ones. Having Larry—he's my lover—helps. But, I still feel the lack, still feel I could be so much closer to another person. But let me make something clear: the lack is as much in me as it is in others. You get what you pay for. And when you sleep with two hundred people a year—and that's not a boast but a fact—and relate to none, it's got to be you as well as them. You are doing something wrong.

What do you think that is in your case?

The fact that you can't go around wearing on your leather and denim a patch that reads: "I Am Sensitive." And if I did, I'd probably go home alone six nights out of seven. Then, too, I'm attracted to the outer trappings of masculinity. I go by surface qualities. I associate leather and denim with masculinity—I always have—and why or how that began I don't know. I dress in it because that's the way I want my partner to look—to be. Masculine. Therefore, I bring an attitude to a cruising situation. I'm setting up an image of who I am before I open my mouth. I am assuming the identity of the very man I want to meet—that super-strong masculine male. But it doesn't work, because if I'm looking for that man and dress and appear like him then I am attracting the male who is looking for the same thing. Do you understand?

It's almost like you are talking about mistaken identities.

Right. I'm looking and he's looking and we think we find it in each other and then . . . boom! A collision. And it's a frequent collision. Yet, on some level it must work, because I keep doing it. The only times it fails is when they think I'm into the heavy S&M scene. If they think I'm going to really work them over, it's going to be a bust. As I said, I'll do some of that stuff but only to a point. I do it to oblige, as it sure doesn't fulfill me. The only part I enjoy is when I'm asked to be dominant. I like that. I like being the dominant strong male. In fact, I play to it and for it. But I really don't want to hurt anyone and I sure don't want to be hurt.

Do you think of yourself as a dominant strong male?

. . . Yes . . . well . . . no. Actually, yes, in comparison to others absolutely. Yes, in most ways, I do. Very definitely. In other ways, no.

But I want to be tough. I admire strength. I admire men who dominate their own lives and others.

Why?

Because to do so is admirable. Weakness or wishy-washiness is hardly desirable.

But why? Why do you admire strength and dominance?

I don't know. Maybe I'm trying to overcome how I felt as a child but that sounds too pat—too psychoanalytical. What's the difference? A search for strength or dominance is hardly a bad thing. The world turns on and by people of strength. I wish I had that kind of power—*inner* power. But I don't think I do and I accept that—accept that I am weak in some area—that I will cry when I feel sad. But I can live with that even though I'm hardly proud of my sentimentality or my sensitivity, as I think them feminine traits.

Regarding your cruising attire—which as you say pushes the strong masculine image—doesn't that automatically put you into a particular sexual role?

Yes, but that's okay. Well, sometimes it's not okay. Sometimes I would like to be nicer to some people than they would like me to be. I would like to be warmer, more affectionate, more sexual even. Like often I'd like to go down on some man who appeals to me, but I don't because if I do, it'll ruin it for him. He wants me to be what he *thinks* I am. It's funny. A lot of guys think I use others because I get blown a lot. But who is using who? Aren't I being used as some guy sucks from me, not at all interested in me but what he wishes me to be at that moment.

How fulfilling then are the two hundred encounters you have a year?

Not so fulfilling as they once were. Obviously, if I must do it that often I'm not being fulfilled in some way. Like if I'm in the bars four, five nights a week, something is not being taken care of. You don't need brains to realize that if you're out cruising on a Saturday after spending all of Friday night fucking that Friday could not have been very fulfilling. Well . . . there seems to be an endless round of Fridays in my life.

What do you think is missing?

The personal interest. The lack of caring for the real me. But, how can I expect what I don't give?

Why do it then?

You must be kidding! Baby, it's about ego. The ego is never satisfied and it never will be. At my age I know damn well sex is an ego trip. I want to be wanted. I want to be desired. That need needs constant reinforcement. Funny how it has altered, though. When I was young, I wanted to be loved. I wanted some man to look in my eyes and see me—love *me!* Now I want as many men as possible to want me but in a purely physical fashion. I don't understand how that changed.

Did you ever experience romantic love as you fantasized it?

No. It just never happened for me, although I still believe that kind of love is possible. Others have achieved it, but something has always stopped me. I think something inside me got turned off at a very early age and I've never been able to turn it totally back on. I get involved but I don't get passionately involved. But . . . I've had many lovers and Larry, as I mentioned, has been with me for twenty years. However, it was never a great love affair and never a great passion. I wish it had been. I so much would have liked to experience that feeling.

Do you negate the chances of it still happening?

Yes, I would not want it now. I couldn't stand to have my life upset. No more. Not at this stage of life. 'Cause if I fell into that kind of love, if I felt that way about someone, I would have to go all the way. I don't want that. I'm too old and too tired for that kind of love. I mean it. It would be too inconvenient for me to pursue. I have a certain kind of life and a certain security in that life. To have a wild passionate love enter and change all that is something I really wouldn't want. But romance . . . that's another thing. I'm always ready for a romance. In fact, I have a few each year.

What is the difference?

Romance is love without commitment. That I can handle. In no way do I want to start over with another man. I couldn't actually— couldn't throw over what I have with Larry. But I do enjoy the romances, the getting involved with someone and feeling all foolish about it. It adds an otherwise missing element to my sex life.

How would you describe your relationship with Larry?

As satisfying. There were lovers before Larry—three in all and I'm still devoted to them in my way—but with Larry it's a whole other kind of devotion. There is no longer sex involved, so I wouldn't call

him my lover. Actually, it's like being married. That's it. I am—feel—
married to Larry. We have so much time invested in one another.
We are comfortable and safe in the relationship. We are like old
married folks. There is a deep caring. Larry does not and never has
understood what goes on inside me—we're not on the same wavelength emotionally—but he cares about my feelings, respects that I
have them, as I respect his needs, although much of what is important to him isn't to me. Yes, we are a married couple and I guess like
many married couples, without sex in our relationship.

But it didn't start out that way?

Oh no. It became that way over the last ten years. Unfortunately.
God how we tried to keep that side of our relationship going! Threesomes, foursomes, groups of all sizes and shapes, but it went. I took
several lovers along the way, but like most straying husbands, I came
home to "mama," so to speak. Whenever it boiled down to who I
was fucking vs. who I was loving, I chose Larry and our kind of loving
every time. And I certainly would today. I have loved Larry in a way
I've never loved another person and I feel he loves me similarly.
When we met, he became involved almost immediately. I did not. In
fact, I wasn't very attracted to him. But he was very devoted to me
and I needed that. He also fed my ego by stating that he thought I
was the world's most attractive man. I needed that too. And, he was
beautiful to look at and absolutely beautiful to know. Larry is a
rarity—a good person. Eventually, his devotion and his unabashed
love won me. I know that sounds self-centered and lousy but it's true.
I was very moved by him. He mattered to me. He still does. I am very
devoted to Larry.

Perhaps I imagine it, but you look very sad.

I am. I damn well am. As I said, ours has been a satisfying relationship. We both became successful—in our respective professions. He
feels secure with me, as I feel secure with him. I know he is there
and that is very important to me. Ours is everything a marriage
should be except for the lack of sex. And I would give *anything* if I
could bring that back 'cause I was the one who threw it away. I was
the one with the insatiable ego need. I was the one who had to have
a cast of thousands admiring and wanting me. He would have been
happy with just us in bed. I was the one to crowd it up. I always had
to have reassurance from people who really had no meaning in my
life. And reassurance of what? My attractiveness. Such bullshit. And

that eventually killed what we had. Larry lost faith in me. We tried, as I said, everything, but it just served to separate us even further. I regret that so awfully. It is one of the very few regrets I have about anything in my life. We have made it on every other level. We own our own home here in town and another at Fire Island—one with a big backyard where I can do my gardening. We want for nothing. And we never will, as the building we own affords us an income. Between Larry and me, we earn $100,000 a year. Neither one of us needs to work another day. But we do. Funny, I've been with my job for the same amount of years I've been with Larry. Twenty years. A lifetime. That staggers me. Initially, I worked to live but now I live to work. I like what I do. My professional work is extremely creative. It uses what's left of my mind. I know I could have been more professionally, but I have a very low creative urge. I'm not about to write the great novel. Oh, once I thought about going into production, but it was just thought. In truth, most of my energies went into sex—the pursuit of it more so than the act of it. But again, I have no regrets. Considering I have no college degree, I've done very well. If I retired tomorrow I could live comfortably.

So once again, you are satisfied *in an area of your life.*

Yes, that is exactly so. Basically, I have a good life. And a secure one. That is very important to me. That perhaps is one of the reasons Larry and I have been together for as many years as we have. Security. Both of us need to know that another person is there. We have that mutual need. Or is it a mutual fear? Both. I don't want to grow old alone. I am afraid of being sick and having no one to care for me. Larry has the same fears. That may be why most homosexuals are afraid of growing old. There is no one there to care for you as you die. No children to comfort and protect you as you once comforted and protected them.

What about friends?

I have very few. In fact, in truth, I doubt if I have any. Larry and I recently gave a party and I remember standing in the middle of the room and thinking at some point how I couldn't care less about any of these people we have known for years and how I was certain that they felt similarly. Gay relationships have a way of being largely superficial. That's another reason why homosexuals fear age. They know they will be alone. The young inherit the earth in gay life. I have already seen a lot of my contemporaries break down, become alcoholics and suicides because of this. That all frightens me. If it weren't for Larry, I would be quietly desperate.

Have you ever tried to make a close friendship?

I think some of my friends would think we are close, but we are not. Mainly, the fault is mine. I think it is related to my not falling deeply in love. I think in childhood that thing—whatever it is—that got turned off prevents me from getting really close, involved, with another person.

What do you think that "thing" might be?

I don't know. I truly don't. It feels like fear, though. I hold back— a kind of reserve. I don't know why I just don't let myself go. God knows I've let myself go in other areas that I never dreamed possible!

What are you referring to?

Sex.

Can you explain?

It's not a matter of "can" but "will" I explain. What the hell, why not. Look, I've tried everything sexually. Everything. Things I thought never even interested me. The only thing I can't do is get fucked. I would if I could but physically I can't. Besides, it really isn't a fantasy of mine. Then, too, it isn't other people's fantasies. Very few guys want to fuck me. Mainly, they want me to fuck them. It's the same as I said before. Most guys want—service me—and get turned off if I want to reciprocate. The guys I meet want me to act and be a certain way and by and large I'll be their fantasy. I'll do what they require sexually.

With no holds barred? Is that what you are saying?

I'll get into anything other than watersports or anything that even borders on the scatological.

Watersports?

Yes. That's the golden shower number. Where you piss on some guy or let him drink your piss. Or piss up his ass after you've fucked him. I mean I've done these things but not by my choosing. They really don't turn me on. I do them to please. Anything scatological, anything involving feces, is definitely out. I find that repulsive.

Would you classify watersports as part of the S&M scene?

I would but I doubt if those into it would.

Then would you agree that you are involved on some level in S&M.

Yes, I am. I slid into it years ago. The truth is I was always attracted to a masculine image and that has always meant the capability of violence. I think of a masculine man as a violent man. From childhood, masculinity and the physical have been interwoven.

Why do you think that is?

I don't know. Wouldn't analysts say it stems from parental figures in one's life?

Do you think of your uncle or your stepfather as violent men?

As a child, I didn't. At least I'm not aware that I did. But now, when I think about both of them, I feel they had the potential of being very violent men. Yet . . . neither ever struck me. But . . . I always felt they could, and would, if provoked. I was always afraid of my uncle. I was a "good child" because I was so certain he would beat me if I weren't. Yet, he had never laid a hand on me. But . . . this is really wild, the more I think about it, the more I feel certain that he was capable of inflicting great pain. Do you know, if my uncle had lived, he would have stopped me from becoming homosexual.

How could he have done that?

I don't know, but he would have. He would have beat me from actively becoming gay. I know this. I was very afraid of him. That's so crazy. Why was I so afraid of him? He never gave me reason to be. He was so remote. So was my stepfather. And angry. You could see that in both their faces. They were unsmiling men. There was a suspicion of rage about both. I remember not caring whether I pleased them or not but I also now remember that I definitely did not want to displease them. I was in awe of them. Awe as in fear. But of what? What was I afraid of? . . . Their strength! Oh my God, that's it. Their strength. Both were towering men. Not just tall but muscular. Big. I was so small as a child. Weak. And they seemed to be like rocks. Nothing ever seemed to hurt or bother them. They were above being hurt.

Are you?

I am now. I really am. I used to get hurt a lot, but I don't care that deeply about people or issues any more. I shrug things off a lot. I care about me. I care about Larry but that's it. And to be quite honest, I think my caring for Larry only goes so deep. It has always seemed to me that to really care about another person is to be responsible for them.

Why?

Because. That is what caring is about. You become responsible for the person. You must supply what they demand. You must come across with you and often at your own expense.

But why do you say that?

Must there be a reason for every feeling? I can only remember that caring for my mother meant doing what she wanted if I were to get her approval. And that's the way it is with most if not all people. We barter. I'll-care-for-you-if-you-do-this-for-me. So most love and most caring is bullshit. Particularly in the gay crowd. We band together. Like pioneers. We make a circle to protect ourselves from the dangers in life.

What dangers?

The abuses life hurls upon all of us. From childhood we learn how to live with abuse. You must or you die. That's something I've learned from the S&M scene. There are those who actually like being abused and there are others who like to abuse. May they find one another.

And you? Are you the abused or the abuser?

I don't think of my involvement as being one or the other. I'm really on the periphery of all of this. S&M is not really my scene, although I lied to you before. I do it but I'm not involved in it. Do you understand the difference? In other words, I've done a lot of things but not because *I've* wanted to but because I would have disappointed my partner if I hadn't. If I look, dress a certain way—with the keys on the right, in leather, chains on my motorcycle jacket—then I am selling a bill of goods. If I don't come across, I'm cheating the other person. So I do a lot of things I really don't want to do.

For example?

I *did* put needles through that guy's nipples. I did do that because he wanted it and he expected me to do it.

What reaction did you have?

None. I personally felt nothing one way or another. I just hoped it made him happy. Isn't that what it's all about?

How do you feel about the usage of pain to make one happy?

To you it is pain, but to someone else it is ecstasy. Who is to say? I make no judgment about it. This summer, I saw one young boy horsewhipped by five other guys, and then, while his ass was bleeding, he was fucked by each of them. To you, maybe to me, that sounds like pain. A horror story. But this kid came two or three times. He was in ecstasy. If there are deep psychosexual overtones to all of this, so what? I am inclined to think that is all bullshit. You see, I saw that kid's face—I saw the face of the guy who had needles through his nipples. They were happy!

Did either episode make you happy?

Yes, in a way. I was happy he was happy. I had pleased him. Like fist-fucking. Okay? Yes, I do that. I do it a lot. I'll get my arm up some guy if he wants it. Do I want it? No. But just because I get no physical sensation from it won't stop me from doing it, because the guy I'm doing it to loves it. He expects me as the dominant one to do it. And to avoid being a cheat, I do it. But I really don't enjoy it. . . .

Why the silence?

I was just evaluating what I had just said and it doesn't ring true. Now that I am listening to myself, I sense that something is wrong in my reasoning. I think I'm lying to myself. I think that on some level, which I'm not in touch with, I must enjoy doing these things. After all, if I really hated doing them, I wouldn't do them, would I? I am beginning to think it must give me as much pleasure to do them as it gives pleasure to the recipient. That kind of frightens me.

Why?

Because that means there's a subsystem at work within me with which I have no contact. I like to think I know all about me. Till now, I thought I did a lot of things I did because I was under the influence of drugs. I've done a lot of LSD, mescaline. Drugs change things. Exactly what they change I don't know, but they definitely release something from within me. Maybe I really want to do those things I described but can't face the fact and use drugs as an alibi. There's little responsibility when you're spaced. You know—the devil-made-me-do-it kind of thing. Jesus, when I think of some of the things I've done . . . if it weren't for the drugs . . . . Did I really want to do those things?

Do you want to talk about them?

No. But I hurt people. I mean I really hurt people. . . . In one of my relationships, a lover, there was a side to it that only worked under drugs. It was the only way I could do the things he wanted. I used to beat him with my fists and when that stopped being pleasing enough, rubber hoses, whips, belts. He loved it. He must have. We were together for two years. Today, sitting here, I want to say that wasn't me—that I could never do those things without drugs, but now I'm not so certain. There is something within me. . . . Yet, I only do what people ask me to do. I never initiate it.

Are there limits to what you would do?

Do you mean have I ever said no? I try to work around a lot of things —like burning flesh, or stringing guys up, hanging them in closets— I really prefer to work around those things. But . . . if the other guy insists, I'll do it. But I really wish they would settle for the fantasy rather than making it into reality. That would make me happier. I'm willing to fantasize. I'm willing to be their strong, dominant man, but I wish I didn't have to do what so many of them require.

Do you really have to do it?

Of course not! You know that and I know that. But I do it because I must believe I am forced into those acts. So who is the abused and who is the abuser? Maybe I really want to be beaten. Maybe I am truly looking for an extension of myself to punish. I don't know. These questions I'm now asking myself, how important are they? How important are the answers? They are not at all important. But I don't think people understand that. All that matters is . . . if it works for you and the other person, why analyze it? Why seek answers if the question poses no real problem.

And you feel relatively, by your definition, "problemless"?

Yes. That's exactly it. I am not unhappy. I am not lost. I am a relatively satisfied person. I have done more with my life than most people do. I *have* more in my life than most people have—homes, money, a twenty-year relationship. I have no complaints. Not really.

Are you happy?

Oh come on! That's a bullshit question. Happy, what's that? I've survived and that's what's important. Happiness? That's a word on a greeting card.

Rabbi Josef Ben Ami

MOST SUNDAYS at an hour he calls "high tea," Rabbi Josef Ben Ami * "officiates" at a Village gay bar well known for its niceties—bright lights and cleanliness as opposed to the usual barroom baroque of dinge and dirt. The rabbi's pulpit is a keg on which he rests his coffee. His congregation is composed of boys and men who may or may not know that the lean, six-foot, blue-eyed blond of rather intense visage, jeaned and T-shirted, is a man of God. Certainly, within the bar, there is no talk of religion. At the bar, Rabbi Josef is solely one of the boys, Sunday socializing and enjoying every minute of it.

He is very much "of the people," which is what "Ben Ami," the name he has chosen as a pseudonym, means. There is nothing of the remote rabbi about him. After sitting with him for an hour, it becomes clear the congregation likes him, and not just because he is attractive.

In his home, the scholar is evident. Certainly no less than 5,000 books (his estimate) line his L-shaped studio. More than 150 plants perch on window ledges facing south. He spends two hours three times a week tending to them. In what limited wall space remains, pictures painted or drawn by his lover Mark and drawings of his own are casually hung, as is the unidentified young man whose picture sits on the rabbi's desk. "He is my inspiration—but not necessarily spiritual," says Josef.

He is not easy to interview, this Rabbi Josef Ben Ami, as he is more given to philosophizing than to direct answers. His emotions run second to his intellect. But he is a sweet man, of good humor, a man who ended his series of interviews (there were five in all) with "You're a very nice fellah. Listen . . . if you're interested, have I got a boy for you!"

When were you ordained as a rabbi?

Twelve years ago in Israel. I was nineteen.

* See Author's Note, page xii.

48

That seems somewhat young.

It is. But as the son of a famous Hasidic rabbi, my education began at three. From infancy, my life was steeped in Judaism. I was raised to succeed my father as a great rabbi—as head of the court. Hasidic Jewry is not unlike a dynasty in that the son inherits the position of the father.

What was your father's position?

He was one of the foremost rabbis in Europe—a great scholar and a great teacher. His importance was such that on High Holy Days people would come from miles around to sit at his table and discuss moral and philosophical issues. Nobody could eat or drink until he acknowledged his cup. Often, more than a thousand cups were raised, waiting to be acknowledged.

What is a Hasidic Jew?

The most orthodox of the Jewish religious sects. He appears different from other people because of his dress. Till I was fifteen, when I rebelled, I wore *peyus*, which are long fringe curls that fall from your sideburns to your neck, and the ritual garb—black leggings, a fringed undershirt, a black jacket, a white *yarmulke*, over which a black fur hat was worn, and a black overcoat. Hasidic Jewry is very isolationist. Hasidic Jews live among Hasidic Jews. I always felt out of the mainstream. Even when I first came to the U.S. as a child, I never adjusted to the American culture because I was isolated from it. I never traveled out of the Hasidic community. Life, whether here or in Rumania or in Israel, was the same, and always with the same restrictions. Prayer in the morning, school, evening prayer, school, as in lessons-with-my-father. As a Hasidic child, I had no childhood. There was no fun. We were not supposed to be children. We were little rabbis.

Do you say that with resentment?

Yes and no. My own son is being raised today as a Hasidic Jew, but he is also being allowed his childhood. In other words, the education one receives—that I received as a Hasidic Jew—is wonderful, quite mind-expanding. That I do not resent in retrospect. But the fact that I was never my daddy's little boy—*that* I resent.

Where did you live as a child?

Everywhere. I was born in Bergen-Belsen. Yes, the concentration camp. It was liberated a week after my birth. We survived because we were *"sheina yiddim"*—the upper crust of international Jewry. My father was world renowned and his family's importance dates back to the early 1600s. Yet, despite his position, he and my mother lost ten children in camps.

Upon my family's return to their native Rumania, the country fell under Russian rule. When I was six, the N.K.V.D., now known as the K.G.B., which is the Soviet Secret Police, interned us in a labor camp for "economic reasons." The crime, in fact, had been my father's teachings as a leading Talmudist scholar. We remained in the camp three years. What we had there was no worse than what we had known. We could not speak Hebrew, although my father taught me the Torah at night. But everything had to be memorized because if the Russians found Hebrew written on paper we would have been exterminated. Fortunately, we were bought out by my father's and my mother's families and followers. We came to America where I spent a year living down on the Lower East Side in Manhattan before we left for Israel.

Do you have any recollection of those years?

Only that our suitcases were always packed in readiness. My parents, no matter where we lived, expected a pogrom. Even in America, we lived with that paranoia. If my father was not home from the temple each night at five, my mother would become hysterical, fearing the Cossacks had taken him. Just imagine: Cossacks on East Eighth Street! That's how deep the scars, and thus the mistrust, went. I inherited that mistrust—that fear of all *goyim.* I learned to keep thoughts very private. We were very fearful for our existence. It was understandable.

Were you happy as a child?

No. My only friend was Avram, my brother who was four years younger. Happy—how can one be happy when one's father never stops believing in God and at the same time beats his children every night except the Sabbath. And I, as the eldest, always received the worst beating. I still have the scars.

Why did your father beat the children?

The beatings were ritualistic and always under the heading, the excuse, of our not having learned our lessons to his satisfaction. He also beat my mother and my sister. God only knows what lessons they

failed to learn. My father was more than just a little crazy. He suffered, I think, from extreme self-loathing. I remember no kindnesses
from him or any semblance of emotion other than anger. Yet, although I disliked him, I loved him and who knows why? Why do
little boys love their fathers? But he didn't love me. He wanted me
to be a certain way—*his* way—and any deviation from the mode he
had in mind brought about his extreme disapproval. When my sister
married outside our faith, my father sat *shiva* for her. As far as he was
concerned, she had died. He never spoke to her again.

Were you close to your mother?

I was, but I no longer am. But I have not disowned her, although I
was tempted to. As a child, I both liked and loved my mother. But
several years ago, when I came out, declared to her and others that
I was a homosexual, she became hysterical and insisted I either see
a psychiatrist or receive aversion therapy. Her attitude became ugly.
It was then I stopped liking her. Of course I refused any kind of
therapy at all. I was not unhappy with my sexuality. It was my mother
who was unhappy with it. She still is. She refuses to understand or
accept that I choose to live as a homosexual. That part of my life is
ignored. But we are in touch. She and her husband—my mother
divorced my father several years ago when she finally had enough of
his brutality—live in Europe. She writes weekly and phones monthly.
When in New York, she phones daily and visits weekly. A Jewish
mother, indeed.

In evaluating what had and what hadn't been with my mother, I
recognized that although I *felt* close to her throughout my childhood,
that closeness was contingent upon my doing things her way or not
doing them. As an adult that was unacceptable to me. And as an
adult, I recognize I still have childlike needs, but I also recognize that
what I want and need from my mother—which is unconditional acceptance and love—I am never to receive. And why should I? I didn't
get it prior to my coming out, so why should it be available now? It
is with pain that I accept that, but it is with joy that I also accept that
I will never give what is wanted of me.

Was your father alive when you declared yourself?

No. Had he been, I would not have, as I feared his disowning me,
which he did anyway. Why? Because I had not become the rabbi, Jew
or man he had wanted me to be. I was not in his mold. His estate was
worth four million dollars. I did not receive a penny.

Why did you declare yourself to your mother?

Because I knew I was to become active in the gay movement and that my participation would probably bring considerable publicity. I wanted to prepare her. I also wanted to stop her from fixing me up with available women. After my divorce she was like a one-woman dating service—the original "Have-I-got-a-girl-for-you!"

At what age did you begin having homosexual thoughts and/or relations?

At nine I developed a crush on a boy of fifteen who lived up the street from us in Jerusalem. My fantasies then were of running away with such a boy and being together. I fantasized about our loving one another, but I had no thoughts of sex. Nor did I masturbate—not until college. But I did have pubescent sex—with Avram. It created a beautiful and lasting intimacy between us.

This may be difficult for many to comprehend, as it was difficult for me to accept, so deep was my incest taboo, but Avram and I continued to make love and have sex for many years. We were not lovers but we loved each other very deeply. Avram killed himself on Mother's Day—how symbolic, yes?—1973. He was a beautiful, sensitive young man who could not stand up to the pressures of our upbringing. He could not say "No." He could not freely live his own life. He could not insist on his right to be.

Avram's death so grieved me that I eventually sought professional help. But I could not stay in psychiatry because I cannot put my life in anyone's hand but my own. Avram was a great loss. He had been my one friend as I had always been very isolated from peers. I was avoided because of my sharp tongue. I could kill with it and often lashed out at fellow students in my rage—rage that didn't belong to them, but who could control it.

But all the talking about Avram won't bring him back. I lived with guilt regarding my relationship with him for many years. But no more. There had been precious little love in our lives other than what we brought to one another. No—no more guilt but still the grief.

Did you feel guilt for your homosexual activity as a child?

I felt doomed and damned. There was always a waiting for retribution, to be struck down, stoned. I felt I had this horrible secret and it preyed on me. It made me different from peers and kept me apart from them. There was only Avram. I grew up feeling I was a bad, even a terrible, person, one who was to be punished for his evil thoughts and actions. That inner, pervading feeling of guilt is what gnaws, and can destroy, every homosexual.

God, then, was very real to you as a child?

Very real indeed. It wasn't until age fifteen or thereabouts that my concept of God changed from a sitting-up-in-heaven, all-knowing, judging, fearsome God, who insisted on my observing all command-ments, to a process in which the focus is on people as members of the human race and as a part of the universe. In other words, my religion is a belief in a process—one which focuses on the order and harmony in the world and on humanity's relationship to nature and each man's relationship to another.

Was sexuality discussed in the home when you were a child?

Only through my studies of Jewish texts. There you get a lot of the who-did-what-to-whom-and-how. Regarding homosexuality, proscrip-tions against it appear in the moral code of the Torah in Leviticus, chapter 18, verse 22, and chapter 20, verse 13. The parties involved in the homosexual relationship are threatened with capital punish-ment.

In Sifra, 9:8, a Talmudic treatise, the Talmud reinforces the pro-hibition but not the penalty, which is limited to flogging in the case of Lesbian relationships. This kind of anti-homosexual thinking cul-minates in the Jewish Encyclopedia, which as late as 1971 reads: "Rabbinic sources advance various reasons for the strict ban on homo-sexuality. . . . It is an unnatural perversion, debasing the dignity of man . . . moreover, such acts frustrate the reproductive purpose of sex, just as do any other forms of spilling the seed in vain. . . . A third objection is seen in the damage to family life by the homo-sexual abandoning his wife. . . . Jewish law, then, rejects the view that homosexuality is to be regarded merely as a disease or morally neutral."

What is the viewpoint today on homosexuality among the vari-ous sects of Judaism?

The progressive orthodox Jew tries to adapt to change. The orthodox rabbi would therefore say, "You are a sinner but you need not be stoned or excommunicated if you work on yourself and change." The conservative Jew would agree but the more liberal among them would add: "It is a sickness. Go get cured." The reform Jew would say it

is a sin and/or psychosis and/or neurosis. The reform see homosexuality as deviant behavior, not only spiritually, as the orthodox
and the conservative do, but also as socially and emotionally deviant.
In 1973 there was a debate within the reform rabbinic leadership
concerning the question as to whether there should be a separate gay
synagogue within the reformed movement of Judaism. One school of
thought believes homosexuals should not have their own synagogue—
that they are sinners and should not be separate but a part of the
community. They are the ones who constantly refer gay men and
women to psychiatrists for cures. The other school of thought says
yes, there should be a gay synagogue because there is tradition to support its establishment. That "tradition" is a European synagogue
established specifically for thieves. This is the school of thought that
prevails. Those who support it are liberals until they find out it is
their rabbi or son who is gay. Then, they can't deal with it. In other
words, there is no place for homosexuals within Judaism.

*Why do you think this is? Why is Jewish law/tradition so anti-
homosexual?*

It flies in the face of the family, which is the building block of all
religions. Who supports religion? People. Without people, religion
falls apart. We are all here supposedly to propagate—to perpetuate
the race. Millennia ago, it involved siring a male child who would
grow up to become a warrior and thus protect the people and their
land. Incidentally, just as homosexuality threatens this structure—
the family—so does the single person in Judaism: the Torah views a
woman without children as "a dead person" who must therefore be
divorced by her husband after a period of time.

What is your view on homosexuality?

That it is as valid a form of sexuality as hetero- or bisexuality. I believe
its cause can be genetic but also environmental, meaning traumatic
events in childhood that disturb a child's development. Regarding
the latter, I believe these traumas can be worked through so that the
homosexual can lead as valid and productive a life as any.

Has your life been "valid" and "productive"?

Neither as valid nor as productive as I would like. When one is young,
one does many things that one would not do again if given the chance
—"things" that were neither valid nor productive but which seemed

so then. Yet, I regret nothing, except perhaps my father's beatings. All else was a learning experience.

Where were you formally educated?

Israel, the U.S., France and Russia. I hold master's degrees in history, Soviet affairs, linguistics and comparative literature. I also have an informal "degree" in drug usage. While attending an Ivy college here in the '60s, I experimented frequently with acid, opium and grass. That experimentation lasted over a period of months, during which I had several positive and no negative experiences.

What, if anything, did you discover with or about drug usage?

That although it is a useful tool to get into one's head, it is not as useful, for me, as fasting and meditation. They, more than drugs, because they are severe disciplines, put me much more in touch with those things that were either hidden from me or which I did not wish to see.

Such as?

Self—who I was. Several acid trips introduced me briefly to the core of me, but fasting and meditation put me right there. I saw that I was a very vulnerable youngster with a need for acceptance and love and with a fear of never receiving either. I also saw I was a person of strength, which I used in order to survive what was often a brutal childhood. I saw how this childhood created a defensive man who set up barriers in order to escape hurt. Lastly, I saw what a romantic, light-headed child I could be. I was in love with love. I was also in love with men, particularly Yehuda, the Israeli boy for whom I had developed a passion when I was nine. Six years later, while studying in the U.S., I met him on the street. He was a student at Princeton. Within the month, we were lovers. We would still be lovers, I suspect, had he not been killed in the Yom Kippur war thirteen years later.

   Yehuda was the most special person in my life, although he was not the only person in my life. During our years together, there was also Kevin, my American lover, who I lived with in New York when Yehuda was in Jerusalem. I loved both men intensely. Obviously I believe that possible. And why shouldn't it be? Why shouldn't one be able to love two beautiful people? And they were beautiful far beyond the physical. But I wouldn't want to experience that again. I don't think I could go through the mental, emotional and physical gymnastics of two concurrent consuming loves again. For part of this time I was also married to Susan. Thus, life was—how shall we say—complicated.

> *When you say you loved both men intensely, why was that? What made them special?*

Their minds. Both were brilliant men. Their interests were myriad. They were both very decent people and passionate about life. Kevin was a psychologist whose greatest strength was then my greatest weakness. He could feel. My feelings had been shut off for so long that Kevin had to pry them open. He used all of his professional skill to do so. He changed me greatly. It is one thing to intellectualize about your life—why you-are-as-you-are and how you *think* about all that has been and what is—and it is quite another to *feel* it. Kevin liberated my feelings. He also liberated me from my body. He was the first man to penetrate me sexually. I couldn't abide that previously. Nor could Yehuda. Anal intercourse is not something Israeli men do as a rule. It's a macho thing—a fear of being reduced to the feminine. The idea of getting fucked repulses them. Or so they think. Then, too, Israelis have this fear of being in another's control. They do not like to be vulnerable. To be penetrated from the rear is to be vulnerable. Again, their fear is understandable. As close as Yehuda and I had been for the thirteen years we shared, he could not even discuss anal intercourse without feeling threatened.

> *Would you and Yehuda have lived together in Israel had he not been killed?*

Probably not, as Yehuda would have married. That is very common in Israel. Gay men never live openly with one another but marry instead and either run around on the side or have an understanding with their wives. Gay men in Israel usually have a series of lovers rather than a series of one-night stands, mainly because it is difficult to meet a wide variety of available men and equally difficult to find someplace to go once you have found them. Single people living alone are a rarity in Israel, which has a housing shortage. So, an Israeli gay usually moves from one affair to another and these affairs can last for weeks to years.

Is there much homosexuality in Israel?

According to the government, there is none. Yet, they keep lists of known deviants; what they do with these lists I do not know. In fact, there is a large gay community in Israel but it remains in the closet. Many gays who accumulate money leave Israel because to be gay in Israel is such a hassle. Yet these men, once free of the restrictions, still live closeted lives once established in another country. That's how deep the paranoia about homosexuality is imbedded.

What about those who remain? Can they live openly as homosexuals?

Very few do. Only those who are immensely wealthy or terribly creative. And even they are barely tolerated. The minute I became known as a declared homosexual, I became a person to be avoided.

Are there meeting places for homosexuals in Israel?

Of course, only they are subtle. In Tel Aviv, there is Independence Park, which gets active with dog-walkers at night, and a few cafés along the Diezengoff, which is the city's major thoroughfare. There is also the park in Jerusalem and a few meeting places along the wharves in Haifa, but everything is very understated. We have no dance or leather or sex bars. Remember. We are talking about a country whose government insists that there are no homosexuals.

Is there an organized but underground gay community?

Yes. Exactly. It meets as salon society in which men from all walks of life congregate.

Is there any organized movement to take it out of the salon-closet and into public awareness?

Not at all. Homosexuals who are "out" are reviled by Israelis, including those Israelis who are gay.

Why?

Because you threaten their existence once you declare yourself—once you admit homosexuality exists. You cannot in Israel call attention to the fact that homosexuals live and breathe. All is done to avoid that awareness.

For the reasons you spoke of before—that homosexuality threatens the "family," God and country?

Exactly, which is ironic as I know of no gay man in Israel who does not deem it an honor to serve in the military. That is unheard of in Israel because of national pride. I also know of very few gay men who do not marry and provide the state with children. So, the whole thing is rubbish. All in all, other than Russia, where I have lived, I cannot think of a worse place to be homosexual.

Did you marry because of the custom you just described?

Mine was more parental insistence. I was nineteen. I had come of age. Tradition demanded that I marry. My father selected a girl for me, whom I rejected, which angered him greatly. I had to be married, with family, if I were to become a member of the Jewish community and if I were to be viewed as a man.

To this time, had you been exclusively homosexual?

Yes, although my dreams as an adolescent were usually about my making love with a woman. But strangely, at point of orgasm, she would turn into a man and I would wake up. I was of course worried about my ability to perform sexually with a woman, but once I married Susan, I had absolutely no trouble. And since the dissolution of my marriage, I have been involved with several women, two of whom I continue to be close to, sexually and otherwise.

Is a relationship with a woman as fulfilling as one with a man?

With these two women it is almost as fulfilling as it almost was with Yehuda and Kevin. I have yet to achieve that totally fulfilling relationship and I know why. It has to do with a lack within myself—a search for perfection and harmony—which I then look for in another. That cannot be.

In truth, sex with a woman is not equatable for me with sex with a man. For a relationship to work with a woman, it has to be on several levels. With a man, it can work on pure lust. With women, there must be a meaning beyond sex. A vagina doesn't turn me on, in itself. A cock does. Another truth: my emotional needs are stronger for a man and better satisfied by a man. I feel more connected, more whole, more fulfilled . . . safer with a man.

You seem to be involved in many relationships.

You noticed that. Sometimes I wonder how I get any work done. But I not only function best in a relationship, I cannot function outside of one. I have been alone for two nine-month periods, and although I did not suffer—was not morbid or lonely—I was not happy. I do not feel fulfilled unless sharing with someone. And I can share with more than one someone at the same time. I don't work well, sleep well or eat well when without a lover. I feel a part of me is missing. I feel unfulfilled. Despite my bouts with promiscuity—and they are frequent and long-lasting—I am a home person, a relationship man.

Are you with anyone now?

Ah yes, and have been for three years, although we do not as yet live together. His name is Mark and like my other lovers he is brilliant. There is an attitude he brings to his work and his life that is astounding. As an artist, he sees life and people in colors, fully, richly. He is a humanist and a very human man. We share the responsibility for the relationship. Neither of us is in control, except of our own lives. We maintain our individual power. We are good together because we complement our respective existences. Our lives intersect often but we are not bound up together. We have what is known today as an "open marriage."

Meaning fidelity is not important?

Is not necessary is a better word. One of my excesses—and it is that —is my lechery. I turn on easily. Yet, I am very jealous of Mark's affairs. So we have our problems but we work at them as best we can. Mark and I are particularly good together because we not only love one another but also respect one another. We like each other. We are friends. That can be all too rare in a love relationship. We also understand one another's weak areas. We both have an inner fear of being close. Mine is based on Avram's and Yehuda's deaths and Kevin's "defection" to psychoanalysis to cure himself of his homosexuality—all of which occurred in the same year! All the people I loved died and left me. After the first five months with Mark, when I realized I loved him, I walked out. I had to. Then, I couldn't risk loving another person who might reject me. But . . . nine months later, I asked that he take me back and he did. I don't think in terms of forever, but he's got me for life whether he knows it or not.

When you did marry, was she of your own choosing?

The convention was not, but the woman was. I met Rachel while working on one of my degrees in France. Physically, she was very appealing, a beautiful olive-skinned, almond-eyed, long-legged girl of ultra-orthodox upbringing, She was quite brilliant.

Did you love her?

No, but I did like her immensely. I entered my marriage hoping it would last. Initially, it was rewarding, as there is something very beautiful and exciting about two people learning to know one another intimately. For a short time, perhaps a year at most, our sex life was good. But then, as I began losing interest in her, I lost interest sexually. And she was demanding. I could not be there for her on that level—or on many other levels as it turned out. The second year of our marriage we lived in France, her native country. Weekdays I would live outside Tours *nervously* with Rachel, but weekends, I would live in Tours, ostensibly to study art and drawing but mainly to be with Yehuda, who was there working on one of his advanced degrees.

Did this double existence have an effect upon you?

If you call feeling schizophrenic an effect. I could never relax with Rachel, never stop feeling I was doing something wrong. And I was. I was being dishonest. The guilt I felt spilled into the marriage in the form of hostility. The more she moved toward me, the more I withdrew. Within a year, I had a peptic ulcer and colitis. In the third year of our marriage, when I was living and studying in Yugoslavia, while she was still in France, I settled into a deep depression. For a month I could not function. It was then I knew I had to make changes. I flew to France and asked Rachel for a divorce. She became hysterical. "But what will my parents say?" was her main concern. Which tells you volumes about her. But then, she had never loved me but did love being the wife of Rabbi Josef Ben Ami, the supposed successor to my father's Hasidic dynasty. Like my mother, who could not let go of me, Rachel, too, had made me the focus of her existence. I was the source of her identification. She did not want to give me a divorce.

What changed her mind?

That great persuader—money. She took me for every cent I had, and I had made a great deal of money—$40,000 per year—as a translator. Then, too, my father had settled considerable money upon us when we married. I gave it all to her. I had to. I could no longer live with someone I didn't love. Our marriage was a farce, a travesty, a setup to satisfy my father and society but not me—not my needs or hers. In that respect it was worth the money to be free. It alleviated much of my guilt. I gave her X dollars for X years. She was satisfied. The "retribution" was just.

Did you ever tell Rachel of your homosexuality?

Yes. After the divorce. She viewed it as an unspeakable abomination. She was very ugly about it. We now have a formal relationship, one that exists only because we share a son who was conceived only months before I decided to ask for a divorce. Our relationship today —mine and Rachel's, that is—is purely legal and economic. I do not like her. Nor does she like me. I would prefer to have nothing to do with her, but my son makes that impossible.

What is the nature of your relationship with your son?

Far different from what I knew with my father. Since his being overseas prevents my seeing my son too frequently, when I am there I listen to Philip, talk to Philip, play with Philip. When I am with him, I *am* with him, loving him in a way quite set apart from the way I love any other. He is being raised as a Hasidic Jew and I am pleased, because the education of the mind is quite extensive at the Yeshiva. But he is not confined just to that world. When we are together, we visit museums, art galleries, amusement parks. I also challenge his "Jewish thinking" and try to help him see things from more than just one point of view. He is being educated for all worlds.

Will you discuss your sexuality with your son?

Someday, because I want him to know his father and since my sexuality is part of me, then he must know it. I worry very much how he will accept it. I would be most upset if he rejected me. You see, not only do I love my son but I like him. He is a good kid on the way to becoming a good man.

Do you have special hopes for him?

Only that he be what he wishes to be. I was never allowed to dream of becoming anything other than a rabbi. I wanted to paint and to sculpt. My mother wanted me to be a modern, progressive but religious academic. My father wanted me to be a Talmudist as he was. It took me years to vow that neither could or would make me into either. Hopefully, my son will be his own person, one who is a thinking, feeling human being, one who is open to ideas and change. I hope he will find his own meaning to life. I also hope he will be kind, nice and most of all, himself. If "himself" turns out to be homosexual, I would try to help him through that crisis—and that's what it is—by being there to support him. Frankly, although I do not care what his sexuality is, I shudder to think of his being gay. I would not want my son to go through what generations of homosexuals have endured—the humiliation, castigation, guilt and rejection heaped upon them by a frightened society.

You say that with considerable bitterness.

I have reason. Do you know when I declared myself to my mother I was a year away from obtaining my Ph.D. from a major Hebrew college. I had to drop out because she was so outraged that I was screwing with whom *I* wanted to screw and with *my* body that she insisted I immediately repay her the $15,000 she had loaned me for my education. Which I did, incidentally. Every penny of it. But upon applying for readmission a year later and after I had helped found the gay synagogue, serving as their rabbi for three months, I was denied entrance. A board of rabbis "examined" me and then sent me to a Freudian psychiatrist. After my consultation with him, the dean told me I would need to spend two years in psychiatry and then, if pronounced cured, I would be readmitted to school. But he would not tell me "cured" of what, although I asked. In fact, he would not respond to any of my questions about my interrogation. Just this: "Get thee cured!" So I never finished my formal work on my Ph.D. I am still angry that it was denied me.

What prompted you to help organize a synagogue for homosexuals?

The need. The Jewish community does not exactly rush to welcome gays into their synagogue. Actually, gays who wish to be Jewish have no place within Judaism to worship unless they deny their sexuality. I felt these gays had a right to a place of worship where they could be both Jews and homosexuals. And it could no longer wait. There were too many Jewish homosexuals who felt cut off from any connection with Judaism. They evidenced their need for that connection. The first Friday night we opened our doors for services, over a hundred men and women came to worship. Today, the largest number of Jews in America to attend the Friday night service does so at the gay synagogue in Soho. And the total congregation numbers a thousand.

How do you start a congregation for homosexuals?

You open your doors and say "Hey, gay!" You advertise in gay publications and spread the word around in bars and baths. News like
that travels fast. Particularly to the straight community. I was severely
chastised for my actions and in particular by my fellow gay rabbis, of
which there are many. All insisted I should have waited until I was
more established, more of a power. It was all bullshit, including the
banishment I felt from the established Jewish community. Suddenly
I was persona non grata. Men who had known me for years—gay and
otherwise—didn't acknowledge me any longer. Particularly those
Israeli gays who were situated prominently within the government. It
was like I carried plague.

So if I sound "bitter" as you put it, you should pardon me. Perhaps
others will be bitter too when they learn there were those within the
Jewish establishment who could have helped the movement but
didn't. Instead, they rushed to their closets and hid. And when they
stopped hiding, they were the loudest of the castigators.

And yet you maintain your Judaism.

And why not? I was born Jewish—I am Jewish—I feel Jewish and I
act within the Jewish traditions. I choose to jew. I choose to observe
those Jewish rites and rituals that have meaning for me. To jew is to
act in accordance with those traditions which give my life meaning.
The roots of Judaism are closely connected to the earth and to nature.
Judaism is a way of life in which one can find not only a social or
economic code but also a manner with which one can approach the
natural world. I observe the High Holy Days. They come at a time of
change—from summer to autumn. I celebrate that change. Purim is
the death of winter; Passover, the birth of spring. I celebrate these
changes with the community. I rejoice in the gift of change that the
gift of nature brings. I fast on Yom Kippur, the day of atonement, because fasting changes my consciousness and makes me more aware of
my commitment to a specific set of values. I examine my values that
day and I atone for my sins—not to God but to me and the world,
or . . . to the process, in other words. My need is to be part of this
process and to feel close to my fellow man. This is why I do not wish
to have another congregation. I tried it for a year—from September of
'72 to September of '73—and I did not like it. I am not a diplomat
or politician. I do not like the distance created by the title of rabbi.

People felt threatened by my title. I want to be with, work with the people. You know, one does not need to be a congregational rabbi but can be a teacher, administrator or bureaucrat. I wish to teach and I have several students now whom I instruct in Hebrew and Russian. I also have conversion students—those people changing from whatever their faith happens to be to Judaism. Teaching is like drawing breath to me. I love it. I need it. I love watching minds grasp meaning.

Are there other things you might do in addition to teaching?

It is not a question of "might do." I am today both a painter and a sculptor. I also do translations of texts from Russian, Hebrew, French and German to English. I have also had published two books of poetry and several short stories. I am currently working on a history of Yiddish theater in the United States and another on the fate of homosexuals in Nazi Germany. Lastly, and perhaps most important, I am preparing a "How to Handle Your Feelings" type of book for youngsters who suddenly find they are attracted to their own sex. Of course, it almost needs no stating, but I will continue to be active in the gay movement, continue to try to effect change and reform within the Jewish and American communities and within the gay community itself.

Regarding the last, what change and reform would you encourage?

Because homosexuals have been alienated, not by choice, from the mainstream, this has frequently resulted in their being alienated from themselves. To survive in a straight world, many homosexuals must hide and lie—must go underground. There is a price paid for such subterfuge and that price is often the repression of one's true feelings. Many gays are out of touch with what they feel. They are naïve enough to think they have escaped without scars from the brutal treatment they have received from the time they were old enough to recognize they were different. The guilt they were made to feel for their sexuality—even before they may have acknowledged that sexuality to themselves—had to go somewhere. Usually, it went within. Eventually, it had to come out. Unfortunately, much of the homosexual's guilt is being acted out upon himself and his brothers. Many homosexuals live frustrated lives without being aware they are frustrated. Collectively, we must look at our gay culture as it now exists. What are we really saying about ourselves as we participate in sex bars. What are we saying about ourselves when we court danger and punishment by engaging in sex in public places. What are the causes and effects of the rather widespread use of S&M? What are we really saying about ourselves, our bodies and those of our brothers when we engage in watersports or fist-fucking? And we must examine our tendency to objectify one another—to seek the fantasy rather than enjoy the reality. We must also look at our relationships with lovers and friends. It begins of course with looking at oneself. And that is difficult. I do not believe the gay community has as yet truly sat down with itself and looked at these issues and sought answers. I don't think we have given ourselves or gained for ourselves self-respect. We cannot expect change in attitude from the straight world until we change within and amongst ourselves.

What about change in attitude within the Jewish community?
I think "*Oi vey*" is appropriate here. That change is not within the near future. There needs to be a complete revamping of Jewish life in order that it adapt more fully to the twentieth century in view of the social changes man has undergone. Jewish life and thought must modernize. Values that may have been valid at one time are no longer valid today. The Jewish view of homosexuality was always invalid. The Jewish community must acknowledge that homosexuals exist rather than deny it. Yet as recently as September, 1976, at the eighty-seventh convention of the Central Conference of American Rabbis, the rabbinic arm of the Reform movement of Judaism refused to confront a resolution supporting the civil rights and civil liberties of homosexuals. The issue was tabled to a committee for further study. The young radical rabbis, straight and gay, who were in favor of this resolution left the conference on written record as "fearful" of a massive witch hunt to rid the rabbinate of homosexuals. And that is a possibility. The answer of course would be in the coming out of all those Jewish leaders who are gay. Then change would happen overnight. But that is not likely to happen. They know that should they come out, there would not be a welcoming committee. Quite the contrary. All this is very upsetting. It infuriates me that there continue to be forces at work that try to make me feel bad, and which do make many young people feel bad, about homosexuality. I believe if any sin is being committed today it is by those within the rabbinical, medical and political professions who could effect change but who don't. They are remiss in their duties and guilty of crimes against mankind.

Yet I know that within Judaism, always the struggle for modernity is slow. I fear that the vast majority of Jewish homosexuals will remain alienated from their religion for many years. Organized gay synagogues are a step but until those in power within the Jewish establishment come to an awareness of the problem, there will be no acceptance.

Do you foresee a gay rights bill becoming a state-by-state occurrence within the near future?

I do not. I am frankly very pessimistic about homosexual rights being advanced in this country. What I am hopeful of, despite the pope's official Vatican position, are changes occurring within the church in its views on homosexuality. There are today a number of priests who are also theologians, who are not being prevented from investigating homosexuality. I do believe the first significant changes in thought and attitude will occur within the church.

I also do not see a consolidation of homosexual forces in the U.S., at least not immediately. There is still too much fear—too much concern for status and privilege for that to take place. It still costs too much to come out publicly. There are still too many retributions, social and economic. Yet, if you think of the power we, as homosexuals, would wield politically and economically if we came out and banded together—demanded our rights—the possibilities are staggering!

Do you have any regrets about having come out?

Not a one! The essential thing for me is to give my life meaning and to bring meaning to my life. I must seek change. I must contribute. My life is about fulfillment. I must be there for others and I must have others who will be there for me. To do any of the above, I must be there, accepting, for and of myself. So I have no regrets. I choose to be me and that includes *all* that I am, part of which is homosexual and part of which is Jewish. I rejoice in both.

Mark Rosen

In a small studio within WBAI, a New York FM radio
station, three men, surrounded by coffee containers and ashtrays
heaped with droppings, discuss "a Jewish gay identity." One interviewee is a sweet-faced, curly-haired young man of medium build who
speaks very softly but with an impact that causes the others to listen
that much more intently. His name is Mark Rosen.* He is a set designer, mainly for opera companies throughout the U.S. He does not
look Jewish. Nor does he look or act militant about his homosexuality.
He is, in fact, ultraconservative in dress and style. His home is a
book- and picture-laden loft in Soho, a Lower East Side neighborhood
in New York. Mark became interested and active in gay rights several
years ago and functioned both as a member and lecturer at the Gay
Academic Union.

When did you come out?

There was no exact date. In fact, it is an ongoing process. I still have
a certain fear of disclosure, as I have seen the hatred in others when
they speak of homosexuality or of someone who is gay.

Have you seen this in New York City?

Of course. But it exists far less in a major urban area than it does in
smaller cities that border on the rural. Recently, my work caused me
to pass through Augusta, Georgia. I walked into a local diner thinking nothing of the shoulder bag I wore. You would be very surprised
at how ugly the name-calling was.

What do you do in a situation like that?

You drink your coffee, eat your pie and pretend the ignorance doesn't
bother you. If you act well enough, summon all your dignity, reflect
it in the way you hold yourself, the taunting stops. But the memory
doesn't. Not ever. There remains enormous oppression of gays in this
country.

* See Author's Note, page xii.

Does there remain oppression of Jews?

Again, not in urban areas but in smaller sectors of the country, yes. My last name, which is decidedly Jewish, attracts a great deal of comment, mainly negative. Even among gays, I am vaguely aware that there exists some anti-Semitism, but I ignore it, just as I do snakes and other creepy-crawlies. Actually, among gays, I am more often than not sought after because of my Jewishness. There is this super-terrific myth—which I wouldn't want to shatter—that Jewish men make the best lovers. I'm sure it was started by a Jewish man.

Are you a practicing Jew?

Not at all. But I am Jewish. My religion is mainly that of a belief in a moral code that governs us all. Also, I see a structure, a form, to the universe. The beauty seems so ordered, so artfully created, that it makes me wonder about its creator. What I do believe in very strongly is the something within us all that is unifying. Man is a part of man. I feel that. What being a Jewish man means to me is more social and historical than religious. But . . . I am a Jew and to deny that would be the same as to deny my homosexuality. I would be denying me.

Do you think of yourself as militant?

God, no! Not the way you mean. I'm no longer active in the movement. And yet, I am. I see my life as a political statement. I see my being a gay, Jewish artist from New York City as a statement with far-ranging aftershocks. I have to defend my place in society for all the things I am. My very existence is political in that society has to be shaped if I am to exist in it. I am still an outlaw in this country because of my sexuality. As a homosexual, I have no place to fight that. I am vulnerable. Thus, my main way of being politically active is the way all gay persons should be: I listen to what the politicians say about gay rights and only vote for those who promise to further what should be mine-without-asking—the right to live and love as I choose.

Do you think the homosexual community is politically aware?

Not at all. Which is unfortunate, because the day we are politically cohesive is the day changes will be radically made. But I fear a plot prevents this from happening.

What kind of a plot?

Take a look around the major cities of this country. An amazing thing is happening. There are dozens of sex bars, truck stops, bushes —all kinds of so-called "freedoms" which are against the law. Now I find that very strange. Many of my friends prefer to think of it as "sophistication," of an acceptance by straights. I think that is bullshit. I think there is a political plot to keep homosexuals promiscuous and —notorious. What is the straight world currently reading about us in magazines? How we fist-fuck. Which, of course, is only a minority occurrence, but the public is led to believe otherwise. How disgusting, they concur, and totally approve therefore that our rights be denied when they come up in a gay rights bill and are voted down, as they are each year.

The plot is to keep us cock-happy. Give the gays their meat—a chicken in every bed—and they'll never focus on the real issues. And that is what's happening. Think of the energy we are wasting in baths and sex bars that could be put to use in gaining real freedom and acceptance. But, until the gay community looks up from the cock it's sucking and gets its head together, we won't move one inch politically. But the day we give up those six to eight inches that fascinate us for the one inch that is more vital to our daily lives is the day we become a power to be reckoned with.

Is your work political? Do you make a statement there?

As a set designer, no. In my painting and drawing—sometimes. But it is not about that. Any statement I would make in my work is secondary to the statement I make as me. Who *I am* is what is important. I try to be honest, try to be me. My very being is a statement. Those people who then discover I am a homosexual and choose to reject me because of it are meaningless. But, there are some who begin to think, "Hey, I like this guy even if he does sleep on the other side of the bed." That's the way true change occurs, by removing the fear and replacing it with knowledge. People fear homosexuals for a variety of reasons. When they see who we are, that fear often dissipates.

From what you said earlier, I gather your coming out was not an easy happenstance. Why was that?

Coming out in this country is seldom if ever easy for anyone. We are not exactly made to feel welcome. From earliest childhood, I have had homosexual fantasies and from earliest childhood I have felt crippling, oppressive guilt because of them. Throughout my adolescence I suffered constantly because of "the secret," which was always denied. While attending Pratt, I came out so to speak. Over and over I wrote on a scrap of paper, "I am a homosexual!" When I stopped to look at it, I began crying hysterically. Although I had never had sex, I knew—without accepting—what I was. I did not like it. The only men I knew then who were gay were campus queens and they were all bitchy, obvious types. I didn't want to be anything like them. I couldn't see that kind of homosexuality leading to anything positive. So, I remained in the closet.

This guilt, felt early in childhood, where did it stem from?

I was programmed from an early age to respond in certain ways to many things. That includes homosexuality. It was an implied no-no. Its very absence from view made it so. Nowhere in childhood does one see two men living together as lovers. Oh no. From early on, you are programmed to believe that marriage between the sexes is the ultimate and that any deviation is exactly that—a deviation. Since my daydreams were always of men, I grew up feeling a deviate, which is such a crippling word and feeling to a child.

A word more about programming. Even my fantasies were programmed. The men I dreamed of were all Supermen types. That kind of man is programmed into our consciousness via print and TV. The Mighty-Man-of-Steel is the ideal. Today I look back on that bullshit with rage. That kind of programming makes it that much more difficult for the kid, straight or gay, who does not look like Superman—let alone feel like him. And in later years, it makes it that much more difficult to relate to the real man and to what makes a real man, which has nothing to do with muscles and steel but with personhood. Today, as I near thirty, I look back on the kid that I was at twenty-one and feel very little connection to him. He was awash in fantasy.

Are you saying fantasy plays no part in your life?

Very little. It certainly holds no interest for me sexually. That is one of the reasons the whole leather and western scene does nothing for me. It is all a fantasy trip. The Stud . . . The Big Butch . . . The Superman. He doesn't exist, but people still search either for him or to be like him. It's sad. For me, the ultimate in sex is not to fantasize my partner into anyone other than he is. The ultimate is in the knowing and then, in the knowing . . . the loving. Which is why I have little interest in sex bars or back rooms in sex bars. For me, there has to be the tiniest drop of love in the briefest bit of sex. Without that feeling, the sex doesn't fulfill me. Like a Chinese dinner, an hour later I'm hungry again.

When did you break free of your youthful inhibitions and guilt to become sexually active?

Very late. I was twenty-two, and my first was a woman despite my fantasizing about sex with a man. But the idea of sex with a man was not only threatening but confusing. I had no idea of what men did together. I sort of thought that maybe they fucked, but I couldn't understand how anyone could get any pleasure by being the passive partner. Even sex with a woman was difficult because I couldn't fathom how a relationship moved from the social to the sexual. In other words, how did one get from the living room to the bedroom? From eighteen on, there were always girls willing to show me how, but I was too insecure.

What "technique" was employed to make you more secure?

I was carefully and sensitively seduced. I had come to England after the most miserable of years of graduate school in New York to earn a design degree from a major English university. I had been so lonely, so cutoff in America, and was truly desperate for human contact. I began having fun in England. Real fun. The English and the Europeans seemed so much more relaxed about sex than we Americans. One of my classmates was a lovely English girl who would walk me to the park each lunchtime and we would share bread, cheese and wine. After several weeks of this, she took my hand one afternoon and walked me to her apartment. I was terrified. I had no sexual urge. But we made love despite my difficulties in keeping an erection. When it was over, I cried . . . from relief. But I was sure it wasn't something I would ever want to do again. Yet, the following weekend, while away in the country, we not only did it again but again and again and again. It was habit forming. I couldn't get enough of her.

And then one day, she was gone; she had run off to Rome with a musician, leaving me the typical jilted lover, bleeding from every pore. That led to my other "first"—Barry. Also a classmate, Barry, too, had just ended a "relationship," as he called it, never identifying the sex of the other person, and was as miserable as I was. So we commiserated with one another. My friends at school kept telling me to avoid him, but I was so naïve that I was unaware he was seducing me until I was seduced. Then, you see, it was beyond me to believe that such an imposing and sophisticated man would be attracted to me. But he was. The "denouement" took place one night when we were invited to a late supper, so late that by its conclusion, all public transportation had stopped for the evening. Since Barry and I were both too poor to spring for a taxi, we stayed over at our host's home. There was only one double bed in the room, which I crawled into fully dressed, maintaining it was cold in the house. By morning, I shed some clothes and enough inhibitions for us to make love. The sex was hardly inspired. In fact, it was dull. A plain old-fashioned handjob. But I was very pleased that it had happened. I had enjoyed the affection, if not the sex. I felt no guilt. Nor, I must add, did I feel any great awakening.

What had you expected to feel?

Lightning, thunder, drums and a Bach cantata. I didn't get it, then or ever, although I sure did get a lot of sex over the next three months, sex that began to improve with age—and practice. Oral sex, when performed on me, I enjoyed. Although I participated, it didn't knock me out. It still doesn't. Even today if I find my head in someone's crotch, I'll do what's pleasing for the other person but it is not a turn-on. Sex is best for me when I can maintain eye contact. I need to see my lover's reaction. In fucking, that's possible. Of course then, my getting fucked amounted to a brief insertion of the head of the cock before I froze and yelled "Halt!" I was a goddamn professional Jewish virgin. It took me years before I could be successfully screwed and then it took a rabbi to do it!

What were your feelings for Barry?

I loved him, although initially I could not admit that to myself. He was very bright, vigorous, actively involved in life and the gay movement. He also exuded sexuality. He was very much in touch with and in control of himself. He was a dominating presence, so much so that after six months I left him. I couldn't handle my feelings for him. Actually, I had begun to leave him after the first four months. It was then I started dating Allison. I was making my last-ditch effort—although I didn't know that then—at a heterosexual relationship with her. But it was not that cut and dried. She was a beautiful, dynamic girl with whom I made wonderful love . . . very creative and exciting and yet, although more sensual than what I had known with Barry, not as passionate. I loved sleeping with Allison. I also loved the relationship—more, I suspect, than I did her. We lived together until one day, after several months, she announced it was over. Again I was left with nothing other than a suicidal-like depression. It's really a bitch being young.

And what of Barry during this time?

He was pissed as hell when I left him. I can't say I blame him. I was callous . . . cruel. But I learned during our separation and the time that followed Allison's leaving that I did love him. It took me months to win back his trust, but eventually we took an apartment and became "recognizable" lovers. In other words, everyone at school *recognized* our relationship for what it was. And I must say, my worst fears about coming out proved to be justified. Suddenly, friends I had known for several semesters cut me from their lives. Then, that kind of rejection hurt me deeply. Today, those people who would reject me because of my sexuality hold no interest for me and thus cannot hurt me—with one exception: my parents.

They do not know of your homosexuality?

They know but they don't know. My father once picked up a Valentine's Day card from Josef.

Josef?

My lover, the rabbi. It was signed "With all my love." So they know, but it is not something they choose to discuss.

That they don't choose to discuss or that you don't choose to discuss?

Both. I have trouble discussing sex, of any kind, with my parents. They were never overtly sexual people. Sex was never discussed, or alluded to, in our home. So it makes me angry that some think I should be discussing my homosexuality with my parents. Why? They never discussed their sexuality or any other with me, so why should I be discussing my own? Telling them would only produce chaos. My mother would immediately assume blame. She would see my homosexuality as some kind of terrible illness.

Yet, there is a part of me that resents my not openly acknowledging to them that Josef is my lover. I feel I should. I feel I detract something from the relationship by not. Thus, as I said, coming out is a long-term process in some cases. With my parents, I've yet to achieve an adult role. A part of me that I do not yet understand is afraid to say, "Hey, I'm an adult who sucks-and-fucks . . . a sexual being." I don't know why this fear exists, but God knows it took me long enough to acknowledge my sexuality, so I can understand my still denying it to them—understand it but not condone it. Furthermore, a part of me continues to blame them for my having denied my sexuality for so long.

Why?

Because of their denial of sexuality which caused me to deny my own. Because of their inability to share feelings with me which caused me not to share my feelings with them, or anyone else. I was always aware of my "differences." My earliest daydreams were of older boys and me together in some romantic way. It was always my secret, one which caused me great confusion and unhappiness. I always had lots of friends, but my "secret" wasn't something I could discuss. It eventually alienated me from my peers even as I continued to be part of a peer group. I was never alone but I was always lonely. I was also never happy. I didn't like me. I thought I was a bad person because I was a boy dreaming about an affair with Superman. Funny, the idea of being a boy in love with another male was so unacceptable to me then that in my fantasies I would turn me into a woman to make the situation less threatening.

Can you trace the derivation of this early nonacceptance of your homosexual feelings?

As I mentioned, when you don't see something about you, you assume it is omitted because it is "Not Good" for you. The absence of men-loving-men in my childhood had me mistakenly interpreting it as an evil. Then, too, one summer afternoon when I was six or seven, we were at Jones Beach when a group of very obvious gays passed us and my mother hooted and howled. That tone, that derision stayed with me. In some way, the child I was knew those men, like me, were boys who loved men. I never wanted to be hooted at in that fashion. So I hid my feelings and truly grew up with no one to relate to.

Did you share any feelings with either parent?

No. I was very affectionate and cuddly with my mother, but I never had a sense of communication with her. Actually, I listened to her, gave her advice, rather than the reverse. My father was a very hard-working man, an executive, with whom I had little to no relationship. By seven and eight, I was already a creative and artistic child, which seemed to alienate me from my father, who was very businesslike and to the point. My mother was much more in tune with my interests. But funnily enough, today, I'm much more like my father. Like him, I have a high tolerance level and am seemingly quite mild. Like him, when provoked, I've got a helluva temper. My father is a very nice man. But when I was a child, I was very angry at him. I was forced into Hebrew school, the Cub Scouts, summer camp and piano lessons—none of which I wanted. But my mother would say, "Your father and I have decided that you *should*. . . ." I always resented the rules of my childhood which she enforced but with his blessings. There were more "shoulds" and "oughts" than any child should ever know. I became a very good boy. Sometimes I think that when I was a very young child they must have said, "Ye shall see and hear nothing of sex." It's incredible that I remember nothing despite my having slept in the same room with my parents until I was six. They must have had sex at least once during that time. I must have heard . . . must have seen . . . but I remember nothing.

Why does that bother you?

Because I think somewhere in that stems my own repressed sexuality. Do you know in all my youthful masturbatory fantasies, sex never occurs!

At what age did your masturbatory fantasies begin?

Exactly when I don't know, but it was very early. But they were always romantic rather than sexual. I was always Lois Lane to Clark Kent or . . . I was always Clark Kent to Lois Lane. In other words, I would shift back and forth and be both persons in my fantasies. Later, as a teen, I used visual materials—pictures of Charles Atlas types—as I masturbated. I know this is incredible, but I didn't start thinking about specific sex acts while masturbating until after I came out.

Was there then no homosexual activity in your adolescence?

There was no sexual activity, period! Although I had crushes on several girls in high school, I didn't date. That wasn't encouraged. We did go out in groups, however, but when it came to pairing off, I never did. I once nearly pledged a fraternity, but I chickened out when I visited the frat house and saw couples, in a dimly lit room, making out. That terrified me. Overt sex of any kind terrified me.

Funny, in looking back I can see a great deal of humor in one young man's repressed sexuality. But then, it was not funny. Actually, until England and Barry, I was in terrible pain . . . awful pain . . . the pain of loneliness, of alienation, of wanting without knowing what was wanted. But when I returned to Barry, when I lived openly with him, when I acknowledged that I loved him, all the pain went away. Suddenly, I felt good. Better than good—I felt whole. All my walls against homosexuality came tumbling down. How could it be bad when love felt so good. By the way, my "coming out" and self-acceptance was largely due to my work—and that's what it was—with LSD.

Was this an on-campus thing to do?

Yes, but I was not involved in the indescriminate dropping of acid. I worked with a woman who had used LSD in controlled scientific experiments at Berkeley to expand her own consciousness. With her, I tripped several times over a period of months. Acid helped me to peek into a lot of dark corners.

What did you see?

That contrary to what I had felt, I was not a horror . . . not an evil person. I saw that I was essentially good but that my warped viewpoint of homosexuality had turned me against myself. LSD helped me to higher levels of consciousness. It helped me reevaluate everything I ever thought and felt about myself. It freed me.

But before the wrong impression is given, I am not pushing acid. I never dropped it for kicks—only for mind expansion. My last trip was three years ago. I will only do it again when I feel there are new corners to be invaded.

Were there any side effects from taking acid?

Not the kind you are referring to. I never freaked out or had a delayed trip. The only "side effect" was the reevaluation of my relationship with Barry. As I sexually freed myself, I was also freeing the other parts of me that had been subdued. I had always assumed a passive role—not sexually but otherwise—thinking Barry, and others, were more intelligent or knowledgeable. In fact, one of my main attractions to Barry initially was his overt coming out—his activity with the movement and with all the people within it. But the damnedest thing happened when we got together. He became inactive. He became a homebody. Which was not at all what I wanted. I had hoped he would introduce me to the gay community. I needed to learn who they were and what they were about. Thus, Barry and I were at odds as to life-style.

How did you solve this problem?

Initially by denying there was one. Until I had peeked extensively into those dark corners, I was overwhelmed that someone like Barry could love me. I still felt very unworthy. That made me compromise myself until I changed. At the end of a year, Barry took off to work for a time in Israel and to his amazement I stayed to take full advantage of a grant I had been awarded from the English Arts Council to do design at a theater in Sheffield. Despite my missing Barry for the year we were separated, Sheffield was a wonderful time of expression for me. I loved my work and it was there that my search for excellence began. It's been a never-ending search, I might add. I never seem to achieve in my work exactly what I set out to.

Which is?

The old clichés—truth and beauty. They are equally hard to find, on a continuum in a relationship, I might add. I joined Barry in Israel immediately after my one-year grant expired. From the moment I stepped off the plane, it was a disaster. I moved to hug him and he gently pushed me away, saying, "That isn't done in Israel." I couldn't believe it. Barry, the Gay Libber, uptight?

But it was Israel, and I soon saw that when it came to homosexuality, everyone was uptight. What a bunch of macho messes! Closet cases, all. Yet, Barry and I lived openly as a couple and we were never hassled, except by one another. We fought constantly that year. I now understand why. I was truly coming out and not just sexually. I could no longer be submissive. When he went to London where a prominent gallery had offered him a job, I returned to New York. Although we never officially terminated our relationship, I do remember feeling as I stepped off the plane at Kennedy as though a huge weight had been lifted from me. I felt free. I liked the feeling.

This was the first time as a homosexual you had been a "single."
Were there any adjustments you had to make?

No. The first year I still felt like Barry's lover, despite his being in England and my being in America. That didn't change until we acknowledged that the relationship as we had known it had ended.

But I was not living a celibate life during that time. I was taking a good look around and learning. I became active with the Gay Academic Union and I joined a gay consciousness-raising group. I began meeting lots of men and enjoying a sexual freedom I had never known. I was finding my gay identity as I was defining me. And it was great. The consciousness-raising group was a mind-blower. And, by the way, that's all that got blown in that group. To keep issues unclouded, we kept sex out of the group. It was incredible—sitting down with a bunch of guys and listening to them talk about real issues in their lives, sharing the experience of being gay in a not-very-gay world. It gave me a connection that I had not had. It made me realize I was not unique—that there were many decent men who had been made to feel indecent and were now coming out of that. It made me angry at straight society for having put us through hell—for *still* putting us through hell. It gave me great pride to sit with these men and *feel* what they had to say. I saw that gay could indeed be good, could indeed be proud. Like with any other sexuality, it solely depended on the person. I saw how many gay men were concerned citizens, fighting to humanize gay society and bring meaning to lives where previously there had been none. The group was one of the most meaningful experiences of my life. It taught me that men can share their souls as well as their bodies and that one doesn't have to include the other.

The Gay Academic Union was somewhat different. Although I both attended and gave several lectures, I never quite found my niche. I did demonstrate frequently, however, and was very much involved in the collective coming out, but eventually my life changed and there was little room for involvement with the G.A.U. Although I am still political, I am more aware today of reaffirming a place for myself in society. My work has become my avenue for doing that. It is enormously important to me and my energies are poured into it.

What does your work mean to you?

Well, previously I spoke of "the quest"—the search for beauty and truth. But overall, it's about communication. In designing for theater, I'm part of a communal effort which I personally find exciting. I often see how the sum total of what five people create is greater than what one can conceive and execute. But my drawings express solely my feelings and experience. Yet I cannot define them. Hopefully, they make their own statement. I think, by the way, that Josef often interprets that statement as "Fuck off!" He resents the amount of time given to a project, often excluding him in the execution. He feels neglected. He often is. But I have learned from both my relationships with Barry and with Josef that I can no longer commit myself entirely. I must hold back a piece of me. A big piece. There are other needs I must satisfy. Besides, I have given up too much of me in the past for a relationship. Josef is a very strong man. He makes his statement from the moment he enters a room. He is a presence. Although I am flexible, I am no longer that flexible. I will no longer sacrifice my needs and my identity to massage a lover's ego.

How did you and Josef meet?

At a party and it was hate at first sight. Josef is a very intimidating man. I also found him a supercilious son of a bitch and totally dismissed him from consciousness. We met again weeks later and again, other than realizing that he was a very interesting man, I still wasn't interested. We mutually avoided one another. On a third meeting, also accidental, we began talking to, rather than at, one another. As I was leaving he growled, "You intimidate me!" I hooted, "*I* intimidate *you?*" And then, matter-of-factly, he said, "I'll call you." To which I said, "Do!" The son of a bitch then replied, "Well, maybe I will . . . I think I will." A week later, he did.

Had you a sense that this might evolve into a relationship?

Absolutely, which is why I was frightened of him. In fact, when we finally did go to bed, I was so wound and bound up by so many emotions that I couldn't achieve an orgasm. In fact, that happened the first three times I was with him, which bothered him but not me. I was absolutely gone on those deep, long-lasting soulful looks into one another's eyes. The lovemaking was far more important to me than the sex.

And sex, incidentally, has been a problem for us ever since. From the beginning, Josef said that because of his feelings for me, he could not have sex with me frequently—that he found it too emotionally draining. That got me nuts. How can sex with someone you love be draining? What also bothered me was knowing he was having sex elsewhere. Josef never pretended not to be promiscuous. He is comfortable in that life-style. I wasn't then but am now. So . . . we had our problems.

Were you able to discuss your problems?

We have always had that ability. Always. We can talk one another blue in the face and blue in the balls. We have never totally worked out our sexual problems or some others either. Basically, Josef is a Hasidic chauvinist. What he really needs is a wife who will stay home, do his bidding, glory in his existence and keep her mouth shut. That ain't me. So we fight like hell, and often I feel I am fighting for my life because I still have this irrational fear of losing me, of becoming the person I once was.

How long have you been together?

We've been on-and-off for three years nearing four. We have had one very long separation after we had been together for six or eight months. During that time, he had been badgering me to live with him. When I finally said that I would, he went running in more directions than I could follow. He panicked . . . ran out, left me without an explanation. Only later was I to learn that he was reacting to some terrible losses in his life. But then all I knew was that one day he was there; the next he was not.

It was a bitch of a time because I kept coming apart. And he didn't help any. Every week or so he would call, despite my asking him not to. It always ended with me in tears. I finally asked him never to call again—to just go away.

How did you deal with your pain?

By cruising every night. Those times I picked up an attractive person, I felt good. Those nights I came home alone, I felt terrible. The worse I felt, the more I cruised. It was a pain-killer. But I hated it. It really is not my style. The quickie doesn't work for me. And it is interesting that most men who are attracted to me seem to be so for more than a quick fuck. I attract the relationship-oriented man.

During this time, did you think to experience women again?

Yes, and I did. Each time it was pleasurable, but there was something essentially missing. Sex with men is just more satisfying for me. Particularly emotionally. A woman, although soft and warm, does not arouse the passion that a man does. I just don't feel that sense of completeness, of union, with a woman. To be downright honest, a woman can't fuck me for the simple fact that she lacks a cock. And I'm not much . . . in fact, I'm not anything at all when it comes to dildos. Sexually, I enjoy being active and passive. I like both joinings with my lover. But most important of the differences, I need a man's love more than I need a woman's.

When did you and Josef resume?

About nine months after we separated we gave birth to a reconciliation that is still taking place two years later. Of course, it happened the night I moved into my new loft—set out on a new life of my own. The doorbell rang and there he stood. I should have thrown him out, but I handled it in typical fashion by falling into bed with him, making love so passionately that Josef fled. The truth! He got so frightened by the intensity of our feelings that he picked up his clothes and ran. He didn't call for a week. When he did, we got together in what is basically an "untogether" relationship that struggles and flounders.

Why?

Because I'm still hanging him for his crimes. I don't trust him. He had said he loved me and yet he damn near wrecked me.

Then why did you agree to the reconciliation?

I was so fucked up and miserable without him that I figured I better find out what's there when I'm with him. But . . . I continue to not trust him, although it is getting better; I continue to keep a part of me separate; and I allow him to put more into the workings of the relationship than I do. You see, I want the relationship to work, but I'm not willing to sacrifice anything for it—not my work, not me. I am still too angry, too hurt, too vulnerable.

What makes you hang in?

I believe he does love me, and I feel a very strong cosmic and emotional connection with him. I also like his image. It's not every day a nice Jewish boy like me gets to hook up with a rabbi.

I also like the private man, the one with that wonderfully quick mind, the rapid wit and the childlike spontaneity. He is also a very sexy man. I am very turned on by his uniqueness. I am also turned on by the fact that such a man is in love with me.

You have not used the word "love" in describing your feelings.

I still have difficulty freely admitting it. It is easier to say he is one-of-a-kind, a genius of sorts, and that I feel "chosen." But all my anger and resentment . . . yet, as soon as he puts that shiny face of his through the door I know I love him. That I do. I can actually view the long-range better than I can the now. I mean, I can see our future together better than I can this interim period. I can see how if my work stabilizes and if Josef stabilizes, then the relationship will too.

Is it possible that perhaps you also must stabilize?

Ouch! Methinks there is a statement in that question. But yes, you are right. I am still learning, still groping toward a greater self-aware-ness. I want to reach the goals I have set for myself and then seek new ones. It's hard to explain, but I don't believe I will ever reach a state of relaxation until death. Nor do I want to. There is too much to experience . . . too much to be, to relax. That's not to say I don't want to enjoy what is, or to pass over it, but now, today, the world and my possibilities within it seem limitless. I need to feel there is always another level of enjoyment somewhere up ahead.

On the today level, I must let go of the past. I see how afraid I am to be so hurt ever again. But that fear is preventing me from a close-ness I really want. But I just don't want any more holes driven through me. Yet . . . to live with barriers is not to live at all. So, I must soon let Josef off the hook and be open to him and us.

I gather you and Josef do not believe in fidelity?

No, although I used to. Now, I can't see where the sex we both indulge in has any bearing on our relationship. Also, at this point in my life, I think it would be unhealthy for me to concentrate all my energies on one person.

The man I call "lover" has a unique place in my life, but he need not be the only person to hold a place in my life. Sleeping around grows me. Relating to others, even on just a sexual level, is a mind-expanding experience. I know that sounds like bullshit but it's true. There's a certain etiquette you learn in bed, a certain sensitivity, a picking up of another's vibrations that allows you to understand others better.

Do you believe what you just said?

In part. I omitted two important factors in explaining why our rela-tionship is not monogamous. We both seem to need the ego reinforce-ment of having others want us and then, too, Josef needs that kind of freedom—he says—and I resent him less if I also indulge. I must admit there is a certain amount of confusion in my mind regarding our openly acting out our sexual desires. This kind of "open marriage" has its dangers. There is always the likelihood that one of us may meet someone who seems to be more "sympatico."

Ultimately, I do want a monogamous relationship, one that just "is" without having to think about it, to worry over, to work at. I'm speaking of a relationship without script where neither Josef nor I try to shove the other into roles we cannot play.

But the simple truth is, I want to be everything to someone without having to be. I want just one man on whom I can concentrate my energies—sexual and otherwise—and my love. I may have all that with Josef. I'm not so certain I'm very comfortable admitting it.

Donald Santini

A LEAN SIX-FOOTER with sandy hair worn in a military brush-cut, Donald Santini * looks like a recruitment poster for the Marines. Without trying, he makes a physical statement. His muscles bulge through T-shirt and denims that fit comfortably but not tightly.

When he was approached to be a subject for this book, Donald was in New York overseeing his first showing at a small but not unimportant Manhattan art gallery. He was courting the art patrons, wooing them with words, and, if necessary, the promise of sex. "Once a hustler always a hustler," he explains, referring to both his former and current professions. In agreeing to sit *still* for several sessions of talk—and for Donald, sitting still is difficult at best—he asked for one consideration: that his anonymity be preserved. "There's lots of small minds out there attached to some even smaller people," he explained. "Particularly in my hometown which is Hicksville, USA."

His idea of "Hicksville" is actually one of the most sophisticated of Southern cities. In it, he is a well-known restauranteur and raconteur, who is frequently asked to address the Elks or the Lions and the Legionaires. "I'm a local country boy who made good," he says, "and I like to talk about it." In point of fact, Donald Santini liked to talk. Period.

What made you consent so readily to these interviews?

I think it is important that people have an understanding of a lifestyle different from their own. Most people tend to think of homosexuals as flaming faggots, which isn't true. No one would ever suspect I'm gay and yet I do enjoy the best of both worlds.

You are bisexual, then?

Yes.

Is it important to you that no one would suspect you are gay?

What I do with my life is my business. I'm not ashamed of my

* See Author's Note, page xii.

sexuality, but I know damn well most people couldn't handle the knowledge with sophistication. They would make snide remarks. But I'm not uptight about being gay. I'm not the least bit feminine. In every way, I am a man. I'm very secure about that. My thinking is totally masculine.

What is masculine thinking?

Logical. Without being ruled by emotions. I'm a doer. I'm an action-oriented guy. I take over. I'm a very strong personality.

Were you always so?

Yes and no. Even as a kid, nobody pissed on me. But then it did matter to me that everyone liked me. I couldn't handle it at all if one kid said something mean about me. I also had to be super terrific.

Why?

Beats me. But I was always out there proving how great I was. On the field in sports or in the field, hunting with a gun. I sure couldn't prove nothing to nobody in school though. My education was lousy and I didn't have a case of the smarts. In the second grade I got messed up with my spelling 'cause they were experimenting with the new spelling. In the third grade, it was the new math and that passed by me too. I wasn't too hot a reader either. But I knew about God and his presence in all these things as I had a Catholic education up until the eighth grade. The nuns told me that if I didn't go on to a Catholic high school and college, I'd grow up to be an atheist.

Did you?

No, but I didn't go to no Catholic college either. By the time I had finished high school, the ecumenical council had turned Catholicism upside down and around and I was as confused about that as I was with the new math and new spelling.

Were your parents religious?

Not in the sense you mean. But my daddy was always setting down these strict moral codes of behavior. It was very important that I be a good Catholic boy and I was. I went to mass daily and I was both a choir and an altar boy. But my parents didn't attend church all that much. My ma did on Sundays, but my dad usually went hunting or fishing with his friends.

Did you ever go with him?

Never as much as I wanted to. He had this best buddy and they'd go off and I'd always feel bad about that as I loved to hunt and fish. We had the woods right out past our back door and a lake ran through it. I was always an outdoors kind of guy. And handy with my hands, too. I built me a tree house when I was a kid which all the other kids envied. But I envied a lot of them cause they seemed to do a lot of things with their daddys.

And you didn't?

Not so much—at least not as much as I wanted. He did most everything with this one best-buddy of his. It made me feel bad—like he didn't like me or something.

What did your father do for a living?

A sheet-metal worker. He made out okay. We were never hungry. We had us this big house right outside the city and we lived nice. We never went on vacations but we always had clean clothes. I seem to remember there being a lot of love in our house. My mama was very affectionate.

Were you close to her as a child?

If you knew anything about Italian-American families you'd know every son is close to his mama. My own thought her son should be king. I was her pride and joy. But she was very protective. Too protective. And smothering. Sometimes she'd embarrass me by thinking nothing of unzipping my pants in public just to tuck in my shirt. That and combing my hair and wiping my nose. She was all over me.

Do you remember that as a child?

I surely do. And I remember how pissed off it would get me. My mother never let me be like other boys. I had all kinds of regulations. And curfews. Like she was the only mother to take her child to the playground and wait for him. Then, she'd walk me home. And if I even fell or got into fights, she'd come running to protect me. I hated it. For a time I held it against her. Then, I moved that resentment to my father 'cause he allowed it. And he allowed her to force him into the same damn thing. Other kids could go to the swimming hole alone. Not me. My ole man had to be there to watch out for me. And I had to wear one of those dumb inner tubes around my waist.

I just never had any freedom. My mother was overbearing and dominating and my father was overbearing and noncommunicative. Rejecting, too. Always going off by himself or with his friends and leaving me with my ma.

What effect did all this have on you?

It just pissed me off. I didn't understand it. But it made me close to my ma because I felt she loved me. I stayed close to her until I was seventeen. Then, I kind of let go of her.

What happened?

I started to date and she would wait up for me. It was like an inquisition. What-did-you-do-where-did-you-go-did-you-touch-her-and-where. She only stopped when my father told her to. She made everything seem dirty—like I was doing bad things. Which was funny, because when I was much younger, it was my daddy who made me feel I was doing bad things. Like when I built me that tree house, he had one rule: *no girls.* He was sure I'd be doing bad things with them. That made me feel bad. 'Cause I was a good Catholic boy and I didn't even know what bad things were. He didn't seem to trust me though.

Why?

I don't know. I really don't. I think now it had to do with my father's own mistrust of himself. My daddy, with all his rules and strict moral codes, it turns out, has had himself a mistress all these years. Which was a shock 'cause I had thought my parents' marriage was a happy one. Actually, they made it work but happiness eluded them. My ma changed according to my dad. She had been a very physical woman when they first married but a hysterectomy changed all that. In fact, if you can believe him, she became frigid. But I don't believe that 'cause the only good stuff I ever heard about sex as a child came from my ma. She used to say it could be a very beautiful thing. Which was more than my father ever said. He never mentioned the word or the subject—told me when I was twelve that there was no point in his saying anything about it 'cause I probably knew everything anyway. Which wasn't true. I didn't know anything. My mother never said what it was about sex that could be beautiful, but for her to say anything was revolutionary in that family. My mother's main concerns were about money and possessions. You still can't buy her enough. But I like buying for her 'cause I love her. I think she has made her own bed and sleeps in it without too many regrets. And she sure as hell is proud of me. She's always introducing me as "my baby who owns that fancy restaurant in town."

That seems to please you.

Damn straight it does. It's a helluva accomplishment. My restaurant has been written up in *Gourmet, Holiday.* We're famous for all kinds of southern dishes.

Is this what you wanted?

It's what I got! I wanted to be a painter, but my father discouraged that. He didn't want no boy of his doing some sissy-thing like painting. To him, a man did tough things. My father beat me into manhood. Literally. I always thought he did that 'cause he thought I was weak. I had to learn to box and to rassle. I could never cry. I had to be strong. 'Cause that was my father. He never showed me no affection or tenderness. But he used to hit on me so I would learn not to cry, even when I was hurt. I used to think I was feminine, like my ma, 'cause I had feelings. Like it was bad to paint and bad to like flowers. Over and over he made me feel a man was like a rock. Even today, my relationships with men are based on my father's image.

Would you explain that?

Yeah, but let me go back a little. You see there are basic differences in a man's and a woman's nature. A mother instinctively loves her child, but a father feels little or nothing until the baby matures. Women are born mothers. They are the nurturers of the world, the stay-at-homes who keep the home together.

The women's libbers will not exactly love the statement.

Fuck them! They're fools. They *think* they want to run the show. I tell every man who has a woman thinking she wants to be liberated to let her run the entire works. Within five minutes, she'll discover she'll never want to do that again and you'll have yourself a helluva woman. A woman is an extension of a man's ego and personality. And they are wonderful in what they do.

What do they do?

Womanly things that us men can't do. Like Dinah, my woman, she is my hostess. All men of position need this. She cares for my home and for me. She sets a proper table, plans a proper menu. And she is beautiful on my arm. She does me proud when we go out. She has replaced my mother in my life. And I used to think that was impossible. I had to have my mother as I could never cook, sew or do any of those things that women do so well for their men. Before Dinah, I ate badly and my underwear was stained. I needed taking care of. I needed *that* kind of love. And only a woman can give it.

> *You could be talking about a highly skilled maid. What's the difference between a dedicated domestic and Dinah?*

Dinah makes me feel like a man. Like when we sleep together, the way she sleeps in my arms . . . I mean, I just hold her. She nestles there and we sleep as one. No pot, no poppers. Just us. It feels real nice.

> *What about your sex life?*

It's good. Not exactly fresh any more, as Dinah and I have been on-again-off-again since I was twenty-one—eight years, since I'm now twenty-nine. Dinah is into straight fucking and size. I take care of her in both departments.

> *How did you meet?*

In a bar. She was with a stud kind of guy and they struck up a conversation. It turned out both were trying to pick me up. I went home first with her and then I went to his place. They both loved to get fucked and they both loved to make me fudge. Only thing that ever got Dinah hopping mad was when I told her he made better fudge than her.

> *Does Dinah accept your bisexuality?*

Totally. But she doesn't accept my whoring around with another gal. That's where she puts her foot down. But regarding men . . . she couldn't care less. And why should she? She's got a damn good thing going. I take care of her. She was some sort of mess when she came back to me for good. She had been strung out on drugs on the West Coast and had gotten knocked up by some cop there. Like me, Dinah has been through her red-whore period. It nearly wrecked her. Like when she came on home, she could barely function. I had to teach her how to live. She's doing fine now—even into her own thing, which is interior design.

No problems then?

Every now and then she gets into this marriage number. She's very much a product of the Ole South and the 1950s. She'd like a big wedding under the magnolia trees. But I don't believe much in marriage unless I decide to have kids. So we sometimes have that conflict. But when she gets restless like she did the other week, I just say, "Hey Dinah, are you having fun? Is there anything you ain't got that you want?" And then she just comes around 'cause she *is* having fun and she's got everything any woman could want.

Like what?

A home, a car of her own, enough clothes to start a dress shop and me.

Does she date other men?

No. She knows there ain't another man who can satisfy her as I do. And I mean more than sex. Who would take care of her? In many ways she's a child.

What does Dinah mean to you?

She's the woman in my life. I am 100 percent me with her. She puts up with my demands and respects what I have to say.

Do you love her?

Oh yeah.

Why?

She is very understanding. And sweet. A really sweet girl. Not very typical of women either. Sitting around exchanging recipes or discussing cosmetics with the ladies isn't her style. She's more interested in sports, not watching them so much as going with me on a hunt or when I fish. We are really kind of a married couple. People in our town think of us that way. And she is the only woman in my life.

You mentioned Dinah has a home, is that yours? Do you live together?

Yes and no. You see I own a large town house, which has eleven apartment units surrounding it. There's a swimming pool in the middle and magnolias grow round the entire house. Dinah has her own unit next to the house but not in it. A lot of nights she sleeps over, but, basically, I live alone and have since 1973 when my last lover went flying out the door—courtesy of my foot. Since then there's been few men in my life, on a steady basis that is. Also, I don't fuck around with lots of guys but with just a few that I get to know well. I prefer that. Strangers make for boring sex and I don't much like to get out among gays. Truth is, I don't much like gay men. Mainly, they're not too sincere.

What are the differences for you sexually between men and women?

Men satisfy me better. No question about that. I'm one of those corny southern gentlemen who put women on pedestals. That's very southern and it goes way back where a man had a woman for wiving and a woman for wenching. Fucking, we now call it. But with me, men are for fucking. Sex with men is more animalistic, passionate, exciting. I can let my true nature out with a man. But sex with a woman is a very gentle and tender thing. Very lovemaking. Sex with a man is nothing like that. It's often rough. It's raunchy. It's all the things you don't do with a woman.

Why can't sex with a man be a very gentle and tender thing?

It just seems downright silly being tender with a guy. Men are about strength . . . muscles. Like I dig punching a guy in his muscle. Not to hurt him but to feel strength against strength. You know, when I grew up, as a kid I mean, you could fuck your buddy, cornhole him as it was called, but you better not kiss him when you were doing it or else you were queer. All my experiences with men were about strength and toughness. Always. Even the church taught me how Mary should be respected but the church never taught me shit about Joseph. Catholicism is about respecting the women. It ain't nothing about the man.

Can you accept tenderness from a man?

I still have trouble with it. I wasn't raised with any tenderness. My father sure as hell wasn't tender with me. Just the opposite. And because I idolized him, thought he was one helluva man, he was the greatest influence in my life—too much of one. He was what I wanted to measure up to—was what I thought I should be. Strong. Silent, too. If my father had feelings, he never expressed them, and I grew up thinking feelings were feminine things, and since I had them, I had to be a little funny. I grew up jealous of my father's buddy and thinking the only way a real man lived was to have a best friend with whom he did everything. I've always wanted a relationship like that for myself. I've always wanted a man to do things with.

Did you want your father?

Always. There wasn't a time I wasn't wanting that man's attention. His affection, too. Even his love. Never got it though. Not the way I wanted it anyway. I did get me lots of lectures on Christian ethics and morality. I always felt my father was disappointed in me. I always thought his lectures were aimed at me 'cause he felt I was bad.

What were these lectures about?

Mainly about being a "good boy." My father gave me a sex education without giving me one at all. He never spoke about sex. Not a word. But he did go on about the no-girls-in-the-tree-house. He made me feel sex was bad and sex with girls in particular was bad. Between what he was implying and what the church was teaching I thought sex was just for procreation. I really thought as a kid the worst sin to commit was to have sex with a woman you weren't married to. I also thought it was a sin if you were having sex not to make a baby. I actually thought it was much less sinful to have sex with a boy.

Did you?

No. Not as a kid. I didn't even know what sex was until I was twelve or so and a priest gave a lecture on sex and marriage. It really got me sick. The idea of a man putting his thing into a woman . . . I was disgusted by it. And the fact that my parents were doing it made me sicker.

Why?

Because both my mom and dad made me feel sex was bad. Sure my mama once said it *could* be beautiful but if that were true how come when I was twelve she was already putting me through an inquisition every time I came home from a party? Her questions made me feel that maybe something dirty had gone on and that I had been the dirty-bird doing the dirty things.

Did you give your mother cause not to trust you?

I don't know . . . maybe. When I was a kid, she used to catch me trying to peek at her when she was in the bath. And she used to whale the bejesus out of me when I'd hide behind her bedroom door, peek through the crack and catch her without her brassiere. She didn't like that. My mother was very modest. Not like my father, who ran round the house naked with that big dick of his hanging out and flapping around. He made me feel real small with that enormous pecker of his, and I was never small. Maybe that's why my father mistrusted me. A six-year-old with a big cock. "No-girls-in-the-tree-house!" Man, if I heard that once, I heard it a thousand times! It really hurt me that he seemed to mistrust me so much. And it was never warranted. Even when I grew up, I only dated nice girls. No barmaids or street girls. And I always had me but one girl at a time as he suggested. In college, when all the other guys were out pussy-hunting, I could never do that because I still thought it was sinful.

At what age did you begin dating?

At eleven I took a girl to the movies. At the same age, I went to house parties. I loved to dance and the kissing games. Sometime in high school, I started necking and feeling up the girls. But when their nipples would get hard, I'd get scared. I wasn't sure, even at that age, if that wasn't one of the ways to get a girl in trouble.

Do you remember your first sexual experience with a woman?

Oh sure. Who forgets that? She was nice gal, a senior in high school. We were in the back of my father's car necking when my dick gets hard. She pulls it out and falls apart at the size of it. Next thing I know, she's got it jammed into her. It felt nice. But the way she went about it didn't. I don't like aggressive women. Like when I was in college, all the girls had discovered the pill and were popping them like peanuts. They expected—demanded actually—that every guy fuck them. And if you didn't, they decided you were queer.

Did that happen to you?

Shit, no! I had me a steady girl and besides I wasn't queer. That came later.

At what age did you begin having sexual fantasies?

Now that's interesting. Do you know I never had me too many of those. I had fantasies but not about sex. More about having a buddy like my father did. I also had these long fantasies about going out on a boat or on a hunt with my father where he would come to appreciate me, love me. Even hug me. At thirteen, even when a buddy taught me how to jerk off, I had no fantasies. I would just pull on my meat but without thinking of nothing in particular. Only how I'd probably be going to hell for doing such a sinful thing. Particularly when I got into circle jerks and guys would want to look at or touch my cock 'cause it was so damn big. Funny, I know most of them guys today and not one ever turned out gay. And all of them were fascinated by my dick.

What about you? Were you fascinated by their dicks?

Hell no! There weren't nothing to be fascinated by. Theirs were downright puny next to mine.

Did you know about homosexuality at that age?

I've been trying to tell you, at that age, I didn't even know about heterosexuality. Now, looking back, I see it was always there. I always had me but one friend at a time and he'd be good-looking and good at sports. We'd do everything together. And I wouldn't allow him other friends or I'd drop him. But sex never entered into it. We would do a lot of rassling though, and I guess at that age, that was my way of having sex. But I never got hard even when I pinned him. Today, if I pin some guy when rassling, I got me one helluva hard-on. Which I then use. I love to pin a guy and then fuck him. That turns me on but I don't know why. Only time it doesn't is if the guy's head gets hassled—if he can't handle it.

What happens to your head when you are pinned?

It seldom happens, but when it does, I hate it, I mean h-a-t-e it. I can't stand being helpless and in someone else's control. I'm not the least bit passive.

Are you then always the active partner sexually?

If you mean am I a virgin, the answer is no. My cherry's been busted. But only when I've been relating to a guy—you know—in a relationship where I do anything if it helps the scene along. But, actually, I only get fucked when the other guy gets uptight about his own masculinity.

Could you explain that?

A lot of men after you've been fucking them, making them feel good, get uptight over that fact and feel the only way they can get back something *they* feel they have lost is to turn you over and fuck you.

How do you feel about being passive?

I don't much like it. Getting fucked is not something I require. Like I get horny a lot, but I'm never horny to get fucked. But when it's about really digging a guy, there is no top or bottom. I can enjoy anything. In fact, in my head, the ideal relationship is being with a guy who doesn't know bottom from top but just does what comes naturally at the time. I think I've always wanted that.

What makes you think that?

Well, at fifteen, I remember *clearly* fantasizing about giving my father sexual satisfaction. I wanted to lie close to him and experience mutual masturbation. A year or two later, I was fantasizing about having his cock in me and mine in him. I wanted him to possess me and me possess him.

Possess?

Yes. Exactly. Possess. Have him . . . own him, in every possible way. I've always known that. Okay? I have always wanted to have sex with my father.

How does that make you feel saying that?

It doesn't make me feel nothing today. But when I think back, it makes me feel sad. I remember the yearning. I wanted my father to love me.

And now?

And now I know in his way he does. The stuff we are talking about belongs to the past. I've been down a lot of roads since then. I've come through a lot of scenes, but one thing hasn't changed. I'm still looking for that buddy-to-buddy relationship my dad had with his friend. I came out thinking I had found it.

When was that?

In college. My best friend, like me, was a football jock. We did everything together. We used to go swimming, get hard-ons and then beat off. That was all there was to it for months until one afternoon when he suggested I pull his meat while he pulled mine. We did and I dug it. Shit, someone else's hand on my cock felt better than mine. But as soon as it was over, he started acting funny. Truth is, I never saw him again. Not as a friend. He was around school and all, but he wanted no part of me. Funny, but the next experience was exactly the same. A friend took me to a gay party, only we didn't know it was going to be gay. We walked in and saw these guys dancing and my friend cut out. I stayed because half the crowd was from my art and architecture classes. There were also several jocks around. Anyway, a truck driver picked me up and we went driving. We went driving a lot for a month before he touched me. He got my dick hard and right there, in the cab of his truck, he climbs up and sits on my dick. As soon as we both come off, he drives me home and I never saw him again either. That puts me back in the closet for about a year. And then came the pro-footballer. I was working as a lifeguard when he picked me up. He was into the rassling scene and we'd come off doing that. We started experimenting. He got into some cock-sucking and then we got into some heavy fucking. I was in love with the guy. It damn near killed me when I found out through a letter he left around that he had some guy back in his hometown. And he had been with him for ten years. So shit, I just pulled out and went back to my college sweetheart.

Did your first experiences embitter you?

I wasn't aware of it then, but now I know they sure as hell did. I became this real ball-buster. A cock-teaser. I'd jam myself into skin-tight jeans which showed a big basket and a T-shirt which would show my chest. I'd turn on as many guys as I could and came across with nothing. Someone in school introduced me to a local photographer who got me to pose for these physique pictures. He'd get me all oiled up so my body shone and photographed it as my dick hung down— just the kind of stuff you now see in *Playgirl*. But he would put me in motorcycle hats and sailor tops—fantasy-ville. I dug it. I think now I was using sexual hostility as a means to express my anger toward my father and every other guy who had fucked with my head at that time.

Why do you call it sexual hostility?

When you're shoving your joint in people's faces without any intention of coming across, that's sexual hostility. And the guys I did choose to fuck with, I abused. I always chose guys with even less rapport with their fathers than I had. I would make them subservient to my will. I controlled every aspect of the relationship. I was the strong one and if they showed any strength, I'd beat it out of them one way or another. Let me tell you, if my father had the best façade of masculinity I have ever seen, I came a close second. I copied who I was from him. I really see clearly how all of my movements toward men years ago were based on the shit-feelings I had toward my father. Man, I had to go through some shit to get rid of that!

That's the second reference you've made to going through difficulties to become who you are today. Would you explain that?

When I left college in my junior year, I came to New York with $60 stuffed in my jeans. But I knew there were guys all over the city who went to bed at night jerking off as they looked at pictures of me and my cock. I was going to find me those guys and get myself set up and then make it as an actor or a model. My first night in town, I scored. A guy in a Mercedes picked me up near the U.N. and for the next four months I lived in a duplex on the East Side. What a pad! This guy fed, clothed and housed me. All I had to do was fuck him every night. But he wouldn't let me out. Literally, I was a prisoner in that house. One night I couldn't stand it no more so I sneaked out. And right at the foot of Christopher Street in the village, I met Tom. That was the end of the duplex and the beginning of the shit. Literally. I met Tom on a Thursday night and by Friday morning my gear was on the sidewalk outside that East Side duplex. I moved in with Tom that afternoon and stayed with him for three years.

What was his meaning in your life?

My first real affair. Christ was I hung up on the guy! He was a ski bum—a really fine athlete—with a great body who peddled his ass to the highest bidder. He also pushed drugs, which I didn't know until I was already with him a month or so. He was into anything that would pay him a buck. And he was into anything sexually. But in particular, getting fucked. We'd spend weekends not even getting out of the apartment. We would just ball all day. His entire life was one big fuck scene. And that eventually started wrecking my head.

Why did his scene wreck your head?

Because he needed me to play out his fantasies. Once he had me going, he started bringing home these black numbers. Big black stuff with these horses' cocks. He knew I hated blacks and he would get off on watching me watching him get fucked.

But you went along with it?

Yes, by then he had me snorting and sniffing. And finally he had me fucking the stud that was fucking him. I tell you the guy did nothing but trick. He never read. He never did anything. He never thought about nothing other than the next dick and the next fuck.

What were you doing during this time?

I was trying to break into modeling. Initially I thought this city would fall at my handsome feet. I sure got a surprise. There's an awful lot of handsome dudes with big cocks in this town. Tom thought I was wasting my time and he got me started in hustling. Not street shit but call-boy stuff. My first client was a famous actor who sat in a dark closet and sucked off four or five guys at the same time. For that I got $25. But I hated it. Luckily, the second job the service sent me on was my last. I scored.

Do you mean you found a John?

Exactly. Let's call him Cory. He is from a very old, very established, and very rich American family, with so much money they don't even know what to do with it any more. He is past being a millionaire. He was married when we met and had several kids. He kept his gay life pretty well under wraps though.

How was your meeting arranged?

I got a call to go to his midtown hotel and ask for a Mr. X. I walked into his room looking very proper in a suit and a tie I borrowed. Cory looked at me and said, "How much you want, boy?" And I said, "Enough to fly home for Christmas, sir." He wrote out a check on the spot and never touched me. When he came back to New York several weeks later, he called for me. We'd go out to plays, restaurants, and he'd give me $20 or $30 and never make me come across. I think four or five months passed before we ended in the sack. By then, he wasn't a trick. I liked him.

Were you seeing other clients besides Cory?

No, I didn't need to. He was taking pretty good care of me and besides I had hit with a couple ads for television. I was trying to make it as a human being but I was having troubles. Tom was heavy into the hard stuff and tricking with anyone to keep his habit going. And every night I'd be part of his tableaus. Me and some black dudes fucking him, beating on him. All the time we're stoned, spaced. Then I began getting these depressions. I started feeling bad. I mean a deep, down bad. Even suicidal. I had this vision once on LSD of me sliding down, down, down. It scared me so bad 'cause I knew I was seeing my own life ahead of me. So I got out.

That simply?

It took three years. You call that simple? I was hurting like some bitch who had a bigger litter than her bones can handle. But I cut from him—lived in a series of dumps with a series of friends and would feel like shit until Cory came to town. He would take me out. We'd go to art galleries and museums. I mean we did things normal people do. It wasn't just fucking. Yes, he was laying a lot of dough on me, but he was also laying a lot of respect. He was really a gentleman. He never made me feel he was buying me. He was a nice man.

Were you in love with him?

No. But I wish I had been. He was in love with me though—but he never pushed it. He seemed to know I was looking for something other than a middle-aged gentleman whose best physical days were behind him.

What were you looking for?

The fantasy. The perfect buddy. I was haunting the bars looking for him. I went through a few hundred guys looking for him. I remember thinking I had found him the first time I saw Richard. We met in one of those "For-Butch-Only" places, the Eagle or the Stud. He was in leather and denim and was a helluva imposing-looking guy. Really big. And I mean big. And in his T-shirt, you could tell he was all muscle. Really a great-looking dude. After we stared at each other for a while, he walked up and said, "How'd you like a ride home on my bike?" I said sure. And when we got outside, sure enough, he had a bike. Not a cycle as I thought, but a bike. When we got home this big stud takes off his clothes and there's the biggest cock I've ever seen—10 inches soft. But he just gets on his stomach and the entire time we dated, he never got off it.

Are you resentful of that?

Damn straight I am! Although I didn't know it then. I hate people who pretend to be what they're not. Like all those queens running around in Bloomingdale's showing off the muscles they've got. But they're not really jocks. They're a bunch of queens who have developed their bodies in the gym. They can't do a fuck with them. They would be lost on a hunt or on a camp-out in the woods. They're phonies. And so was Richard. I'm thinking I've finally found the other side of me—my no-top-no-bottom guy—but nothing could be further from the truth. But I stayed with him for a couple months—don't ask me why, 'cause I sure as hell don't know. Maybe 'cause he was a great fuck and maybe 'cause he was an education. Richard had his own scene. He would make me costumes to wear. Like one night I'd be an S.S. trooper, another I'd be an M.P. or a policeman, prison warden, sailor, anything but me after a while. He would have me handcuff him to the bed, spread-eagled, and then fuck him. Eventually, he made me a hood in which just my eyes, my nostrils and my mouth were visible. I have no idea who he fantasized me into but he sure got off on it.

You seem to put all the responsibility on him. Couldn't you have said no?

Yes, but I didn't. I allowed it because a part of me, I guess, dug it. Richard would get so fucking carried away when I got into these uniforms that I'd get turned on. He was totally in my control. Do you know what it is like to have a man under you who is writhing and moaning with pleasure? And that's your cock he's taking deeper and deeper inside of him. You might say I got sucked in. That's a joke.

I'm glad you told me. It didn't sound like one.

Shit! I guess it wasn't. It got to be a terrible time with Richard. I'd be wearing his goddamn hood, fucking his brains out, when suddenly I'd feel like I was all alone in the room or worse—not even there. And I wasn't. I mean *me*, the person, I wasn't there. Just some stud in a hood. I began thinking whose brains were *really* getting fucked. I said to him once: "Richard, is all this really necessary?" but he pretended he didn't understand. But I did. I understood that something bad was happening to me. I began getting the shakes. I started getting those depressions again. I felt like I was falling apart . . . losing me.

Could you explain that?

Who was I? Richard didn't know. Richard didn't *care*. I was beginning to wonder if anyone did—including me. I felt so fucked out. I was tired of the dinner parties which ended with pot, poppers and gang bangs. When I got to New York, I wanted everybody to want me; I dug having everybody sucking on my dick or fucking on it. But that's *all* they wanted. Nobody seemed to give a damn about who was attached to the meat. It could have been anyone's joint. I really think I would have flipped out if it weren't for Cory. Yeah, he was grooving on my body but it was strictly secondary. He was doing something nobody in my life had ever done—grooving on me. He treated me like a person. I meant something to him—something more than just a big cock.

What does the size of your cock mean to you?
Why do you ask that?

Are you aware of how frequently you make reference to its size?
Am I doing that? Oh shit! You know I didn't think any of this— the questions or talking about my life—were making me nervous. But it must be because the only times I lead with my cock today is when I feel insecure. When I felt like a nothing, I knew my cock was a something. It was always an object of admiration. It damn near made *me* into an object of admiration. Actually, it did so, forget the damn near. But today, I don't usually go on about my cock. I'm successful in enough other areas and feel good enough about me not to do that. So I must be nervous.

But does a "big cock" have a meaning for you?
Well, I'm glad this boy has one rather than not. It feels good knowing you got something special in there and as you can see I don't show it off any more. My jeans fit loosely. Years ago, I did think having a bigger cock than most made me a bigger man or more of a man. But no more. Not really. In getting around I discovered my eight-and-a-half ain't exactly the Big Time I thought it was. There's lot bigger in this world. Initially, my dick opened a lot of doors for me. It got me into modeling and it got me into free dinners, free weekends at Fire Island and trouble. But my dick also closed doors—mainly the ones in my head. Until I started falling apart, I wasn't using any part of me above my waist. I wasn't thinking. I wasn't dreaming. Most of all, I wasn't working toward anything. That's all changed.

But on the same subject, regarding the men you are attracted to, does their size matter to you?
Yes, I like well-hung men. I get an extra off on fucking a guy with a big dick. I know I'm giving them something they can't ordinarily get.

Why do you say that?
Because the way it is set up among gays, the guy with big dong usually does the fucking whether he wants to or not. A big butch guy

has trouble getting himself fucked. He can't even admit he wants it or he looses his standing as a butch—with himself as well as with tricks. I dig meeting this kind of guy and then satisfying his fantasies. I dig taking a guy who has trouble admitting he wants to get fucked and then practically making him beg for it. I'll tell you a story about that. It's sort of what I'm talking about. A year or so ago I met a guy on the street, a really handsome dude, and took him home. It was dark so I didn't recognize him. When we got to my place, he stripped and immediately got onto his hands and knees. No warm-up. Nothing. Just hard-core fucking. I was in him and at him a full thirty minutes before I reached for his cock and when I had hold of it I couldn't believe it. Bigger than Richard's. Bigger than anything I had ever seen before. He was one of the biggest studs in porno films. When the fuck was over—and it lasted more than an hour—he turned and said, "I really needed that." And I dug it. I knew what he meant. A guy hung like that is usually doing the fucking rather than getting it. It's just really hard for a butch guy to get himself fucked.

What does fucking a "butch" male mean to you?

It must mean something because I can jerk off nights thinking about it. Earlier, you asked about my childhood fantasies. Well, we are now talking about my favorite adult fantasy.

Would you describe it?

Yeah but you better watch out. I get horny just thinking about it. Anyway, in it, I'm with this super-butch stud who is having difficulty admitting he wants my cock in him. I overpower him and get my dick a little up his ass. He fights it but the more he fights the more it slides further in. Finally, after one big struggle, I shove it all the way up and he screams. Not with pain but with pleasure. He goes with it. He raises up his ass and squirms to get it in deeper. When he comes, it is like nothing he has ever experienced before. And then he wants more but he hates wanting more—hates the whole idea of what has happened. And that's it. That's my fantasy. It's also pretty much the pattern of my sex life. I usually do find a butch guy who is pretty well hung and having trouble getting himself fucked for the reasons I mentioned before.

Is there a face to the man in your fantasy?

It is indistinct. But I kind of know who he is. Like he's married, or with a woman, and he likes the outdoors a lot. He's a man like my father's buddy. That's still my ultimate fantasy—to have a relationship similar to the one my dad had with his friend. Actually, one of the few things that shakes me up sometimes is thinking the guy in my fantasy is my father.

> *Why should that shake you up when you have admitted that you wanted to have sex with your father when you were younger?*

I don't know. But it does. I often think about my dad and his friend. I don't know if they were having sex with one another or not and if they did, who was doing what to whom. I used to think it didn't matter but now I think it does. Yet, I can't imagine wanting anything—least of all sex—from my father today. What I would like though is that kind of relationship I imagine he had with his buddy— one where there is no bottom or top but where each is both.

> *Have you experienced this?*

No, but that doesn't mean I won't. There is a guy now who I think can handle it. I think he can be in that place where there is no upper or lower berth. So far, it seems he can handle the bottom without getting all shook up over it. He has no trouble admitting he likes being fucked and he doesn't seem to get into being the fucker to prove his masculinity. I think I may finally have gotten lucky. I think I may finally have found another me. Shit! In listening to me I just realized how much easier this poor boy's life would be if my dick was just another four or five inches long and bent the other way. Then I could fuck myself.

> *Is fucking your sole interest sexually?*

Yes. Cock-sucking doesn't do much for me. I'm not the least bit oral. Getting sucked feels okay but because I'm so big very few guys can give good head to me—at least where I get any kind of good sensation from it. I think I've come off maybe a dozen times in my life through a blow job. And I think maybe that's about the amount of times I've taken off some other guy. I'll suck a cock but only to warm a guy up for where I want to go. Like when I'm sucking, I'll get a finger up his ass. Then two fingers. When I got four in there, I know he's ready for my dick. But sucking, in itself, gives me no pleasure. Also, when fucking, I just want to mention here that I'm solely a dick man. No dildos and no fists. Actually, the guy who has traveled that far where he is into those scenes doesn't interest me. As mentioned, I'm more into the virgin territory—the guy who doesn't get fucked very often.

How do you feel about fist-fucking as a sex act?

I don't. I don't feel nothing about any of those things. They're just not my scenes. Like the other week, I was at a dinner party at somebody's house and there were lots of famous people there. Other actors, lawyers. The Who's Who of the gay world. Well, I left with this guy. Who wouldn't? Half the country wants to fuck with him. Anyway, he wanted me to piss in his mouth. I wouldn't. Watersports don't interest me. Nor do drugs. Like at a party the other night. Here is one of the most successful attorneys in the U.S. and he is doing all kinds of drugs. He not only uses, but he gives them to the jocks he imports for his orgy scenes.

Imports?

Right. The guy is so rich he flies in the studs who pose for *Playgirl* and other magazines like that. He gets them snorting—gives them some pills—and then its gang-fuck time. I've seen some pretty famous jocks —pro-football players—do some pretty wild things on mesc and cocaine. Now I don't dig taking advantage of some guy who is spaced but this lawyer does. Okay, that's his scene. I don't judge it. But I don't participate either.

When the actor wanted you to piss into his mouth, did you feel anything?

No. What am I supposed to feel? Look, I keep my emotions out of my sex life. I learned to do that. I learned to go through a lot of that shit as though I weren't really there. Man, if you start feeling everything that's going on around you in this fucked-up world, you can go crazy. Particularly in this city. Back home at least you can get away from all that. You can just take yourself and go off in a little rowboat.

Are you saying then that you are two persons sometimes?

Exactly. When I'm playing, when I'm out there being trashy, I know it is a game. I know the requirements. I take none of it personally. No more. But my work is another thing. In my restaurant, I'm all business. And dedication. It's one of the best in the country because *I* make it one of the best. Now, as a painter, I haven't had three showings in three years because I fuck good. Hell no! I paint good. The best of me goes into my painting. Everything I have seen and experienced is there on canvas. I think of my painting as my pulpit. I'm preaching through it. I'm telling every young stud to beware. Now I know that sounds pompous but that's it. I work at my art. I make it a point to wine-and-dine the right people. I've even made me a list of the top one hundred in the art world. You know what? I've met more than half. I hustle. Right! That's the word. Only it ain't about hustling dick no more. I hustle to meet and cultivate the people who can make or break you as an artist. So . . . the me that's in a gay bar is one person—actually just part of a person if you know what I mean —but the me that's at home, with Dinah, in my restaurant and in my art; that's another person. And he's a full one. I'm proud of him. I rescued him from a garbage heap. I put him through New York University, earned him a degree in fine arts.

How did you manage that financially?

By deception, dishonesty and what's the word Jews use . . . *chutzpah*. When I left Richard I became very steady with Cory. I was his only sex. When he was in New York we'd be together constantly. We also went off to South America and a whole bunch of places together. Had there not been money involved—or had there been love instead of money—we'd have been lovers. Cory took care of me. And I, in my way, took care of him. Let me say again, I cared for him greatly. But I took care of him in another way. I stole from him. Actually, stole is the wrong word. I *charged* Cory for every lie I caught him in—2,000 bucks per lie.

How did you manage this?

Simple. First of all, it started when I once asked Cory for some money and he told me he didn't have any cash with him. Later, when he asked me to get something out of his attaché case, I found $5,000 in $20 bills. That pissed me off. I decided then and there to take $2,000 every time he held out on me or lied to me. Now you ask how. I learned to forge his name and I took what I needed, and then some, on his Bloomingdale's charge. I also forged his name on checks. But I never took much—not enough for the people in his office to think anything about. They were used to his spending $1,500 a month at Bloomingdale's. What the hell, Cory had so much money that the stuff I took was nickle-and-dime shit.

How much "nickle-and-dime shit" did you take?

Altogether about $100,000. That put me through school and got me the down payment on my restaurant.

How did you feel about what you were doing?

Great! I was living good and helping some others to stay alive too. I never had any guilt feelings about it. In fact, I wound up telling Cory and he just laughed. I mean *laughed.* He was actually proud of me. Truth is, what he was proud of was my being enrolled at N.Y.U. A lot of other dudes would have taken that money and run. But I had me a purpose. I wanted to be something and a thief wasn't it. An artist was. I know where you and others could think what I did was wrong. Maybe it was. But Cory never made me feel it was, and although I can see that it was legally wrong, I don't feel bad about it 'cause I know what I felt for Cory and what I was doing with his money. You see, that was years ago and Cory and I today are even closer than we were. And it ain't about his money no more 'cause I don't need it. But I do need him, his friendship and his caring. He is so sick now. Heart. All that money and not a damn thing that can be done. I'm sick over it. And the family won't let me see him. Oh yeah, they know about me. At one time Cory tried to pass me off as an illegitimate son born in Europe after the last world war. But his brothers put on private investigators and they turned up the whole mess. They tried to buy me off but I wouldn't take a dime from them. They never understood—still don't—what Cory meant to me. He read to me. He spoke to me. He gave me back my dignity. Shit! He was the daddy I never had. Okay. Okay. There was sex involved. Let me tell you about our sex. It was a joke. He didn't like oral sex any more than I did. He wanted to fuck me. The first five years I wouldn't go that route and when I did I discovered he's a thirty-second pop. And that was our sex life. A real fun-filled orgy.

What you are saying is that there is something beyond the sexual with Cory?

Far beyond. Even today he is the most significant man in my life. Through his help, I'm a millionaire today. He educated me to investing. But he's so ill and I can't see him and in that respect all of our combined money doesn't mean shit. I don't know if I've made you understand about Cory. He was one of the few people in my life who never made me feel bad about anything and least of all about me. And I made me a lot of mistakes. Without him, I don't know that I could have jumped from the speeding train before it crashed. He really should have been my father. I should have adopted him!

What of your father? Do you see him today?

Do I ever! He lives part-time in one of my apartments.

Is he separated from your mother?

Not really. No more than he ever was, it turns out. My father uses one of my apartment units for assignations with his mistress. She's younger than me and has him like a tomcat going after the pussy. My moral daddy. He's having his wenches on the side. Always has. Ain't that something! Keep-the-girls-out-of-the-tree-house-son! He had his own stashed all over the place.

How did you discover this?

I didn't. He told me. Two years ago he fell apart in my arms. Just sobbing and crying. He kept going on about his imperfections and weaknesses. I didn't know what the hell he was talking about. How could *my* dad be imperfect or weak? He just rambled on about how my mother had been frigid—how all desire left her after her hysterectomy several years ago—and how he was a physical man with human needs. He laid all this on me without taking a breath but blubbering how he was afraid I would now hate him what with my being so close to my mama and all.

And did you hate him?

Not at all. Just the opposite. For the first time in my life I felt close to that man. I was able to hug him, hold him, be there for him. My biggest problem was watching him cry. He hadn't allowed me my own tears when I was a kid and it was hard for me to allow him his. He always taught me any emotion of any kind was weakness. I grew up thinking I was a disappointment to him because I had me these emotions. I used to blame my mama for them.

How did this turnabout with your father make you feel?

Shaky but okay. Shit! We're all human. But, truth is, I had a selfish reaction. I felt free. I felt more manly. I felt my own person. My father and I became quite close after that, but I must admit he initially misused that closeness. He took my not condemning his women as a condoning. He started bringing them around to my apartment. I didn't like this. I was afraid that if ever my mama did find out about my father's running around, she would think I was helping him. I knew she would be hurt bad—powerfully bad. It was a problem for me for a while. He was just playing at his leisure in *my* home. He seemed guiltless about the whole thing. He didn't care that he was making me a party to something I didn't want to be no party to. Eventually I got pissed. I couldn't paint. I couldn't look my mama in the eye. So, I gently got him out of my own apartment and set him up in his own. I just cautioned him that discretion is the better part of valor. I didn't chastise him none though, as I didn't want to lose this new closeness that we were sharing late in life.

What do you think the overall effect of all this has been on you?

As I said, I've come into my own. My father no longer is the power or influence he once was in my life. He also sure ain't the ideal. He is now just another person rather than a god. And shit, he is better as a person than as a god. I finally got some form of father. He respects me today and shows it. He no longer makes cracks about my painting. He has an understanding of what I am about.

Do either of your parents know of your homosexuality?

No. Why should they?

Is that not part of what you are about?

But only a part. My sexuality has something to do with who and what I am, but my parents don't relate to me sexually so why do they need to know about that aspect of my life. It would only confuse them. They live by very middle-class conventional rules. In that society, a man can take a mistress—take several—and that's within bounds. But a man taking a man—that sure as hell ain't. That's considered perverted, which is strange 'cause I don't think of it that way at all. I'm really a very conventional kind of guy—even middle class. I'm not looking to screw the world. I'm looking for one guy. I'm ready to settle down. I've done sown me all the wild oats I care to sow. I look at my life and I see that I am the product of everything I've been and done to date. And I've done a lot! But I don't regret that. I've profited by mistakes. And some of them I'll live with forever. Like the physique pictures. They're still around to haunt me. But I understand today why I did that. I understand too my promiscuity. I don't have those kinds of ego needs or deficiencies today. I did some cheap things in my life but now I know I'm not a cheap person. I used my mistakes to become first class. I have success and more important, the respect and love of my parents and peers. I am painting and enjoying it. I am also receiving some good notices for it. I have a woman with whom I've been engaged in a one-to-one relationship for several years. And now there is this man. Now the world, and in particular my parents' world, would judge this as abnormal. They'd be sick over it. They just wouldn't and couldn't understand. So I ain't about telling them. Not from fear, but there just wouldn't be any point to them knowing things they just aren't sophisticated enough to handle. They're just setting there hoping I'll marry Dinah. And the truth is . . . I might. Why? Because I'd make me a fine papa to some boy.

How would this affect your new relationship?

You mean, with Bob?

Yes.

It wouldn't. What's one to do with the other? If it sounds like I want my cake and intend to eat it, too, that's just about it. And why not? Bob may be what I've been looking for most of my adult life. He just may be that. Frankly, I hope so. I'm tired of living alone. The truth is I want to live with a man more than I do with a woman.

Where does Bob live now?

In one of the apartments. He's just relocated from L.A. We've known each other a while and have commuted back and forth. Finally, it was either shit-or-get-off-the-pot-time for both of us. Since there was nothing really hanging for him in L.A., he came here. And if one can trust first impressions, I honestly do think the man in my life today will be the last man in my life.

What makes you think that?

Because Bob is just about everything I could want in a man. He is big. Big everywhere. Okay? He's also kind of a rough guy. He looks like rough trade. But underneath he's a pussycat. Like me. A big, warm lovable guy. And like me, when he's revealed the soft side of himself, he's been rejected. He's had to play the stud 'cause nobody's wanted the real person. Well, he's played that game ten years longer than I have and he's ten years more tired of it. He is ready to stop.

How do you relate other than sexually?

Good. It's going to get better 'cause I'm learning. Bob is the first guy I've ever known who lets me be. He just seems to dig me as I am. He doesn't ask me to give up my painting and he doesn't ask me to give up Dinah. He also doesn't ask that I give up my friends or my need to sometimes get off by myself. We both kind of know that what we are to each other is a combination lover, father, friend and brother. No one role is constant. Bob, like me, has had his own father problems. Like me, he's been through the shit. Like me, he's ready to hear the roses and see the breeze.

Is there tenderness in your relationship?

Shit! What kind of a half-assed question is that? Maybe tenderness is *your* need. Our sex isn't tender. We do anything and everything sexually. Both of us believe that anything that is needed to make it work is okay. I can go anywhere Bob wants to go. He is into fantasy a lot. And I've discovered so am I. We tell each other what we're into on a particular night. We make up situations and act them out.

Could you give me an example?

Sure. We may get into jockstraps and rassle with a winner-take-all prize. The "all" of course is the top position. Or we may pretend one guy is a policeman that the other is going to forcibly fuck. We usually have a lot of rough stuff. Rassling and rape I call it. But nobody gets hurt. I know how far to go. So does Bob. I have fucked him into his ultimate orgasm—have made him beg for it—and he, in turn, has done the same with me. I've never known such sex.

Do you love him?

I wish you hadn't asked that. I have trouble with that word. I can't use it easily, particularly with a man. When I was young, I said I loved Tom. But love when you're a baby-fart doesn't mean shit. Today . . . I can't put that kind of label on what I feel for Bob. I want to live with him. I want to be with him. I am better with him than I have ever been with a man. But I work at that. I don't want to wreck this relationship and I could . . . easily.

What makes you say that?

I know me. I tend to dominate. I tend to suffocate. I tend to castrate. I don't mean to, but the nature of my personality makes me try to take over—run the show. I blast away at a guy's ego. I got a lot going for me and it's tough with a guy who has less to feel anything but subservient to me. That always kills it in the end. That and my own intrinsic strength. That rips at his. With Bob, he's come down a long road to be where he is. He knows himself. He knows me. I think he can handle my shit and stop it. I don't think he'll just let me take over. I don't think he'll want me to take care of him without him reciprocating. I'm really trying hard not to rape Bob of his independence. I can be such a bastard that way.

But why?

Because I need to control. I need to remove men as threats. I must be better than them. I'm still proving to my daddy that I'm as good as his neighbors' sons. Goddamn! I've come all this way, through truckloads of shit, and I still can't stop proving to my dad that I'm one helluva man.

Bob Lawson

I T IS MORE THAN the drawl that gives Bob Lawson * away. Everything about him—from what can only be termed a courtly manner to his gentleness in speech—says "Old South." He is indeed from an old southern family and the traditions are deeply inbred. Despite his ten-year love affair with New York City, Bob will never be a New Yorker. Not really. He wouldn't know how to be that kind of rude.

Simply, at six-foot-one, 175 pounds, Bob is tall, dark and handsome. More important, he looks happy. His life is filled with Big City activity: opera, theater, dance and concerts. Weekends are frequently used to explore the various music and dance festivals that abound in New York State.

His home is within an old building on the Upper West Side of Manhattan. His high-ceiling apartment is filled with memorabilia of theater and opera. But among the autographed pictures of Beverly Sills and Rudolf Nureyev sit pictures of his son and daughter. There is also a picture of his former wife.

Often, in speaking of his life, Bob wept. Sometimes it was in sadness, other times in joy. "Why not?" he asks. "'I've had thirty-eight years of both."

Why the big smile?

I was thinking how seven or eight years ago it would have been impossible for me to discuss my homosexuality with anyone but a psychiatrist. That thought led to others about recent changes in my life. Believe me. I have reason to smile.

What were you and your life like seven years ago?

Well, I wasn't smiling much. I was coming to the end of my marriage and saying good-bye to my two children—a son and a daughter. I had just recently arrived here in New York and begun living openly as a homosexual rather than furtively and guiltily as I had during my marriage.

* See Author's Note, page xii.

Had you been a practicing homosexual prior to your marriage?

Yes and no. Mainly, it was brief encounters in not-so-terrific places. I would drop my pants and get blown. Despite my loneliness, I never saw any of these men more than once.

Why was that?

I couldn't imagine that any kind of relationship between men who "liked" men could be wholesome. Besides, I wanted to be married. I had always wanted that. It was a childhood fantasy to be with one woman in a house filled with kids.

When did you first become aware of homosexual tendencies?

The word was foreign to me as a child. Once I heard my parents speaking about a "queer" and I asked them what one was. They answered "a pervert." That I looked up in the dictionary and it seemed very ugly. But then anything to do with sex seemed ugly because of the Victorian attitude toward it in the southern mansion we called home. I say that somewhat snidely because the yelling between my mother and father could be heard all along the banks of the Mississippi. I can remember fantasizing about how that would never happen in my own home when I married.

But, what's strange is my masturbatory fantasies. From childhood, they were about boys. At thirteen, I engaged in adolescent sex play with my cousin. We would masturbate one another. Then the damnedest thing happened: He got interested in girls, while I remained interested in him. Several years later, but while still in my teens, I discovered those places—in parks and public johns—where some men go to have sex with other men.

During this time, did you date?

Yes. Quite a bit, actually, but Marge, who I met in college, was the first woman I ever slept with. And . . . she got pregnant, which is some kind of beginner's luck. Marge was from a very old southern family. She was terrified that "Daddy" might discover her indiscretion, but she was even more terrified of an abortion. So we decided to marry, which was fine with me. I not only liked Marge but I loved her . . . as much as I was capable of loving then. Then, too, marriage had been my goal. And lastly, marriage might take me out of the homosexual encounters I so much hated yet seemed to need. I actually entered my marriage in good faith. I intended to be faithful. I remember thinking "It can work because you want it to work."

Did Marge know of your homosexuality?

No. And at the time of her pregnancy she was so desperate that had she known, it would not have made any difference. Uppermost in her mind was getting down that aisle without "Daddy" knowing his little girl had sinned. Well, "Daddy" gave his consent for our marriage provided that we wait for a proper church wedding. Which we did and I swear Marge was then quite pregnant but didn't show a damn thing when the man said "I now pronounce you man and wife." One day later, as we flew up north to where I was to be stationed for three years as part of the military's Special Services, she blew up like a balloon. Some months later the baby was born and our marriage began its slow death.

Why was that?

At Marge's insistence, we gave our baby up for adoption. You see, had we kept it, "Daddy" would have known and, at all costs, "Daddy" must never know. The "cost" was Marge and I, our relationship. The day we gave that baby away, Marge became frigid. She did not have one orgasm all the remaining years of our marriage. Prior to that, our sex life had been pleasant. The rift between us, caused by giving up that child, never healed. Between my resentment and her frigidity, I was back among "the boys" within the year. I hated that. I think I blamed Marge for that too. I had so much wanted to be straight. I had hoped my homosexuality had been just a phase. I used to wonder what would have happened had we not given the baby away, had Marge not turned frigid. Could we have? Would we have? I doubt it. I believe now that eventually my homosexual needs would have to have surfaced.

Were your homosexual encounters in and around camp?

Yes, but never with the other servicemen in Special Services. And there were plenty of opportunities. We were all trained musicians and there is a large homosexual populace within the classical music and opera worlds. But I was too much in the closet to play close to home. Instead, I did the bushes and the johns. I sneaked around and felt dirty. But that's how I then viewed homosexuality. I also felt that as a married man and a gentleman that what I was doing was terribly wrong. I was constantly guilty and all the guilt combined to keep me fairly dull and sterile sexually. I was still what's known as trade. And then when I did start reciprocating by going down on some stranger, I would really hate myself. Anal intercourse was out! Intercourse of any kind had been difficult enough with Marge. Not that I couldn't get it up, because I could, but because of my attitude initially. As a child, when my mother became pregnant, instead of her or my father telling me how a child was conceived, they gave me a book to read. My child's mind believed a man put his pee-pee into a woman's pee-pee and then they pee-peed all over one another to make a baby. I thought that pretty disgusting, which is why I was hung-up about intercourse until I discovered how cozy and warm it was inside Marge. And that, by the way, is how our lovemaking felt—cozy and warm.

What was your marital life like initially?

We struggled from the moment we gave the baby up, but we seemed to be surviving. Marge worked at a job she liked and we had a lovely off-base apartment. Had there not been this distance between us in bed, we could have been happy. We had sex occasionally but it was not very good. And strictly in the missionary position. Once I went down on her and she was horrified . . . repulsed even. Yet, she would perform orally on me but to avoid intercourse, I think. It was awful. It was fucking awful or perhaps awful fucking best describes it. I wanted desperately to arouse her . . . make her passionate . . . make her come. I had an incredible need to prove that I could fulfill her . . . to prove that I was a man.

How did you feel toward Marge at the time?

I felt many things, including pity, anger and hostility. Yet, I also cared about her. I still do. Although she is remarried, we remain close friends. She is a very special person . . . a good person who is very giving but who has trouble receiving. But then, I felt love and hate and this pressure to make my marriage work.

Is it possible that part of this "pressure" was to avoid your homosexuality?

Absolutely. I was very afraid of becoming committed to a homosexual existence. I was afraid it would swallow me up and I would become another poor, pathetic faggot.

Why that choice of words . . . "poor, pathetic faggot"?

Because that is how I then viewed homosexuals. So many of the men I knew then were so sad, so lonely. Their dreams seemed destined to failure. I didn't believe then, based on my small-city upraising in Mississippi, that a relationship between men was possible. I thought society would jail the men before they'd allow it. Playing around was one thing but to openly live that life was courting disaster! Obviously, I had not come to grips with my homosexuality or with anyone else's. I was a guilt-wracked wreck.

When did you have your first non-anonymous sex with a man?

Somewhere toward the middle of my second year of marriage I met Charlie in the library near the base. He was a college student, very bright and very beautiful. I brought him home. Right! I brought him to the house and the bed I shared with Marge. Insane? Yes. And the insanity went on for several months. We even fucked in that bed! He simply guided me into him one day and all my taboos about anal intercourse vanished. It was beautiful. And what was also *beautiful* was my getting from Charlie what Marge was denying me in that very same bed.

Could you have had sex elsewhere?

Of course. We could have gone to hotels, but I wanted it in *our* bed. I always knew there was the possibility of discovery—of Marge coming home ill from work and finding us. A part of me wanted that. A part of me wanted her to see me in bed with this boy. I wanted to punish her with it. I wanted to hurt her. I wanted to bust her balls the way she had busted mine. I wanted her to feel as inadequate as I felt.

What, if anything, did you feel for this boy?

I liked Charlie very much. In fact, when he completed his schooling and went back home, I felt very hurt . . . rejected. I was not in love with him, but I felt very loving toward him. He was very nice to me. After he left, the pain was such that I avoided any similar type situation for many years.

Did your relationship with Charlie have an affect upon your marriage?

Yes. It increased the tension between Marge and me because now I knew sex could be beautiful. It also made me even more guilty toward Marge and the guilt made me more resentful. I was slipping around town more and thus slipping further into guilt and subterfuge. I hated my life. I was constantly tense . . . torn. It takes a helluva lot of energy to lead a double life. Part of my guilt was for not directing that energy toward saving my marriage. You see, at the time, I still wasn't certain which sex was more fulfilling. Being with Charlie had been wonderful. But being with Marge *had* also been wonderful at one time. I kept deluding myself, thinking, "If only she would be different." I wasn't ready to accept then that I was already "different" and had needs that she could never fulfill. It was easier to sneak around, risking military discharge and scandal if caught, than to face reality. Yet, I wanted to stop. Every day I vowed to be stronger. Every *other* day I would return home determined to be a better husband. I kept wishing "It" would go away. I felt like two people, neither of which was having a very easy time of it.

Did you have anyone to talk to about your difficulties?

No. I was much too guilty and closeted then to speak to anyone about my homosexuality. I was not raised to be open. Feelings were never shown or expressed in my home. For example: When I called to tell my parents I was getting married, my father said "We love you." He couldn't say "*I.*" But just the fact that he said "We" made me cry. He had never said that before.

Frankly, I'm such a textbook case on homosexuality that it is boring. I had a totally passive father and a dominating, smothering mother. The ole lady looked to me for all the things she should have received from my father. I was her companion and her emotional support. I was also her "little angel," her "special gift" from God. She would tell me I was the perfect son and how "I just don't know what I did to deserve you." She would top that with "And I just know you'll never do anything to embarrass me." What a guilt trip! What a goddamn setup. Everytime I, the "perfect son," masturbated, I was guilty for weeks. What would mother think! Special, she called me. Well, I don't know how special I was, but I sure became different. Other boys my age disliked me. I was precocious and an all-around smart ass. I didn't question their not liking me because I didn't much like me either.

Why should a child not like himself?

Because I was already so guilty for my thoughts. I was very curious about sex as a child but I didn't know all children were. I became aroused very easily. Again, I thought that only happened to me. Although the Methodist church wasn't as fanatic about the pitfalls of sex as some religions are, there were enough sermons about those thoughts and feelings you weren't supposed to have, but which I did have, to make me feel the sinner. Very early on in life, I was in conflict sexually. In other words, I have been burdened with sexual guilt all of my life. It began with the "queers" my parents spoke about and continued on with the moralizing of the church. Had this not happened, I think I would have sought a man's love much earlier on in life. But I subverted this need for many years and that subversion caused me terrible pain.

When did you realize that your marriage was not going to work?

I had that realization many times but lacked the strength to act on it. In retrospect, I wonder with considerable amazement how we managed to stay together for as long as we did. Given the hostility I felt and the frustration, I was really a glutton for punishment. Yet, the idea of divorce crossed my mind shortly after Charlie left. But Marge got pregnant and the baby, which arrived one week before my discharge, seemed like a miracle of miracles. I was so proud of that baby. I took my family home, which was down south, convinced things would now be different. But they weren't. With the baby, Marge had even more excuses for not having sex.

Did Marge ever ask for a divorce?

Oh no. "Daddy" would have been horrified. Divorce just isn't something a respectable southern family experiences. But also, in fairness to Marge, although they were few and far between, we did have some good times. We always liked each other and that was enough to hold her. I wish that hadn't been true.

I was back at school working on my master's degree in music, sneaking around and feeling like a piece of shit. I was killing myself. How can you do this, I would ask, when you have a wife and a child at home. Again I thought of divorce and again Marge got pregnant. This time with our daughter.

Were there any significant outside relationships during this time?

Only with a woman who was attending a seminar. She was in the process of divorce and made it very clear she would like to have an affair. I wanted to but was afraid. Suppose I went to bed with her and it was a disaster? Then there would be no doubt that I was a homosexual. I wasn't ready, still, to face that possibility. Which is so ludicrous since I was cruising the notorious johns on campus daily. Of course the inevitable happened. I was entrapped one day by the vice squad. I did not fall apart when it happened. In fact, I was very cold about it—which is not the same as being "cool." Somehow I realized that getting caught was what I had always wanted. I needed that punishment. My guilt forced me into dangerous situations which made sex that much more exciting. I wanted to be caught . . . to pay for my sins. And I was, only I wasn't. With my one phone call allotment, I called the school chaplain. He came immediately, heard the facts and simply said "How unfortunate." I was remanded in his custody. He in turn placed me with a local psychiatrist.

Retrospectively, that entrapment experience, which was humiliating and terrifying in all its ramifications, was the best thing that could have happened to me. It was a turning point in my life. I began seeing the psychiatrist three times a week and also attended his group. By the way, although Marge never learned of my reasons for being in therapy, I did persuade her to try it. She went once and never went back. She was very shaken about what had transpired in her hour. She remained hostile toward therapy the entire time I was in it.

How would you describe your therapeutic experience?

As mind-blowing, painful and eventually freeing. I remember the first time I broke through the repression to realize that instead of loving my mother, I hated her, hated how she had castrated, used and abused me. I also saw how angry I was at my father for not having stopped her and . . . for not having loved me. That pain had me shaking for weeks. But later, I dropped it. I got tired of that pain.

It took me several months before I could admit before the group that I was homosexual. When I did, the damnedest thing happened. Nobody threw rocks. In fact, nobody seemed to give a shit. That surprised the hell out of me. Suddenly I saw, and accepted, that I did not have leprosy, that I wasn't this awful "perverted queer." In my final year of therapy I realized I wanted to lead an exclusively homosexual life. That was no easy realization as I am very family oriented and my nature certainly isn't to shirk responsibility. But I saw how my life was actually hurting and not helping the very family I wanted to help. My resentment of having to be what I was not— a heterosexual husband and father—had to go somewhere and it was going to the very people I didn't want to hurt but who I wrongly felt were hurting me. They weren't. It was me holding me where I was. It was me hurting me.

It was a terrible time of pain, of conflict and growth. I was now working in public relations, earning excellent money, and the owner of a fine home in an old and respected section of Houston. Yet,

summers I would take off to sing with the various light opera companies that toured around. There were always little affairs with members of the troupe. I saw very little of my family during those times.
The last six months with Marge were terribly strained and in that
entire year, I think we had sex maybe a half dozen times and then
only at my insistence. There was no feeling between us—not in bed.
But there was always the tension and the fighting out of it. My son
has neuroses I'm sure he'll never shed because of the way Marge and
I acted toward one another. He hated to see us fight and I'm haunted
to this day by the vision of this little kid trying to act as a peacemaker
between his mommy and daddy. It is so fucking unfair that an innocent kid has to suffer because his fucked-up parents can't keep their
fucked-uppedness away from their child.

But eventually I came to see very clearly, during a period in my
therapy, that I could no longer live both as a hetero- and homosexual.
I asked Marge for a trial separation and she agreed. The plan was for
me to come to New York, check it out for work and then, if
we wished, she and the children would join me.

Why did you choose New York?

Primarily because I knew my kind of work would be available here—
and it was, as I began singing with the Philharmonic and American
Symphony almost immediately—and also because I knew if sexual
freedom existed anywhere, it would have to be in New York.

And did it?

Yes. I was initially like a kid let out of school for summer vacation.
I went around feeling, touching and tasting everything. I thought
then I was being very wanton. Looking back, I know I never was. I
have never been engulfed in gay life. I have never been to the baths
or the truck stops. I know the sex bars exist but I have no interest
in them. Actually, I find them repugnant. There are areas of gay life
that distress me. I don't need the freedom to be licentious. I just need
the freedom to be gay. There is a difference. One is freedom with
dignity, while the other is not.

But it wasn't all "summer vacation" and fun in New York. The
first weeks I was miserable. I would frequently cry myself to sleep. I
missed my kids terribly. In fact, after the first six weeks, I asked
Marge to come up, but she refused, having decided she didn't want
to raise the children in New York. Then, four months later, she
called to say, and I remember her exact words, "Although I love you,

I don't want to be married to you any more." An incredible thing had happened to and for Marge during the separation. She found she could make it on her own, that she would not fall apart, and that she could tell "Daddy" to mind his own business.

What was your reaction to her being the one who asked for the divorce?

Relieved, and then, like a true neurotic . . . rejected. And then relieved, again. However, I wasn't the only one with conflicting feelings. The night before the divorce became final Marge called to ask me back. But by then I couldn't. By then I knew what it meant for me to be gay and that within gay life is where any hope for my fulfillment lay.

Did you ever tell Marge about your homosexuality?

Yes, and I had been right—she had never suspected. I was glad I had told her. I wanted her to know the responsibility for the marriage's failure was not hers alone—which was what she was making it. She was not repulsed or judgmental. She, too, had suffered. We both had, with feelings of hostility and inadequacy. Both of us had felt frightened . . . unhappy . . . resentful. Now, at last, there was some freedom from such unnecessary binds.

Regarding "freedom," did you feel free once you were divorced?

Well, there was no freedom in the monthly sum I agreed to send for child support. It was a rather large sum but I had a rather large amount of guilt. I also had a large amount of the "What-to-dos." I went through a long period of adjustment. Suddenly there was no anchor around my neck and I was faced with discovering what it was I wanted to do with my life. Often, I felt very lonely and alone. Often, I felt very frustrated in not finding someone to be with. It wasn't until I realized that I was looking for some guy to share my problems . . . to make me happy by filling in the missing pieces, that I stopped searching without and started looking within. It wasn't easy. I questioned what I had done with my life to date and there were times when I thought I might have been better off with Marge and the kids—secure within a family framework—than on my own. Then, too, there were the hours spent wondering whether I had been selfish, whether I had hurt the children by leaving. Ultimately I realized that you must be selfish if you are to make your life work. I had to make my own life better before I could do that for my kids or anyone else. Had I hung in the marriage, I would have been miserable and would have taken that misery out on those around me.

Eventually, I did begin to feel free. As mentioned, I was never overwhelmed by the amount of sex available. But I certainly did get involved in a number of relationships which both I and they endured. And believe me, *endured* is the right word. Name the type and I was involved with him. Name the mistake and I made it. Which was all good. The experiences defined and redefined what it is I want in a relationship. I'll never settle again.

Had you "settled"?

Often. I didn't want to be alone and being with someone was preferable to being with no one. You have to make it with yourself before you can be alone. It took me time. I'll never sell out for "protection" again. I don't need another person to feel safe, although I admit I feel safer within a relationship. Today, I can live alone—and do—and like it. But I function best when with someone. But that someone would have to possess the same ethical, moral, intellectual and spiritual values—the same standards that I maintain. And mine are pretty damn high. Thank God I have such a someone. His name is Carl and we have been together, although we do not as yet live together, for more than a year.

When and how did you meet?

Across a crowded room at some cocktail party given in honor of a recently published book written by an old friend of us both. Like in the movies, our eyes met and that was that. Except nothing happened. He was attached. So we were like two ships that passed in the night until we collided at Philharmonic Hall a month later. It took five more collision-course months before we went to bed. It's a corny story but every word of it is true. There is no other man who holds any interest for me.

What makes this relationship . . . this man, special?

He does share the same values I spoke of before. We also share many of the same interests and attitudes. He is an artist and sees life and people with that special sensitivity most artists have. He colors everything around him with vitality. With Carl, I feel freer than I have ever felt in my life. It is hard for me to describe this freedom because until I met him I didn't know of its existence. The best I can offer is to say that within his love I feel whole . . . complete, as though I can move and do anything. I can share freely, particularly my soul as well as my body. I have such pride in this person . . . so proud to be a man in love with *this* man. He is one of God's rare creatures . . . a talented, refined, sensitive human being who cares about himself and others. He is more than my lover. He is my best friend. I've never been friends with a lover before. I am so proud of what I am with him . . . to him and of what we are together. I never knew there could be freedom in loving and in being loved. I also never knew—and I know many people will not understand this—that I would feel more masculine than I have ever felt in loving this man. I am the total me with him. There is no role-playing whatsoever, not in bed or out. For what? For whom? We are what we are. We do sexually whatever we feel like doing without premeditation. Our sex is a spontaneous expression of where we are at today. He is the first man with whom I am capable of performing all aspects of sex. For the first time I am allowing myself to be vulnerable sexually and I like it.

Do you think of yourself as "married"?

Engaged is a better word. If within the year we continue to feel as we do, then we will live together. Then, we will be married, as you say. This is the man that I want to be with. If certain problems can be solved, I will be with him. Carl just recently entered therapy to work out certain things that gnaw at him, things that affect us.

Do you worry about the relationship not working out?

Yes, but should it not, I won't be destroyed—just hurt and disappointed. But I'll survive. There is something I now know about me . . . that I have incredible inner resources—strength. I have managed to stay on top of all the chaos in my life. I don't know where that strength comes from but I do thank God for it. I have gone through long periods of doubt and despair but I regret none of those periods because they brought me to this place in time. I had to travel those roads to reach the here-and-now. Had I not, I'd be a frustrated and bitter man.

Are you secure within your homosexuality today?

A year ago I would have said "almost." Today I can say "yes." Within the year, I experienced EST training. I went in supposedly to work out a few professional problems but found somewhere during the seventy-two hours that I felt strained . . . uncomfortable. I felt outside the two hundred people in attendance. I knew it was my feelings about my homosexuality that were setting me apart. So I stood up and came out before one-and-all. I accepted the responsibility for my sexuality. I stopped blaming my parents and opted instead for a statement of self. "This is what I am and I like it. This is my life and I like it." It blew the damn place away. I was crying and so were others. Many came to just touch me; some just to say "thanks" or "hello." It was one of the most beautiful and significant moments of my life. Since then, I feel no shame, no guilt. I just feel loved and loving.

When you say you have dropped the blame, has that altered your relationship with your parents?

Yes and no. I see less of them than I ever have but I can see them if I wish to. I've let go of the hate and hurt I felt for so long. I also let go of the needs they cannot, and never could, fulfill. Thus, I don't take any shit from them. Like if I do see them and my mother starts running one of her numbers, I stop her. They still don't know of my homosexuality and I wish they did. But I know my mother. If I told her, she would lay such a guilt trip on herself . . . a real "Where-did-I-go-wrong" kind of thing. Too bad. I really don't want any more secrets in my life. I am only sorry that I must still hide professionally but . . . I have heard my employer pontificate on the subject of "queers." Unfortunately, I need my job or I'd tell him to shove it.

Having made your peace with your parents, where are you today with your religious beliefs?

The church no longer serves any function in my life and hasn't for many years. My relationship with God needs no intermediary. I have a direct line to him. We all do. And I do believe in him. You cannot love someone as intensely as I love Carl or be loved as intensely as I am, without feeling God in that love. That kind of love between people is holy. In that love you know that all the rules imposed on man are *by* man and not by God. He does not make such negative rules. No. He makes beauty and order.

Do you feel beauty and order in your life?

Very much so. I'm two years away from forty and instead of being regretful about the age, I feel good. I'm proud of my years and I have no fears about the future. That I *might* grow old alone never enters my mind. That is not a particularly homosexual happenstance. You can be straight and face your old age without a partner. If that ever became difficult for me, I would take my own life. I don't ever want to live past the point of enjoying my life.

The beauty and order in my life has a great deal to do with my years. I'm past the point of lying to myself and others. Today, I want all the shit up-front where I can deal with it. No more games. Life is the only game in town and if you cheat at it you cheat yourself. Without the lies, there is beauty . . . order.

One of the accusations often made about the homosexual life is that it is selfish. Have you thoughts on this?

Assuming it is, so what? Selfishness is not necessarily bad. Frankly, I'm more afraid of the self-sacrificers than I am of the selfish. They make those they sacrifice for pay, pay and pay. I firmly believe we should all be at the center of our lives. We should not live for our spouses, lovers or children but for ourselves. Because if one does live "selfishly," for oneself, then one can truly give to others out of his own contentment. My life is not a selfish one today. I give something every day in the way I talk to people, in what I share of me with them.

What will you share with your children?

You must be reading my mind. I was thinking of them as I spoke of what is, and what isn't, selfish. Marge remarried a few years ago and shortly thereafter, she and her husband—a really nice guy who loves the kids—asked that he adopt my son and daughter. My initial reaction was *never!* Not *my* kids. That was selfish. It took me a lot of soul-searching before I realized that to prevent his adopting them was not in their best interests but was an ego need of mine. The kids needed to feel part of a family unit. Their best interests demanded that they grow up in a house with a father with whom they shared the same last name.

I'm not pretending it was an easy decision. A major part of me did not want to do it but I did. *That* part of me felt good. I believe I did something very constructive for my children. Certainly, it hasn't changed my feelings for them. They are still, and always will be, my kids.

Now about what I will share with them. There is only one thing that I can . . . me. My son will be spending a month with me before

school starts. I'm excited and nervous. I haven't seen either one of the
kids in two years. I couldn't. It was too painful. It hurts like hell to be
with them and it hurts even worse when I leave. Well . . . you can't
have everything. But seeing my boy . . . he's not so little any more.
Almost a teenager. So special. I had been guilty toward him for many
years. The divorce caused him great pain. When Marge and I split,
he was old enough to be affected. My little girl was not. That first
year, no one could get to my boy—not me, not his mother or his
teachers. He was so hurt. I did everything I could to assure him that I
loved him and that the change would be good for us all but how do
you convince a young child of things he cannot understand?

Do you feel he ever did come to grasp the situation?

I don't know. That's the pain.

Is that why the tears?

Yes. You see, he's such a gorgeous little guy. I feel such love for him
. . . such a bond. We are very much alike. He's had a tough time of
it and I wish to God that hadn't been so. He has had difficulty adjust-
ing to Marge's remarriage. He felt very rejected when I left. I wanted
to spare him that, but how? Despite all the explanations, the bottom
line was "Daddy went away and left me."

I'm sorry. I didn't mean to come apart. It just happened. But he is
so much like me. Not just in looks but in temperament. I look at my
son and think "Oh Lord, what you will have to go through." I think
he will be gay, and I hope if he is that he will have an easier time of it
than I did. There have been many societal changes in attitude but
hardly enough.

What makes you think your son will be homosexual?

There is an aura about him . . . a special sensitivity. It is not that he
is delicate but there is a delicacy about him. He is shy, mild-mannered
and loves beauty. I really can't explain it further. It's just a feeling I
have.

*What do you feel about the likelihood of your son emerging as a
homosexual?*

If it means his happiness, fine. That is all I care about. A few years
ago, I would have answered your question by stating I would prefer
he be straight. But now that I know such inner peace and have found

such happiness as a homosexual in love with a homosexual, I can only wish my son find equal happiness with whomever he chooses.

What advice, for want of a better word, would you give your son if he were to become a homosexual?

The very same Polonius gave to Laertes . . . "to thine own self be true." It is your life to live so live it as you see fit and not as others do. I would not pretend to him that it is easy to be gay in a straight world, but it is also not easy to be straight in a straight world. There is no "easy life." There are always the outside pressures telling you what you should and should not do or be. I would tell him not to listen to any voices other than his own and if that means living alone in the woods, then do it. But don't compromise yourself.

I would also want him to believe there is no reason to do anything but rejoice in who and what he is. I would never want him to feel like a second-class human being because society puts that label on homosexuals. I hope he would have the strength to tell that society to "Fuck off!" And lastly, I would hope he finds someone with whom he can share his life *if* that is what he wishes.

Will you tell your son of your homosexuality?

Yes, but I don't know exactly when. I feel he is still too young to deal with it successfully. He doesn't need any more confusion in his life. But he will be told. I love this child and want him to love me. If he doesn't know me—all of me—then he really can't say he loves me. I have very little fear of telling him, although I do worry about his acceptance. If he were to reject me, I'd be very upset, but I would hope that time and maturity would change his thinking.

We have spoken only of your son. What of your daughter?

Although only a year separates my daughter from her brother, that year seemed like five when I left. I cannot pretend that I feel the same closeness to her. She is very different from her brother. She has made a marvelous adjustment. She loves her new daddy.

Do you plan to speak as openly with her one day as you plan to speak with your son?

It will be more difficult, but yes, I do. It just seems more important to tell him because of the possible confusion he might one day feel about his own sexuality.

Have you considered the possibility of your daughter becoming a Lesbian?

Not until this exact moment. But, again, I would only hope that whatever she becomes that she be proud of it. I've become very simplistic in my old age. I believe the world was put here to enjoy. Suffering is a bloody bore.

Are you enjoying your world today?

More than I ever thought possible. If there are any married men who read this, who share the problem I once had, I can only hope they will be moved to make changes in their own lives. To hold a marriage together for the sake of the kids is to do them a disservice. Kids feel a parent's frustration and resentment. And they don't know what to do with it. Often, they mistake it as a failing on their part that has caused it. But even more important, I honestly, sincerely believe one must live one's life. There are some men who stay married because they cannot accept who and what they are. They deny their lives. I feel terribly sorry for them because I know of their pain. Until they are ready, they will never believe me when I say they would be so much happier if they would accept their homosexuality rather than continue to hide it behind the cloak of marriage. I just don't think there can be any peace, any real happiness, until you accept who you are.

I enjoy being a homosexual. I am sorry society condemns me for being who and what I am. But I now look at it as their problem. My life belongs to me and I live it as I should. Am I excited about my life? You bet your ass! I'm excited about me. Life is filled with goodies. From people, books, plays, opera, dance to Carl and me. But mostly, it is filled with me. I have everything because I have me.

You are smiling again.

Yes . . . I hear myself . . . feel myself and I know . . . I am happy. . . . I am *really* happy.

Kjell Eriksson

I T IS A wonderful face, beautiful as it reacts to the music his hands create from the keyboard of the baby grand that fills his studio overlooking the East River in Manhattan. With his eyes closed, Kjell Eriksson * begins to sing. His voice, belying the 140 pounds that barely fill a six-foot frame, is enormous, yet sweet. Somewhere, in another place, Kjell Eriksson is happy, consumed by his music.

As abruptly as he began, Kjell Eriksson stops, slamming his hands furiously down on a final chord. As if returning from a trance, he enters the present, looks about the sparsely decorated room—mainly rich woods covered with rough but richly textured fabrics—and there is but the faintest trace of tears in his blue eyes. He nervously brushes back his long blond hair, lights a cigarette—which he quickly extinguishes after a long drag—and collapses onto a couch.

"I'm trying to quit," he says of the barely smoked cigarette. "It's lousy for the voice. Besides, it gives cancer and cancer kills. Thank God something does," he adds. "Christ! What a melodramatic remark." He settles back and speaks of opera—his passion—and the singing career that still might come. At forty-four, he is waiting for many things.

Including the Messiah.

Do you believe in His coming?

Baby, if he is between twenty-six and thirty-one, with a smooth, hairless body and a big, thick cock, I definitely believe in his coming . . . right in my mouth!

So much for religion. I gather you are a "non-believer."

Wrong! I was born a Baptist and raised a Methodist. At eighteen I converted to Catholicism. That eight-year romance ended when I became a metaphysician. Today, I'm anti organized religious *anything* but a great believer in the Christ consciousness that lives within us all. It is a spirit of godliness and once it is found, it must be kindled

* See Author's Note, page xii.

129

and cherished. It is about love, the possibility for which is within us all.

Have you found it?

Found and lost it. It comes and it goes. It was there a while back when I was singing. But then . . .

Then, what?

Look, this really isn't a good day to talk about God and love. It's buried under a pile of shit. This is one of those black times when I feel I would like to die soon—see what's ahead because what's been till now hasn't been all that terrific. I'm forty-four and tired . . . damn tired. No self-pity here 'cause that's a fucking bore. But after a while, worse than cigarettes and cancer is loneliness. That really kills. And I've been lonely a long, long time.

Did anything in particular happen to trigger this mood?

Yes, my life! Specifically, last night . . . cruising. I don't make out. I may be the only man in town who can spend a night at the baths and not get laid. And I don't know why. The mirror tells me I'm still a pretty good piece of ass but it just seems the people I dig don't dig me.

When that happens, how do you react?

Like a petulant child. I get depressed or enraged. I could stamp my feet, hold my breath, and all because I can't have what I want. Do you know I've broken three phones from sheer frustration? Seriously. I'll call a guy I've gotten it on with and he won't remember me or he'll put me off and that kind of shit sends me up and off the god-damn wall.

Since, as you say, the mirror tells you of your attractiveness, what is it you think men see when they look at you?

I only know what they tell me. Like when a guy finally does react to my come-on, he'll say that from a distance I look arrogant . . . un-approachable, as though I think I'm God's gift to gay life. Like last night, the kid I met—the one who turned me down—said, "You look as though you don't need anybody." Christ! If that were true, what would I be doing cruising Central Park? I could stay home and fuck myself.

So their words have little meaning for you.

None. I am not self-sufficient. I do need somebody. Emotionally, I have never so much wanted and needed support. Not the kind you get from a friend but that which only a lover can give. Friends I have plenty of, lovers I have none. And it terrifies me that I might always have none. But I should stop this shit. Really, it's just a bad day. I mean it's pretty difficult to feel sorry for someone who earns $25,000 a year, at his own time and pace in a field he loves. Look around you. I've got everything I need except a lover. So I should shut up.

Would you like to stop talking?

I'd like to stop hurting. It's that fucking experience of last night. And it is so damn dumb! I'm shot because men seldom pick me up. I'm upset because men don't see me as fuck-stuff. They approach me, talk to me, and most times excuse themselves and walk away. And the ones who don't walk away, all they want is to fuck me. There is something about us blue-eyed blonds that makes everyone think we're fuckable.

Aren't you?

Oh sure. I can get it on that way, but it's not my specialty. I'm a cock-sucker . . . one of the best. Always have been.

What do you mean by "always have been"?

Do you know what my first childhood recollection is? And I mean just that—my first! Sucking cock. Through the bars of my crib. Maybe I was two. Maybe younger or older. I have no idea whose cock it was, but I distinctly remember being very excited and liking it.
    You look shocked.

Not shocked . . . disturbed . . . no, shocked, too.
Who was the man?

Damned if I know. We lived near a rather large racetrack in the midwest, and we took in gentlemen boarders during racing season. I assume it was one of them.

What do you feel about that experience in retrospect?

Not what you would expect. No outrage or sense of "rape." Still the excitement and the fear. Yes, the fear. That was transmitted to me through the "gentleman boarder." Again, although it was many years ago, I distinctly remember the experience . . . the excitement and the knowledge that I should not be caught doing this.

Do you recall till what age you were nursed?

Let's not get into that Freudian mumbo jumbo. As far as I'm concerned I was born gay. I have never felt victimized by that man's craziness. It had to be there, already working inside me, for me to have enjoyed it as I did. I do think the son-of-a-bitch could have picked someone a little older. Not that I exactly pick mature types. My taste in men seems to run to children—those between twenty-three and thirty. Hardly peer material. But then I've always had trouble making it with peers. As a child, my friends were always much younger. Boys my age frightened me.

By the way, my second sexual encounter occurred at four. The boy was ten and he pissed in my mouth and I swallowed it. What's more, I liked it. I still do. Now you do look shocked.

Is your mission therefore accomplished?

I'm sorry. I think I was testing you.

Do you do that in cruising situations?

Sometimes. Just to shock the shit out of somebody, or to turn them on, I'll say something outrageous.

Is it then that they walk away?

Sometimes but then sometimes not. Look. I'm sorry about the way I came on. It's just my mood. But what I told you is true. I can get into the piss scene. But only—are you ready?—with all-American, healthy types. It's got to be in the spirit of . . . good, clean fun.

Can you explain why the "piss scene," as you put it, is pleasurable?

I think it's part of my fetish for big things. Like in opera, I like *big* voices. I like *big* sounds, *big* lavish meals, *big* cocks. With me, bigger is better. Like the more a guy can come, the more I dig it. So what's even heavier than a heavy load of cum? A big flow of urine.

So there you are . . . "My Thing" by Kjell Eriksson. Only here's the real *pisser*, it's not my thing at all. It is but it isn't. I've had two lovers in my lifetime. Neither had better than a six-inch cock. And it didn't make any difference. Nor did what we did in bed make any difference because we did everything and it was wonderful. Only now that there is this endless parade of faces, this anonymous, meaningless sex, have my habits become somewhat S&M. But when I've loved . . . been loved, it has been nothing like that. And dammit! That's the experience I want. From childhood, all I have ever wanted is someone with whom I could communicate on a permanent basis.

Was there none within your family?

Next to none. One brother is many years my senior, so we had very little communication. The other is five years older and at that age resented the little brother who tagged along. Kids my age I avoided. I always felt this sense of inadequacy. I wasn't good in sports and other than music and art, I was only fair scholastically. I was very alienated as a child. I began gaining attention in the tenth grade because of my expertise at the piano but that only made me more separate.

You are speaking then of an unhappy childhood.

Do you know, people always spoke about my sunny disposition. I had this really terrific smile that I could turn on and off at will. I gather it must have been a dazzler. Company would come to the house and they'd say. "C'mon kid, give us one of those famous Kjell Eriksson smiles." And I did. Until I was eight. Then I said to my mother, "I'm never going to smile again unless I really want to." She said that was fine with her and that I should always do what I feel.

You're smiling now.

Yes. I was thinking of my mother. She is seventy-four and still gets up off her sagging ass to get around the old town and make life work. She's always up on the latest films. She loves making trips to Burlington, where my brother lives, and New York. She's quite a great ole broad.

Were you close to her as a child?

Too close. I felt smothered by her and actually asked her to stop hugging and kissing me as often as she did when I was about ten. Again, she listened to what I had to say and complied with my wishes.

And your father?

He's dead now, although he was dead to me most of my life. I was never close to him. We never shared anything. When I was nine, he left my mother for a younger woman. He never said a word to me—

just was gone one day. I hated him for it—hated him for making her cry and scream—which she did for days and months at a time. And then when I was thirteen he came back, and although he tried then to be a father to me, I wouldn't give him an inch. I treated him like shit and that didn't change until I was sixteen or so and then somehow a truce was declared.

What did you want to be as a child?

Exactly what I was . . . the town's cock-sucker. From about age six till age thirteen I blew every boy who would let me. But not enough let me. They were too frightened. And I became frightened because I began hearing words like "fairy" and "queer" and I knew from the tone in which they were said that they were very bad things to be. So at thirteen, when I began high school with all new kids, I stopped all sex play. I wasn't about to risk that kind of embarrassment or rejection, particularly since I already had so few friends from grade school and felt so apart from peers.

Was there no sex throughout your teenage years?

There was masturbation, three and four times a day. Also, in my junior year, with a bunch of guys I became friendly with, we would gang-bang this very willing girl. But in truth, it wasn't fucking her that was exciting. It was watching the other guys and then putting my cock where theirs had been that really got me off. As far as I know—or allow myself to know—I've never experienced any real sexual feelings toward women.

How did you feel about your homosexual feelings during your childhood and adolescence?

I hated them. I knew I had to hide because discovery would have meant humiliation. I always loved men, loved the sex with them, but I always hated the feelings that followed—that I could be rejected. That's why I was able to channel all my sexual energies into my music during my teenage years. That was safe. That was also encouraged by my parents who scrimped to put me through a good music conservatory. Only I didn't want to go.

But why?

Fear. I remember clearly telling my parents that I thought their money would be best spent by sending me to a psychiatrist because I was obsessed with sex feelings toward men.

What was their reaction?

They were incredible . . . just incredible. No shock. No sense of horror or shame. With me, they went to their minister and spoke of the problem. He said it was "normal" for boys my age—I was then eighteen—to have sexual feelings toward other boys but that once they socialized in the world, these feelings matured toward members of the opposite sex. We believed him. We wanted to. And I attended the conservatory, which turned out to be one big coming out party for me. In fact, I came out so often that I finally came out of the conservatory. I figuratively and literally blew it. All that sex and no work makes for a dull boy . . . in class!

But my parents were wonderful. Really super. They never made me feel badly about my homosexuality. Both accepted it. If I bring it up, my mother today will discuss any aspect of it. But she'll never pry. The same was true with my father.

And your brothers?

The eldest is gay but in the closet and is quite miserable living there alone. But since he won't come out, but waits for someone to join him there, I think he'll be forever unhappy. I love him but I can't get near him. My other brother is a fucking gem. He is married with five kids. When I was twenty I took him with me to a gay bar. He sat, observed and finally said: "Frankly Kjell, I don't understand and can't pretend that I do. It not only turns me off but kind of sickens me. But, you're my brother and if it makes you happy, I'm happy. Just remember, should that ever change, and should you need me, I'm here."

As I said, the guy is a fucking gem. I wouldn't mind having a lover exactly like him even though he is five years older.

Can you explain your attraction for young men?

Sure. I'm a dirty old man. And shallow, too.

Granted! But beyond that?

I like smooth, young bodies with hard lines. Men my age usually are sagging, physically and mentally. They're dried up. The young have a spontaneity, an excitement about life, that special childlike enthusiasm, that just . . . well, it excites me. Life with a younger man is never anything but current. Not dull or dormant. But maybe after my last two affairs I'd be better off with dull and dormant. Certainly, the way I've been feeling lately, emotionally and professionally, I've got to make some changes.

What kind of changes?

I'm not certain but I have the feeling that my own life is getting away from me. And that frightens me. Music is my sole security. I teach music mainly to very talented students but I really want to sing. That makes me insecure. New steps at my age are frightening. Then, too, I'm still searching for that *something* or someone to make me complete . . . whole. That's also frightening. When does the search end?

Was converting to Catholicism part of your search?

Exactly. Shortly after getting bounced out of the conservatory, I began my conversion. My brother was in the process because he was marrying a Catholic girl. Together we found "God." Only I really did. I truly fell in love with "him" and Catholicism. I felt a part of something . . . at last. The feelings of separateness that I had felt from childhood vanished in the church. For the first time in my life I wasn't lonely.

What did you do with your homosexuality?

Promised continually to give it up and confessed constantly because I couldn't. But I was always forgiven. I was never damned or excommunicated as long as I promised to try to abstain. You see, as a child, in church, I had been told during Religious Instruction that boys who played with themselves were boys God couldn't love. And I always wanted him to love me. But I was always masturbating.

You want to hear a cheery story? My uncle caught me at it one afternoon—I was eight or nine—and said little boys who do such awful things grow up to be axe murderers. I believed him but I still couldn't stop masturbating although I would try for days, a week even. Sooo, if you ever read of an axe murderer running loose on the East Side of Manhattan, you'll know who to look for.

If I understand correctly, you were a practicing homosexual while you were a practicing Catholic.

Yes. And it was a constant conflict. I had begun living with a man— a foreign diplomat—whom I didn't love but who would blackmail me into staying with him.

How so?

He would speak of his heart condition—he was only twenty-eight—and how my leaving would kill him. So I stayed for three rotten years. Then, I was very passive and I never challenged what people said but accepted their word as though it were the gospel.

In the meantime, the gospel is telling me I'm a sinner—that all homosexuals are sinners. So, I was torn twixt hell and hell. Some choice! But I must say, not one priest ever threatened me—told me that I was the Devil's Doing—or any shit like that. As long as I confessed my "sin," I received absolution. In all other ways I was a very good Catholic. And why not? I was so grateful God would love an unworthy like me. I was sorely tempted to join the priesthood but the Army got me first.

What was your military experience like?

Bad. So bad that after training, when my unit was about to be shipped out to Germany, I declared myself—told the Army doctors I was a homosexual. Yet, my homosexuality was not my problem in the Army. I had sex with no one. What was worse was my inability to relate to the men my age. I was again alone . . . alienated. And that made me feel very frightened . . . panicked. I was afraid of cracking up. They were very understanding and I received a discharge with honor . . . from *them*.

Why do you stress "from them"?

Because I killed myself over what I had done. For eighteen months I went through a depression that no one and nothing—not even my beloved church—could break. I crucified myself for what I felt had been my weakness. It makes me sad just remembering how that child suffered. And so needlessly.

Was it time, or some specific action, that relieved the depression?

Both. Mainly my music was my salvation. I had been accepted at a good music school and was studying composition and theory when one day during class I just casually began to sing. Within a month I switched to voice with not only the approval but the push of everyone in the music department. They felt I had a natural bent for singing—and I do. But I got sidetracked. To support myself and my lessons, I began taking music students of my own. Initially, it wasn't meant to be anything other than a part-time job—you know, like the way some kids wait on tables to put themselves through college. But I also had a natural bent for teaching and before I knew it, I was singing less and teaching more. But I was young, in New York, in love with the city, with my music and with sex. In other words, I lost my concentration. I allowed myself to become distracted from my real pursuit—which was singing.

And there were other distractions. My Catholicism collided constantly with the young men coming in and out of my life. I wanted to be loved by a *real* person more than I wanted to be loved by God. Or so it seemed. For eight years I was torn between my physical and my spiritual needs. I went less and less often to church until finally, when someone took me, by chance, to a meeting of metaphysicians, I gave up Catholicism entirely.

What did metaphysics give you?

A very different religious belief. To look for the God within me. To make me my own God because he lives within us all. Metaphysics was a very positive experience, because it stressed you, me, everyone can have things as we wish. I had always resisted formal therapy because I felt it only dealt with problems. Metaphysics only dealt with solutions. I liked that. Metaphysics was about *willing* your life to work. It was finding and accepting your uniqueness—enjoying your individuality. For the first time I felt at peace with my homosexuality because it was me. I found I could like and enjoy it because I didn't have to be like anyone else.

Another very strange but wonderful thing happened through metaphysics. I forgave my father—and my mother, too; but she was never the problem my father was—for being a lousy parent. I understood that both gave me *all* they were capable of giving. It wasn't that they intentionally denied me companionship and communication, they *couldn't* give it. I realized that they were no older at my birth than I was at that time and if I were still so uncertain and fucked up in many ways, why should I have expected them to be perfect?

But we do expect our parents to be perfect . . . to love us as we would have them love us. They couldn't. It was then I began to know my father. Before he died, we achieved a kind of warmth, a closeness —although we were never close—that we had never shared. My relationship with my mother altered totally. I became much more friend than son because that was the relationship with which she was always most comfortable. I have great love for my mother today, as I know she has for me.

Are you still actively involved in metaphysics?

The problem is I'm not actively involved in anything. Not metaphysics, not sex, not my music, not life. Months ago I went through EST training, hoping that would give me some further answers. As you can see . . . always the search for something, anything, to keep me going. Anything to ease the loneliness—that inner barrenness that often makes life unbearable. Like today. That's how I feel . . . barren. On days like this it is an effort to teach . . . to breathe . . . to just be alive. On days like today I look out at the brilliant blue of the sky falling on the East River and don't see it. Or see it but not feel it. I lose the miracle of life . . . the wonder of being alive. And you see . . . life really is a miracle, a wonder. There really is so much beauty. But I don't *feel* it although I can tell you about it. Funny, that reminds me of the Gay Encounter Group I attended until they kicked me out after six months. I'd sit there and bawl over everyone's pain, but when it came to talking of my own, I'd be calm and dispassionate.

As though you didn't need anybody?

Oh my God! Exactly. It was the same thing as in the cruising situation. People kept blasting me because I was always so "together." That is so funny. I mean, that is really funny! Me, so together.

Listen. I'd like to stop now. Could we pick this up another day?

Most of the patrons at the outdoor café at Lincoln Center take notice of his arrival. His blond hair is flying competitively with the scarf loosely tied around his neck to protect his throat from a chilling early autumn breeze. He is carrying two containers of coffee and looks very much at home in what is to him "native surroundings."

Is Lincoln Center really the home of the gay mafia?

Now that's funny! Yes, I suppose it is. Probably. The opera, dance and concert world is basically dominated and, I suspect, even controlled by gays. It is a very tight circle, one which is much more difficult for a straight to enter. Many jobs are achieved through "sexual favors" but no more so than in any other profession. But being gay certainly makes you "preferred" in this field. But not among singers. Many administrators of opera houses throughout the world are vehemently anti-gay. They'll reject a gay tenor. So . . . even with the control gays exert in the music world, we still suffer from discrimination. But we do get even.

This gay mafia is composed of a very dangerous group of people. Probably the most deadly mouths in the West . . . and the East, too. Awful, bitchy people mainly. I avoid them.

> *But certainly there are heterosexuals gainfully employed in the opera/concert world.*

Many. And they are very different from most heterosexuals. They are very sympatico. Maybe because they are exposed to gays and see we are not a "disease" or a "menace," they relate to us comfortably as people.

> *How do you relate to them?*

Also with comfort. My friends are equally divided among straights and gays. In fact, I'm even more likely to be fixed up by my straight friends than I am by my gay ones. At a dinner party I'll often find my host and hostess have gone to the trouble to find me an "eligible." It's really very nice and I'm very lucky. In my isolated world I've never encountered that terrible prejudice many gays come up against in their professions. I have never known the feeling of the "persecuted homosexual" in my field.

> *What about within yourself?*

That's a terrific question and I congratulate you for asking. Before you and I began this bit of masochism, I would have said "All Clear." I really thought I had it together regarding my homosexuality—was fully at peace with it. But since we met, I can't make my brain turn off. I find I am not as together with it as I thought. If I were, I wouldn't be so repulsed by the people who march in the Gay Lib parades. I always thought it was because they seemed crude—like ranters and ravers. But now I see that's untrue. I'm still in the closet in some ways. I do not want to be affiliated with the movement because I am comfortable in my work. I am not threatened. But, should I come out, be irrevocably exposed as a homosexual, I fear retribution. Like should I ever want to sing professionally, it could be used against me. But it is more than that. The truth is . . . as alone as I am, I don't want to risk being even more alone. I view public admission of one's homosexuality as the ultimate test of rejection. I feel too rejected already to take that risk.

But speaking of rejection, one of the things I have come to realize between the times we've talked is how I set it up. I have had two lovers; one was twenty-five and the other twenty-six. In both cases, I was fifteen years older because one followed upon the heels of the other. In fact, retrospectively, I see I had but one lover. The other was the "sugar substitute"—the pacifier to get you through the night.

The boy I loved came to me as a student. He was the lover of a man considerably older than himself and although nothing happened between us for three months, we both knew it would. And it did. As they say in the movies, I fell madly in love. And for good reason. He was beautiful to look at and an incredibly intelligent as well as talented young man. He was everything I had waited for. He told me he loved me and just needed time to break off with this other man. Months and months later, he still needed time. At the end of a year, as we sat in United Nations park, he was still insisting he needed time. And in that park of peace I punched him in the mouth and left. He remains, to this day, with that man. I see him around but I can barely say hello. The pain still cuts that deep.

Rather than live with the pain, I took up with Barton. That lasted nine months. What a prick he was! So what was I doing with him? Filling up my bed with someone. I needed to have a young, beautiful person there, with me. And he stayed for nine months and during that time there was no communication—no real giving on his part. I'll explain. He had a very high sex drive and he would fuck me daily and I would blow him at least once a day as well. But in the nine months of "togetherness," I think I had maybe a half dozen orgasms. He just didn't care whether or not I was satisfied.

So why did I hang in? That would be your question if I wasn't rattling on. Because I had just "suffered" my fortieth birthday. God but that particular event is a killer! Suddenly you feel your age. Forty! My God. More than half your life has been lived. It's strictly downhill-time. All that negative stuff gnaws at you, so . . . you grab the first goodie that comes along and you hold on tight even though in the holding you are drowning anyway.

I was lonely. I was frightened. I was forty. I took in Barton not to be alone. I made believe I loved him. I even believed in *his own way* —don't you love that rationalization?—he loved me. It was all horse-shit! It was with Barton that I allowed myself to be abused. I let him fist-fuck me. I seduced him into pissing on me. I let him do with me as he wanted. If only he would stay! Desperation makes you do dire and desperate things.

Well m'love, since our talks, old Kjell here, forty-four moving toward fifty, has seen a lot of light. Sure I still find young, gorgeous men appealing, but I know now that if I'm serious about wanting a real relationship, I better stop playing with children. I need a man who has also walked through shit—smelled it—and now wants a rose instead. So the rose might be a little wilted. It still smells better than shit. Enough of the self-torture. Enough of unfulfilled needs. Do you know what I realized when I sat myself down to think about it? My relationship with both boys I loved—or thought I loved—ended when I exposed my deepest need: to be held, to be treated with tenderness, to be loved. It was more responsibility than a child could handle. So . . . it's no more raising of children for me. Little birds eventually spread their wings and fly the coop. There must be men my age who have not allowed life to defeat them, who are still young in thought if not also in body.

Now I must run. I'm teaching a lesson in five minutes. And I haven't even asked how you are. How are you?

He dashes off and leaves a rose on the table. Two weeks later, when I enter his studio, roses sit atop the baby grand. He is singing an aria from *Tosca* and his face again has that special glow. His hair has been cut short. He looks younger . . . happier. He acknowledges my presence by nodding his head as he continues to put Puccini's "Mario" where he is, "out front."

This is my life, you know. I have no other real interests. I read some, but, basically, music is my all-consuming passion. And I'm never bored with it. In my fantasies, I still dream of becoming this great Wagnerian tenor. The talent is there and I have decided to pursue it. I cannot just give up teaching to concentrate on singing, however, as I have been very foolish with money. Frankly, I haven't a nickel because if there is a concert or an opera I wish to hear, I go. And . . . I take my penniless, starving-artiste friends with me. Why not? They would do the same for me. Besides a brilliant performance means so much more when you share the experience with someone. It becomes so much more meaningful.

Do you feel your life will now be more meaningful with your decision to pursue a singing career?

Yes. Singing is the lover that I should be giving myself to. For in giving me to this lover, I feel the most me. If only I had given to this lover what I so stupidly gave to others, I'd have given and received so much more in life.

I am glad you heard me sing. No one can know Kjell Eriksson unless he hears him sing. Only then the real man emerges. Only then are his life experiences shared. When I am singing, as I sometimes do at parties, a hush will fall over a room. People *hear* me. More, they *feel* me. They sense my sensibilities. But then, when I'm singing I'm not afraid of being me. I feel so centered when singing . . . so in touch with me, the person. I like me so much when I sing.

Kjell, why are you crying?

Because I don't understand why people . . . men, can't hear or feel me unless I sing. What doesn't come through? Where do I lose me? Why do they continue to think I am things I am not. I'm not so strong. I'm just me.

But who says otherwise?

Last night, again, in a bar . . . lots of bars, I cruised. Nothing. Finally, one young man talked with me a while and then excused himself. I went after him. I had to ask . . . had to know, why? Why are you leaving? And he said something about my strength being overpowering. I kept wondering who had he been talking to that he had gotten such an impression.

Kjell, why do you expect your song to be heard in a cruising situation?

Where else is it to be heard? Do I rent Town Hall and give a concert for potential lovers? Where does one go to *sing*—to meet a nice man. There are no gay matchmakers. But God knows you are right. One's song isn't heard in the baths or the bars. No one listens to anything but their own voices there. Or their own crotch. All those places are about sex. Well that's fine. I dig sex. As I told you: I'm a cock-sucker and a damn good one. But what I didn't tell you, it is the person whose cock I'm sucking that's important and not the cock itself. I'm a goddamn nineteenth-century romantic. I believe in love and I believe in giving your all when in love. Worse, or better, depending on your own orientation, I love tenderness in sex. Just to stroke someone you care for . . . ah, but I'm finding it very hard to be a homosexual in my old age.

Do you think it would be less difficult if you were heterosexual?

Over the past weeks I've allowed myself to explore my heterosexual fantasies. They aren't frightening any more. I'd like to try sex with a woman. I've also asked myself if I would prefer to be straight . . . wondered if my life would be more simple, more content. But the truth is, although I like women and find many very beautiful, I am not truly attracted to them. And if I turned toward women sexually I don't believe my life would be better. You see, I don't believe my problems are necessarily homosexual. I have pain . . . anger, which I frequently turn against myself. Feelings of inferiority. All those "pretty" things all people feel from time to time. What ails me is not my homosexuality but my *being*. The faith within me, in myself, that Christ consciousness, comes and goes. When gone, what difference what sexuality you are? I mean what difference who pisses on you . . . a man or a woman? What matters is . . . you allow yourself to be humiliated. That is what I am intent on stopping. Why should I allow some guy, or, if I were heterosexual, some woman, to slap me around in bed or do things to me that I consider perversions? Why should I allow anyone to put me down? In the past weeks, in soul-searching, I've discovered I hate that shit. I'm not frightened by my masochistic tendencies but . . . and here's the change, I don't want to play them out any more. I don't want any more punishment. I refuse to feel useful only because I am allowing some man to misuse or abuse me. I am demanding *I* treat myself better. I have received the names of several therapists and I will talk to them. I have a life to live and I intend to live it. I am almost positive that if I can get in touch with what I feel, I think I could be a great singer. What stops me, sometimes, is the invisible shield I erect between me and the world. I still keep Kjell very separate, very protected. And that affects my singing because I can no longer bring that shield down at will.

What is that shield protecting today?

Me! Some days I feel like an onion skin is all that's between me and coming apart.

What does "coming apart" mean to you?

Crying.

So?

But I'm afraid I'll never stop, which is why I haven't wanted to feel my pain—why it's been easier to break telephones and curse God for having forsaken me.

Can you define your pain?

It's in never having loved or having been loved as I would have wished . . . as I have needed. And I am capable of giving and receiving that love. For all my bravura about my skills at cock-sucking and how much I enjoy cock, do you know, when I've been involved, I have never had sex with anyone other than my lover. It simply doesn't interest me. To be honest, I am incapable of understanding the need for other "cock" when in love. 'Cause when I love, when I'm making love with a lover, the feeling inside me is akin to when I am singing. It is pure, joyous me. I am at my freest. But I have known that so infrequently and now, not for four years.

And you fear not knowing it again?

Yes. Exactly. It does get more difficult as you move past forty. We are not as physically attractive as those who are twenty or thirty. But I do not intend to compete on that level any longer. Nor do I intend to seek love among the young—or among the "ruins" either. But somewhere, in between, there is someone, my age or thereabouts, with whom I can share a lifetime. Oh I'm sure, knowing the way I react to youthful beauty, that I'll fall in lust several more times but that's what it will be seen and accepted as.

It sounds as if you are pinning your entire life on finding a lover.

Well . . . the prospect of living alone in the future does bother me. Hell, that's bullshit! It bothers me now! I will always have my music. I will always be sustained. But if my life evolves to be only about music, it will be a waste. And you know why? 'Cause all this talk over the past weeks has made me look inside and you know what? Living there is this really nice human being. But between him and another human being is this pile of shit which I now fully intend to wade through, sort of flush away. I'm going to open those formerly closed doors and look even deeper inside Kjell Eriksson. I must. Who is to hear my song if I cannot truly sing it? I mean . . . if there is a beautiful flower growing in the middle of the desert, how is one to know of its existence if one can't see it?

Lee Brown

"**M**AN, CUT THAT SHIT!**" says Lee Brown,* feigning annoyance as people compare him to his lookalike, Richard Roundtree, "I'm a much prettier-looking dude." Certainly, the night of our first meeting at a black, sexually mixed disco, he is as pretty-a-dude as you are likely to see. He is wearing a white suit but no shirt. His smooth brown chest gleams from sweat and draws numerous admiring glances from the people who hustle and boogie about. Says one young woman, "Brother, you are a brother!" Lee grins and asks her to dance. And does he dance! In, guess what?—red shoes!

The next day in Central Park's Rambles, the "beautiful dude," wearing sawed-off jeans that barely cover the essentials, parades proudly before the admiring glances of the young men who have come to take the sun and one another that late summer afternoon. To many he says "Hey!" in friendly greeting and response to their equally friendly glances. Yet, when he settles down to talk, Lee Brown becomes oblivious to his surroundings. At the disco, despite a beat that threatened to beat down the walls, he concentrated solely on the interview. In the Rambles, despite the ramblings of the men cruising back and forth, he again tuned into the conversation as he tuned out the distractions.

At our last meeting, he was edgy. A plane awaited to take him back to his current home in Jacksonville, Florida. He did not want to leave New York, a city in which he finds an admiration he does not get in the South. Toward the end of the day's interview, he became restless and began pacing. Then, he faced the mirrors which composed one wall of the room, and boogied. As he concluded one very intricate and sensual routine, he stood tall, looked at himself in the glass and said: "Just looking at my own self makes me know black is most definitely some kind of beautiful!"

Does being black and homosexual pose special problems?

Let's say I'm not thinking about converting to Judaism. Two out of three is enough. But special problems, you ask. . . . Do you know,

* See Author's Note, page xii.

146

I've experienced much more prejudice toward gays than I have toward blacks. No one has ever called me a nigger, but I've sure heard a lot of that "faggot" shit. But it's like anything else. If you choose to look at it that way, being black *and* gay can be a bitch. But I've never had no problems with either. I dig being black and I dig being gay.

Is it unusual to be a black man and to have reached twenty-five and not have been called "nigger"?

Perhaps. But I didn't have the average black upbringing. My father was an important man in the South. He was a businessman whose work took the family up north six months of the year while the other six months were spent down in the South. He was a very big man among black folks. Whites also treated him with respect. Wherever we lived, he was known as *Mr.* Brown. And I was always *Mr.* Brown's son. No one dared call me "nigger."

Of course I'm not exactly stupid. I know you don't need someone to call you that to hear it. You can smell it. You can *feel* it. People— white and black—resented the way the Browns lived. We always had a nice house to live in and a new car to drive. I think "uppity" was the word most often used behind our backs. But I never heard it or if I did, I paid it no mind. I grew up feeling good about me. I never felt black or white. I just felt me. Since we lived six months of the year in Alabama and six months in Jersey, my friends were black and white. I was very popular as a child. I never had no negative vibes about being black. That didn't happen until junior high school.

Were there "negative vibes" about homosexuality?

That began early on. In one of the towns we lived in a bunch of black drag queens paraded around in long dresses and parasols. Sometimes their "husbands" would be with them. Funnily enough, the drags were accepted. People didn't bother them none and people didn't bother with them none. But . . . if a macho male was caught carrying on with another macho male, the whole town shook with righteous rage.

Why was that?

Blacks think of homosexuality as weak shit—something for the white man to do. They're only first getting around to seeing it in themselves. It goes back to your first question: blacks have enough problems just being black. They don't want to add what they think is another negative to their lives.

Did you experience this firsthand?

I sure did and very early on in life. When I was a kid—and I'm talking like four or five—I began doing what my family considered to be "womanly things"—like dressing up in my mama's clothes and playing with dolls. I also used to love cleaning up around the house. Well, my father, the Mr. Brown, once caught me running around in my sister's skirt and he like kicked my ass around. Then he and my mama had this long rap about me and they were going to send me away to my aunt in Virginia, thinking maybe a change in scene might help me. But somehow, I never went. I just went on cooking and a-cleaning.

Was sex or homosexuality ever discussed in your household?

No. But not at all. And my mama had many children, of which I'm the youngest. You'd think someone would have dropped a hint along the way.

Was there any sex play among the children?

Shit, no! The brother nearest to me in age—and he was seven years older—he took me with him everywhere. We also slept in the same bed, and although he would cuddle me, it ended there. He wanted for me to be an athlete real bad. He went through some kind of changes when he thought I might be gay! I wish he was. He is one handsome dude and hung! That runs in the family. And speaking of the family, my experience seems to be a lot different than most people's. I felt a very special kinship to everyone but my father. I still do. We Browns were something! We had to be. My mama insisted we all do our schoolwork, dress neat and be ladies and gentlemen. She took no messing with. We all learned and we all behaved. I was a very happy child. I have always felt my mama loved me dearly. I still do. My mama did most of my raising and I always wanted to be like her—have her values. I always considered my mama to be strong, elegant and beautiful. But, like I said, she was no pushover. Ours was a very loving but strict upbringing. The only bad news was the fighting between my mama and my father. They had separated several times before I was born. They got together one more time and had me. I remember their fights. I guess that's when my hatred for Mr. Brown begins. He used to hit my mother and once I found her covered with blood. I remember thinking—and I'm only maybe eight at the time—that if he ever hits her again, I'll kill him. And sure-as-shit, somehow I would have. I've never had a good feeling for my father since that time. And why should I? He never did a goddamn thing with me.

Have you no fond memories of your father?

Not a one, man. I never felt love from him. Only once can I remember him taking me with him someplace and that was to the fields. He didn't tell me we were going there to shoot a cow for a barbecue. I was maybe four and didn't know about death and dying. When he shot that cow, that poor beast started screaming and so did I. I kept right on screaming and they had to put me in a hospital for a few days until I cooled out. Now, what else do I remember about *Mr.* Brown. Well . . . he was one handsome dude who dressed in beautiful threads. He always had diamond rings and shiny new cars. He smoked big cigars and no one ever knew that he had never learned to read or write. And it didn't matter none because we were rich. Or so we thought. Then one day, the man from General Motors comes to repossess our two trucks. My mama keeps saying there has to be some mistake. There was, but it was hers. It turned out my father had gambled away thousands of dollars. And what he hadn't spent gambling, he laid on his women. My mama threw him out.

But I remember him coming back—driving up to the house with this juke-joint chick sitting next to him, dressed like the whore that she was, and him going in to get some money from my mama. They had a fearsome fight. He hit her. She took a razor and cut him up bad. I never saw him again—never had the desire to and I still don't. My mama somehow managed. The brothers and sisters all worked and we never suffered for anything.

Did your mother remarry?

No. Early on she took us all aside and said there would be no stepfathers and no "uncles"—if you get my meaning—and there weren't.

Did your life change after your father's departure?

Only in that we stopped traveling north for six months of the year. And I kind of missed that. Even at that age I realized the northern schools were better than the South's.

Why was that?

Up North, I went to primarily an all white school. In Alabama, we were segregated. We got the oldest books and the oldest visuals. But my grades, both places, were always at the top. And don't think that didn't buy me some bad news. Even when I was a kid, there were blacks who wanted to lay a trip on you if they thought you were going "bougie." And whites, they couldn't deal with a black boy who wasn't shiftless and lazy. Man, I messed up a lot of folks' minds! But the real racial shit I didn't see until I went to an integrated junior high school. I ran for class president and the shit went flying in all directions. No black boy was supposed to do that! That was the first time I saw hatred because of color. And I didn't like it. You see, all black folks have bad news stories but they don't mean nothing until they hit you directly. Like my mama told me how her father—a foreman—was shot down and killed by whites because he was preaching for some kind of reform that whitey didn't like. But that was just a story to me. But when a couple white boys busted my ass for *calling on the telephone* a white girl, that's something else. By the way, she and I were co-chairmen of a dance and I was calling her to check out some shit. But *she* decided no black boy should even call her on the telephone. So I got my ass kicked in. And about a year later, when I'm playing on the football team, another white chick takes a shine to my black bones. This time, the entire team tries to kick my ass. But I kicked most of theirs all over the goddamn locker room. I was the one who got suspended, but I learned something then. After that fight, after I said "Enough of your shit!", most of those guys became my friends. I never had no trouble again. And that's how I feel about being a black man in this here life. You gotta take your position and defend it. You know what I hate? Black folks who take shit without shoveling it back where it came from. When I see a black man today, begging for pennies or lying around drunk on the street, I want to shake his black ass and make him fight. I want to scream, "Up goddammit. Don't you lie down for no man!" And that's how I live my life today as a black and a homosexual. I don't lay down for no man unless it is to lay down and fuck.

When did you first, as you say, "lay down and fuck"?

When I was seven.

Obviously a case of arrested development.

But I didn't know we were fucking. The little girl next door—she and I crawled into the back seat of my daddy's car and started playing. Suddenly she found herself this big new toy. And I somehow found where it fit and that was that. But I honestly didn't know what we were doing, just that it felt good. And I started making my-self feel good every chance I got after that. By eight, I think I must have been masturbating seven or eight times a day. Before breakfast, during lunch, at piss-break at school, after school. I would get real worked up in school because all the kids always paid so much atten-tion to my cock. It happened at a piss-call. One of the guys noticed how big my dick was, and after that all the kids always wanted to see it. And I was always happy to show it. Even in class, when I'd get these hard-ons, I was never embarrassed. Actually, I'd be so proud, I'd find some reason to get up and show it off. I still do that. I've got a very big cock—big like in h-u-g-e—and I like showing it off, like the attention it gets. And it does get attention! Anyway, as a kid, I was always getting worked up so I would have to work it off. I think I spent half my childhood locked in the bathroom jacking off.

Why "locked" in the bathroom?

Somehow, without being told, a little boy knows that jacking off isn't something you do in front of your mama.

Did you have masturbatory fantasies?

Yes. Sometimes about girls but mainly about me. It excited me then to think about my body, my cock, and I would watch myself in the mirror. I still do that. I still get off on watching me whack off. But it always struck me as strange that the first time I ever came—ejaculated—it was after school and I had sneaked into my mother's bed. No one was home and I knew I shouldn't be there. I don't know why I did it, but it sure was exciting.

Did you ever have homosexual fantasies?

No. I didn't have the time. I went from jacking off, thinking about little girls, but mainly me, to screwing my cousin Calvin. I was maybe ten—so was he—and I think it was more kids' play than anything else. Other than the fucking, we didn't do anything "fancy," if you get my meaning. That went on for a year or two and then there was nothing till I turned fourteen and then with a bunch of the guys on the football team we would get blown by a few "queers" we knew in town. Some of the guys would also fuck the "queers." But we were never "queer" ourselves. Oh no. We were all getting blown or fuck-ing, but we were straight. *They* were the "queers." And I'm sorry to say I think that is still the attitude of a lot of men who play but play on only one side of the fence.

When did you actually come out?

At fifteen. A dude in local government—important, handsome—he was making me know he was turned onto me. And that's something no one teaches you. It's a sixth sense. Like everyone, including my sisters who were hot for him, thought he was straight. But I knew as soon as our eyes made contact that he wasn't. Of course, since he wasn't responding to any of the women who came on with him, he was suspect. Still, no one knew for sure. Funny thing is, I don't remember exactly how or when he and I got together—just that we did and that it felt good. But I didn't mark it in my mind as a particularly noteworthy event. What I mean is . . . sex always came kind of easy and natural-like to me. I really don't think I had or have any hang-ups about it. So you see, exactly when I first went down on a guy or what my reaction was, that's just not in my memory. What I do remember is refusing to swallow his semen because I had read somewhere that to do so would cause warts or blindness. Then I read that it was pure protein and good for the skin. Well shit! Soon I just stopped reading and started swallowing.

Did you experience any guilt feelings about your sexuality?

No, but I tell you, it sure put some of my family through their changes. Like one of my sisters followed me to this man's home one day and then busted in on us. So happens we were dressed, but she is waving this gun around, threatening to "blow your head off, boy, if I ever hear anything funny about your sexual preferences."

What was your reaction?

Best as I can recall, amazement. I mean it was funny that that poor girl was going to Nut City just because I was gay. But did you ever notice how it is always the people around you who get more fucked up with your being gay than you do? It's their fucked-upedness that can really take you out there if you let it. But whether it came from my brother or my sister, I never let anyone's shit make me guilty. The only thing along those lines I can recall is deciding to be careful— to make sure not to bring any discomfort to my mama. And I haven't.

Does your mother know of your homosexuality?

Although I've never told her directly, she knows. All mothers know, whether they admit it or not. Now me . . . I am kind of glad she knows. When I am in her house, I live her way. But when she comes a-visiting me, since she knows, I don't move out of the room I share with my lover, if I got one. No way.

What was the attitude toward sex and homosexuality within your religious upbringing?

Whatever they were, I never paid me no mind to that shit. I mean, the church and I never did mix. I mean, shit, the preacher man is up there damning everybody to hell and back for fooling around with their neighbors' wives and daughters and all the time he's trying to get into my sister Jean's pants. And listen, if sex was half the sinning that preacher man said it was, half that town would be walking round through hell now. Led by the preacher himself. So, I never bothered with that shit. I believe in God, that he exists within us all, but I don't believe he thinks homosexuality is bad. Since I think he is the creator of all things, then he must have created sex feelings between men. I think God only cares whether a person is good or bad—whether he hurts others or treats others decently. I don't think God gives a shit who you ball. Religion can mess with people's minds because so much of it isn't about God but what man *interprets* as God. There's an old expression—Don't knock it till you've tried it. Let me tell you, if you've made *love* with a man you know it can be just as beautiful as making love with a woman.

Then you have made love with women?

I have and I do. I had a steady girl through most of high school. I have a woman now, Laurie, who I am thinking of marrying. So I know what I'm saying. Lovemaking can feel good no matter who it is with. So can sex. But there is a special something added when it is about love.

Who was your first lover?

A very influential black businessman. He was middle-aged; married and the father of children in college. He became my unofficial guardian. I lived with him and his wife on and off for several years, leaving when I joined the Air Force.

What is an "unofficial guardian"?

Actually, he wanted to adopt me but my mama said no. However, because he had money and influence she let me live with him, thinking it was nice that a fine man would take an interest in her son. He bought me clothes, a car and would have put me through college had I not decided to go into the military.

Wasn't this somewhat of an unorthodox arrangement—his wife and his lover all under the same roof?

No one that I know of complained! I was happy. I was loved. I was cared for. And I loved loving him. I liked his wife very much and she liked me. To this day I doubt if she suspects that something "funny" was going on.

How did you meet? Did he approach you?

Yes. Again, I knew he was interested from the way he looked at me when he and his wife would come to pay their respects to my mama. And I was very interested in him. I had a thing for older men. I think it is because I never had a father. But he had to do the approaching. People still do, if they want me. Not because I'm conceited, hell no. I'm shy. I can't handle rejection but at all! If someone doesn't come onto me in a bar the first fifteen minutes I'm there, I start to fall apart. Worse is when someone does come on to me and then walks away. That wrecks my head. Although that seldom happens—shit! I'm one fine-looking dude!—when it does, I'm devastated.

What made you join the Air Force?

I had to get away from him. I stopped being in love and he couldn't accept that. Besides, I couldn't decide what I really wanted to do. He wanted to send me to a fine black college but I had no goal. I was immature. In the Air Force, I saw and learned a lot. In fact, those were some of the best years of my life. I was stationed in the Far East and since there wasn't much to do, we began doing one another. And that was some joke! The military gives us all these lectures on the evils of homosexuality and then sticks a bunch of horny young boys on an island that is pretty much without women. Now I'm not saying everybody was *out there,* but there was some mighty fine swinging.

One thing really pisses me off about that though. Those same guys, stateside, would pretend that nothing happened. They'd go out of their way to avoid you. The world's filled with that kind of bullshit —the I'm-really-straight number.

But I had a good time. My second year on the island I met Wally. He was an enlistee, married and cool. I didn't particularly dig him

—not sexually—but he courted me. And this boy just loves to be courted. Flowers, phone calls, all of that shit. I just love it! And it is hard to find. As much as I like passionate sex, that's how much I love lovin' . . . being touched, caressed. But very few men can do that. They get fucked up with tenderness. They think they got to come on like Charles Bronson or Jim Brown. All that macho bullshit. But not Wally. He just took his time and well . . . soon enough, we became lovers. We still are but we're not. He lives in the North with his wife and two kids—he's very successful, going somewhere in his field—and I see him rarely. But there remains a bond between us. He once said I was the only man he ever trusted. That's a helluva nice thing to hear from someone.

Wally was like my mentor. He pushed my black ass into the university I needed. I did three years there while I was in the Air Force. I majored in psychology and minored in English. Wally wanted me to go pre-med. He still does. And he'd pay the bills. But then I wasn't interested, and now I want to have a buck in my pocket.

After my discharge we toured the Orient together. We were gone three months and I had the kind of *informal* education a lot of folks dream of. I'll never forget the parts of China and Japan we saw. And . . . I'll never forget those times with Wally. He has been *the* man in my life. I never did finish school 'cause as soon as the plane landed in New York I fell in love, again, only this time with a city. I've had a hard-on for Manhattan ever since.

What is special about New York?

The excitement. You really ain't nowhere unless you are here. I always wanted to be a star. Truly. In New York I am that. More folks want my body here than anywhere else I've been. I like that. It turns me on to turn on people. I like sex. And I like a lot of sex. This is the place for that. But this is also the place for fine clothes and beautiful cars and *things*. I love *things*. Like someday I'm going to live in one of those sky-high penthouses. I'm going to flash a few stones from Cartier. Truly. New York was made for living. Getting dressed and going downtown to boogie, that's a trip here. In Jacksonville, where I now live, it ain't nothing at all. But then nothing ain't nothing unless it is in New York. But if you haven't got the bread, you're better off living elsewhere. I spent two poverty-stricken years here, wound up in debt, and you lose half the fun when you're hassled by money.

Did you work while in New York?

At one of those very chic department stores. As a credit manager.
I wore a suit and tie daily and was called *Mr.* Brown. But I think
after two years I was taking home, *after* taxes, about $100 a week. I
never seemed to get those promotions that were available to the white
boys. By the time I paid my rent on my one big room on the West
Side I had about enough left over to live it up big at MacDonald's
three times a week. So I figured, shit, let me get my ass somewhere
else, make it there and then bring it on back home to New York.

Where did you "play" in New York?

The question should be where *didn't* I play. That would take like
no time to explain. Man, I played everywhere. I did it all—from the
baths and sex bars to the porno houses and discos. I did threesomes
and orgies and had me a ball. But there is no big deal about that.
I think it is the same with all good-looking young dudes in this town.
Group sex is a blast. Instead of having one guy playing with your
ding-dong, you got two or three or seven. I got enough to go 'round,
so why not? Only thing I care about is . . . does it feel good. Remember I said that I don't have no hang-ups about sex? It's true. I
do everything and I don't find nothing shameful. Like people sometimes get all shook up when I talk. 'Cause I call things as they are.
Like I dig sucking, fucking, rimming and a few other things. Now, if
those words put you in Nut City, that's your trip. To me, they are
just words of *things* I like to do and have done. Fun *things*. And the
things I don't like—that don't feel good—I don't do. Like drugs.
Smoking pot I dig, but I'll only smoke with certain guys because
others, when they turn on, forget who you are and fantasize you
into somebody I-don't-even-know-who. Well shit, I want whoever
I'm balling with to know it is me! I gotta be some guy's trip and not
the drug.

Do you find the usage of drugs prevalent?

In New York, yes, and in Jacksonville, where I live now, no. And in
New York, people, straight and gay, are popping all kinds of shit,
from qualudes and Valium to mesc and cocaine. Like my girl, Laurie,
lives in New York, and although she doesn't use anything stronger
than grass, when we went dancing at a straight black disco on the
East Side, they were dropping-and-popping all over the place. But
not the oldies-but-goodies, as I call them. The dudes doing drugs

seem to be under thirty. By the way, something that might interest you . . . at that "straight" disco, I'd say almost half the guys there were bi. And that's a new black phenom!

Does Laurie know of your homosexuality?

Absolutely. I refuse to live with beards—cover-ups of any kind. Actually, she pays it no mind. She said once, "If you're as good with guys as you are with me, no wonder they chase you." Then, too, Laurie is honest enough to admit she digs a big cock. And she sure got that in me!

> *Lee, you keep making references to your size. Is part of, much of, your identity in a "big cock"?*

Look man, people, *all* people, are attracted to pretty and not ugly. If they say otherwise, they be liars. Most men dig big tits on their women. Right? Check out any chick or dude and if they be honest they will tell you that *pretty* usually determines what you are going to get in this here life. I got a big cock. A pretty cock. But my self-esteem is not about my cock. But my cock is part of my self-esteem. I dig being hung. Ask any guy who is hung and he'll tell you he stands a helluva lot taller because his joint is a helluva lot bigger than other guys'.

Every lover I have had—man and woman—has grooved on my body, and particularly on my dick. I dig that. I've already told Laurie, as I've told every man I've been with, if I marry you, I'm your husband but I'm not your possession. I like being wanted. I like fucking around. That's my nature. I make no apologies for it and I refuse to let someone lay a guilt trip on me because of it.

Like I got a fine black boy sharing my home in Jacksonville now. But he has to get his black ass out 'cause he's been hassling my head. Although he said up-front he could handle my running, he can't. And those jealousy and fidelity numbers I don't need. Should I marry Laurie, I will be her husband but I will not be hers. Should I shack up with some man, I'll be his lover but not his to keep. That doesn't work for me. I'd have made a lousy slave.

> *You mentioned somewhat casually that you do have a lover today.*

That's all it is worth—a casual mention. We're splitting, like I said. He doesn't understand that I can be with one guy, loving him, while still screwing with others. To me, one has nothing to do with the other. A lot of people don't see it that way and that's cool. That's their trip. But don't lay it on me. But my problem with my soon-to-be-ex is deeper. We are, as they say, sexually incompatible. You see, most black men are hung up sexually. Generally I much prefer to have sex with whites because they are much more liberated. The brothers usually got this thing about getting fucked. It fucks with their head, their so-called male identity. That's true of my friend. He hates getting fucked. His not doing it, fucks me. Black men still have this bullshit going about being passive—that it makes them less of a man. Well shit, if your head is still into that kind of wind, get your face out of mine. I can't be bothered.

Could you elaborate on why you prefer having sex with white men?

In addition to the fact that they are a helluva lot more sexually free, I like the mental sex that goes with the physical.

What do you mean by "mental sex"?

Many white men, although they're not conscious of it, continue to think of us black folk as dumb or "inferior." It's an attitude they give off that a black dude feels. Man, I can spot that kind of mental superiority trip coming at me from one hundred feet! But I play with it . . . put them on and sooner or later, they dig. But often that kind of mental battle goes right into the sack. I enjoy coping with that kind of shit and proving it wrong, in bed and out. I'm a lot keener around white men because I'm on more toes. Whites are more conniving. They don't talk as straight as blacks. But they are more interesting because their interests and horizons are much wider. You'd be amazed by the amount of southern blacks who still think *we* shouldn't make waves but should keep our place. That attitude sucks! Where are their aspirations? Seems to me now that they're earning a decent dollar, they stopped dreaming. And if you stop dreaming, you might as well be dead.

What do you dream of, Lee?

I sort of told you already. Coming home to New York. And I do think of New York as my home. If you can get it together in this town, you can have the best that life has to offer. I'm working toward it. My job in Jax, managing a dry-cleaning store, isn't exactly the I.B.M. corporation, but I do my job well. With pride. The folks like working for me. My boss, the man who owns the franchise, digs me. He and his wife have had me to dinner. They're good people, good white people. He's taken an interest in me—helped me—because I'm good. Not because there's anything "funny" going on between us. I'm going to work that job into something bigger. Maybe Atlanta will be the next stop. But in a couple years, I'll be home.

Funny thing about "being home," I'll have to really make the bread to live as well as I do now—two hundred dollars per week, *before* taxes, goes a long way in Jax but in New York, earning that kind of money, there is no way I could live in a two-bedroom apartment, with a swimming pool in the courtyard, as I do now. And I'm not coming back until I can live in a high-riser, with a doorman, a dishwasher, a washer/dryer and air conditioning. It's "bougie" as hell but so what? It's my life and if I dig "things," t'ain't nobody's business if I do. I like pretty things as much as I like pretty people. I like having money and I hate not having money. One makes me feel free; the other trapped. And I hate being in anything or anyone's control.

Even in sex, if a guy's trip is about controlling me, he can forget it.

Could you explain how a man might try to control you sexually?

Sure. I like to get fucked. I'd rather fuck, but I can go either way and get off on it—except when it isn't about having fun but is about power, being in the control of some dude who thinks he is one up on you 'cause he's in the driver's seat. He's the kind of guy who feels more of a man because he is putting it to you. He's the guy who is putting you down as he puts it to you. He is seeking to dominate with his cock. To that kind of guy, as soon as his vibes come in loud and clear, I say "See ya around." I don't dig his trip. Yet, if some guy wants me to control him for a night, two nights even, I'll play because I'm not giving up anything. It's his scene.

What do you think the particular "trips" you have just described are about?

I don't "think" about them. I don't give them any meaning. You got to understand something: I don't look for any deep psychological meanings. I'm not a very deep person and I know it. I'm not interested in having my head messed with. The whys and wherefores just don't interest me. I couldn't care less why I'm gay. I just accept that I am. What I do care about is having fun, enjoying life. I have very simple needs. See, I learned something this year. Two friends of mine—neither one of which was forty—just upped and died. In other words, there ain't no Prudential policies guaranteeing any of us life. So, I believe in living it. If there is something you want to do, do it. If it turns out to be a bad trip, retrace your feet and go another way. I've eased on down a lot of roads and I regret none of the experiences, even the ones I'm not interested in having again. But I've done them. They're out of the way. Afterwards, I just said, "Did it feel good or bad? Did it hurt anybody?" Simple shit. But it works for me. I don't dwell on angers or hurts. None of that negative shit. Like when a love affair is over, I take myself home, have me one helluva cry, maybe even bust up some furniture, before I settle into a hot tub and wash myself clean of it. Then I get dressed in my best threads and take me to a place where I can boogie.

Are there places to "boogie" in Jacksonville?

One or two. It isn't New York, but we have a drag bar, a cruise joint and one or two discos.

Is there generally a community acceptance of homosexual activity?

When it is confined to a bar, yes. The only time there is any police harassment is when the cruising takes place in a public area. Actually, Jacksonville isn't uptight about the gay scene, although there is considerable tension between blacks and whites in the bars. Not that there has even been a racial incident that I know of, but you do find that people still tend to stick with their own. Blacks mainly mix with blacks and whites with whites. Of course we got our dominoes, our Oreo-cookie couples and nobody hassles them either.

But that hesitancy between whites and blacks is a fuckup. That whole black awareness trip of the '60s, although good for a lot of black folk, has also messed with a lot of minds. I was only fifteen when it began but I can remember how whites and blacks then kept their distance. Today, there is still distance, but I don't think either side wants it. There is just this uncertainty about how to approach one another. We've been apart for so long that to come together means maybe saying, or doing, the wrong thing. Shit. Wasn't only a few years ago that if you were making it with a white guy, you were copping out. The attitude was, nobody who is really black would make it with a white man. B-u-l-l-sheeit! But that's all changing now. Folks are doing what and *who* they want. To which I say, "Hey!"

Even back then, in the '60s, I didn't hold none with black militancy. I was disinterested. I see all that shit as robbing us blacks of getting what we want and need. I don't want to be separate. I just want to be. Counteraction to the shit that is thrown at you changes things. To fight back . . . that's what matters. I believe changes for the black man occur when he gets his program together and takes it out there for the world to see. By the way, I feel the same about gays. I don't want to be separate. I want acceptance. I'll earn it by being me and standing tall. Again, it's counteraction to the shit.

Are black attitudes toward homosexuality different from whites?

Believe it! They haven't changed all that much in ten years, which is why I still prefer making it with white men. The black man is still, mainly, uptight sexually. He can't do most anything in bed. He is still akin to his brother of the '6os who would let some guy blow him but not kiss him cause that was sissy-shit. Black dudes in the '6os would fuck a guy and then put him down for doing it. Today, more black dudes are into a give-and-take number but most still can only pitch and not catch. Black men worry about their balls. They're afraid of losing them. I dig. If you ain't had them, and then get them, they're hard to give up . . . if you think being gay is giving them up.

Would you explain what you mean?

Society has castrated the black man over the centuries. De-balled him . . . made him feel less of a man. Well, a black dude who is trying to make his program work doesn't want to lose his balls again. To the uptight black gay, being gay, getting fucked, is losing his balls. Society says so, which is why most blacks—men and women—see homosexuality as another cross to bear, one they don't need. Just as it was in the '6os, it is still very difficult to be a declared macho homosexual in the black community. If you come out, generally you are put out. Funny, in all other areas but homosexuality, blacks are so much more out there than whites. We party so much bigger and better. All we need is some wine and a disco beat. Whites talk you and themselves to death! They come up short on just having fun. Man, that's why I never understood that talk about achieving a positive black identity. I never wanted to be anything but black. We be fun folks!

Do you feel the same way about being homosexual?

I'm comfortable being gay. I think I always have been. But it is a helluva lot easier to survive if you're a macho gay. There's a lot of shit out there for gays. Sometimes I think there's even more than there is for blacks. People can get you crazy, hassle your head because you're into men. I hear them because they speak in front of me thinking I'm straight. I usually let them go in their rap for a while and then I blow their minds by telling them I'm gay. They don't know what to do with that because I don't fit their mold.

Do you usually declare yourself?

No. But I don't try to avoid discovery either. I just don't go around talking about my personal life. It isn't anyone's business. But in that situation that I just described, I feel I have to open up. I can't let people talk that shit. 'Cause it hurts me if I do. I gotta stand up and be me! But it does hurt. It would be easier to be straight. But I'm not. And being gay is not something I chose. I don't think anyone wakes up one day and says, "Hey, I'm going to be gay." It's just something you are without having much to do with it. Now if I wanted to, if I feared discovery, I could marry Laurie right away and have a bunch of kids, but what would that prove? No man who is gay can just shut off the hots he has for guys and turn straight. Besides, although I *may* marry and raise a family because I think I *want* that kind of life, it will have nothing to do with discovery or going straight. I am not ashamed of being gay. I'm saying, however, that life would be a helluva lot less hassled if I weren't. But not because of *my* head but because of where society is at.

How seriously are you contemplating marriage?

Very seriously. Laurie is a fine woman. Beautiful. We lived together my last year in New York and we seem to make each other happy. There are no lies. She knows my scene and says it's cool. I like having a woman in my home. I would like to be a father to a mess of kids.

Is sex with a woman as fulfilling for you?

That depends on where I'm at. If I'm really into Laurie, who she *is*, it's fantastic. But those times when I feel the need for a man but climb in the sack with Laurie instead, it just doesn't work as good. Orally, it is never as good. What I like most about sex with Laurie, or any woman, is the softness of the female body. And it is the hardness of the male body that turns me on to men. I am only attracted to very masculine men, just as I only dig very feminine women. Sex with men is generally much better for me because there is more mystery involved. I never know who is going to do what to who. It is also much less inhibited. I have very few taboos with men. I've tried some of the kinky stuff, but I'd just as soon leave it. Mind-blowing sex for me is screwing a guy who has his program together—a guy who can handle his getting screwed and then can put it to you. I think that's why most of my relationships have been with married men. They're guys who get off on being men with men. I also think they function better because they know they can get it on with women.

Previously you stated you generally prefer sex with white men to black. Does that apply with white women also?

No way! In fact, there *is* no way I'll ball a white chick. I give them lots of room. I believe all this racial shit was caused by the Scarlett O'Haras of this world. Down South, Scarlett ain't quite dead yet. There are still a lot of white women who get all wet looking at some black dude, but they'd rather have him lynched than put in their beds. I've long felt that the white woman's nonacceptance of her attraction for the black man has resulted in a lot of hostility.

What about sexual hostility between white and black men? Is that in your experience?

Yes. But I don't dwell on it. Sure there are a lot of white dudes who want the Black Stud. One guy, in the middle of my balling him, got carried away and said "Give it to me, black boy." I walked out, which was giving it to him in quite another way. There's an awful lot of shit being played out, particularly when some guy wants you to use your cock as a weapon, but I ignore it. I figure it's his trip. Humiliation—giving or getting it—just doesn't interest me. But I do think times-they-be-a-changing. Most of my experiences have not been like that. They've been cool. Or maybe I should say, they've been "hot." But here is something funny that I just thought of which ties in to what we are talking about. Although whites are more open and skilled sexually, I get far more affection in bed from a black man. There are just certain vibes that pass between brothers that don't seem to exist, at least not yet, between a white and a black man.

Lee, do you think in terms of a long-lasting relationship with a man?

Yes I do. No I don't. Yes, no and mainly no but in truth, yes. But I have a feeling it is a-ways off. I like being with a man but not exclusively. I like being with a woman but not exclusively. So I think I'm not ready to settle down in the ways most people want to be settled down. I'm a whore and I like it. Although I love a home,

I'm not a homebody. Someday, I suspect I will be, but shit, I'm only twenty-five. There's an awful lot of stuff out there I still want to play with. I want to have me a good, good time before I check out. I mean I don't know that I'm coming back this way again, so I intend to do it all in this here lifetime. Some gay guys worry about growing old. Not me. As long as there is plastic surgery, I'll be fine. I'll take an inch off my waist and add it to my cock. Shallow man, that's me, right? To the end! But you see, to the end I'm going to boogie. I'm just going to have me the best time life has to offer because until someone can prove it otherwise, that's what I think life should be.

Mr. Dino

VERY PINK. Very gold. Very ugly! Yet, it is one of the better beauty salons in New York. Royalty and the wives of heads of state have been clients, but so have glitter-groupies. One of the establishment's stars is "Mr. Dino," * a Newark-born Sicilian with the body of a mini Greek god. Very mini. He is five-foot-six, but on that small frame are some very large muscles. "Mr. Dino" knows his audience and how to play to a crowd. His pants are snug and his shirts, open midway to the navel, are form-fitting. If-you-got-it, flaunt-it and "Mr Dino" does.

On stage at the salon de beauté, "Mr. Dino" makes an appearance only three days a week. From the moment he picks up scissors or blow dryer, he appears to be a spirited performer. His charm is continuous. In the privacy of his home, a one-bedroom apartment on New York's West Side, which he shares with Michael, his lover of eighteen years, the charm remains, although the performance ends.

Does one have to act to be a good hairdresser?

Constantly. If the job were just about cutting hair, it would be a lot easier. But most women go to a hairdresser more for their heads than their hair. In the course of a day, I become Ann Landers, James Beard and Masters *and* Johnson. The mental pressures are enormous. Daily, I listen to the world's most inane garbage. I *must* listen whether I wish to or not.

What kind of "garbage"?

Which shoes should I wear with my pink dress? The silver or the gold lamé? And, do you think lemon yellow or seascape green would look well on my living room walls? *That* kind of garbage. Most of the time I want to yell, "Madame, I don't give a flying fuck" but I don't. Tactful, I'm always tactful.

Why the bitterness?

Because it's an unbelievable strain. Nobody sitting in your chair ever

* See Author's Note, page xii.

gives a fuck how you feel. You're there for their pleasures. For that reason, a good hairdresser must always be up. He is not allowed to be in a bag or into himself. Each day, he must become totally involved with each client if that is what the client wants. And that is what the client wants.

Is it a strain?

It is such a strain that I've got my work load down to three days a week. I can't take any more. Working another day would break me again.

Again?

It got the better of me for twenty years only I wouldn't admit it. I was a drug addict without thinking I was. But, if you take "ups" every day to be up for your clients, then you're an addict.

Were you on amphetamines?

Until last year, yes. I quit by accident, but I remain off the stuff by intent. Actually, I got mugged a year ago—a few teeth got moved about and a few ribs got busted. I was a week in the hospital and went through severe withdrawal. But once off the shit, I decided no job was worth being on the stuff. It would get me up all right but when I came down . . . crash! So, I work three days a week, earn two hundred and fifty bucks and feel way ahead of the game.

Do you dislike being a hairdresser?

Not at all! I like my work. Like any job, it's got its problems but unlike many jobs it is creative, stimulating and often fun.

Do you have to like women to be a hairdresser?

It helps. A hairdresser and his women enjoy a unique relationship. As mentioned, he becomes all things to her, including Father Confessor. Many women become very possessive, almost like a jealous lover. If they suspect you give another client more time or attention, they become bitchy. Still others will tip you ten bucks just so they can bust your balls. These are the angry women, the ones who are abused in their own homes and have no place to vent their pent-up hostility—except on the hairdresser.

How do you cope with that?

You try to remember that their discomfort has nothing to do with you . . . that they are in pain. But sometimes you want to belt them.

Do you dislike women?

Shit, no. Women are people.

Would you explain what you mean?

Just because some women are ball-busters doesn't mean all women are. I don't lump women into one bag any more than I lump men into one bag. Some I like; some I don't. Similarly, because I'm gay doesn't mean I'm going to like all gay people.

Are you comfortable with heterosexuals?

Very. Heterosexual is just another label. They, too, are people, about 80 percent of the world, I guess. At Cherry Grove on Fire Island this summer, there was a movement to ban the straights, which I fought. (1) I don't like ghettos of any kind, and (2) some of my best friends are straight. Why should I be denied their presence just because some gays haven't worked out their thing.

That really answers your question, by the way. Any gay can be comfortable with straights and any straight can be comfortable with gays if he has worked out his own sexuality. I'm comfortable with me so I can be comfortable with any man. Like at the gym, there are lots of straights there. We get along fine. I don't threaten them because I don't come on with them. I'm not interested in seduction or one-way sex. So I can talk with a straight guy without either of us getting uptight. And I don't have to talk baseball to relate to him.

Being comfortable with yourself, was this learned?

It is still being learned. What I meant is I am comfortable with my homosexuality. Whatever problems I have, and I have them, have nothing to do with my sexuality. As a matter of fact, homosexuality saved my life. I'm not so certain I might not have been a teenage suicide or a homicide statistic had I not found gay life and with it the acceptance, kindness and love, even, that I never had.

You are referring to an unhappy childhood?

A very unhappy childhood. My father died when I was four, which is no big deal, because my only remembrance of him is that of a man who shunned me but adored my sister. My mother was forced to work at a factory, thus leaving me to be raised by the streets and my sister, who was only two years older than I. That, too, is no big deal. My mother was a stupid woman and an unkind person. She constantly threatened to send me to an orphanage or a reform school, which is a terrible thing to do to a child. I can only remember feeling bad as a kid and never being certain if I would be sent away or whether my mother would run away and leave me, which she also threatened to do.

I didn't like my mother then, but I was just a little kid and so I was terrified of losing her. But she never gave me a damn thing. If I went to her for affection, she'd push me away. On Christmas and on birthdays, she never bought me a thing. I still don't like my mother, but today I understand that it wasn't me, my ugliness—and she used to look at me and say: "I wonder where we ever got you from"—but her ignorance, her lack. She simply couldn't give anything to anyone. She should never have had children.

Were you close to your sister?

As a child, yes. She was all I had. We took care of one another. When my mother would refuse to buy my sister a dress or shoes for school functions, I'd shovel snow or wash windows to earn the money and buy the dress. I loved her a lot as a kid.

And now?

My sister eloped at sixteen. She has now been married a hundred years, has had four sons and smiled a lot as her husband became a millionaire. I never see her. I never will. She knew I was gay at twelve. When she began having children, she didn't want me around. She was afraid I'd contaminate them.

Is this difficult for you to talk about?

It is many years ago, but I can still feel that kid's pain and loneliness. And his fear. God was I frightened as a kid. A lot of that rejection has never left me. I still need constant reassurance and approval. Most of my sex life today is about my need to prove that I'm attractive . . . wanted. It's a hang-up. I even dress bizarrely to attract attention. Yet, when I do, I become shy. I'm afraid if people look too closely, they'll spot the imperfection.

Do you feel imperfect?

Yes and no. I like me. I know I'm a nice person, a kind man, one who basically likes people. But I still feel people won't give me a chance, will reject me. It's a carry-over from childhood when no one looked at or saw me, except in a negative way. *They* made me feel inadequate and a part of me still suffers with that feeling. To prove that I am attractive, lovable, I search for attractive, young bed partners. In other words, I look for the acceptance, still, but among the young and beautiful. Being physically attractive is very important to me—too important. I tend to think of myself, at forty, as that ugly little kid from Newark. I never disbelieve my body, which I know is good, but is it *as* good as people say?

With all this accent on the physical, how does the prospect of aging affect you?

That, too, is a two-sided coin. Losing my physical looks fucks with my head. One of my great fears is reaching an age where it becomes difficult-to-impossible to lure someone to bed. And it is my body that lures first. Most of the time I dismiss this kind of thinking from consciousness. I let it lie, hoping it will disappear as so many other problems have disappeared with maturity.

And that's the good thing about aging. I like being forty. I find it very comfortable. I wouldn't want to be twenty or thirty again. Life today is much more relaxed. I'm less frantic. I live a quiet life and like it. I no longer have to be everywhere at the same time. Even at our home on Fire Island, Michael, my lover, and I may do the disco scene but only once on a three- or four-day weekend. Yet, at the island is often where my insecurities grab hold of me. So many humpy guys are there and I need them to reassure me of my attractiveness. And if they don't, I feel inadequate. That feeling has been with me since grade school. There, to get attention, I was rebellious as hell. I was really bad and that got me noticed. By junior high I was gay and running with a straight gang, cutting school, buying beer and shooting pool. Sometimes we'd jump motors on cars and go drag racing. I was always small but I acted big.

You said you were homosexual in junior high?

I knew I was gay at five, which is when I began masturbating and always with the image of men in mind. It has never been about girls for me. I've known where I'm at sexually ever since I can remember. I've never had sex with a woman, never had the urge to. I think my ole lady killed that early on. I was *that* repulsed by her. But I have no regrets about not having had a heterosexual experience. I don't feel I've missed out on anything. Maybe I would if my own sex life was not fulfilling.

Since you experienced homosexual feelings quite young, did you have any difficulty achieving a sexual identity?

If you mean did I know which end was up, I didn't. For years I was confused as to whether I was a boy or a girl. At twelve I had shoulder-length hair, which wasn't done in those years, and wore makeup. You see, at that age, I was already associating with gay people. With my cousin, who was also gay, I'd come into the city and hang out where gays then congregated, which was at the skating rink at Rockefeller Plaza. When you're young, the types you meet tend to be outrageous. So you become outrageous too. Mainly to fit in, to belong. Also, I think I wanted to be like my sister—everyone seemed to like her because she was so pretty.

Till what age did the effeminate period last?

Only a year or so. It ended the night I got up in full drag and came into town for a party. I hated the feeling of being a girl. That wasn't me. So then I went the other way, became this big butch number, or as big and as butch as a fourteen-year-old who is only five feet tall can be. Those were difficult years but they were good years. The experimentation made me realize I was male. There is no doubt of that in my mind today. And I like being a man. I think it is the best way to travel through life.

How did your classmates react to you during your effeminate period?

Because I ran with a tough gang, I was left alone. But I heard the abuse they would hurl at other effeminate boys. Words like "faggot" and "fairy" were well known to me by ten. The environment told me at an early age that to be gay was not cool in most people's eyes. But I never got hung-up. You see, till I actively became gay, I always felt on the outside looking in. At twelve, when I met all those other gays, I finally felt I belonged somewhere. In other words, a lot of guys grow up with their awful "secret," and thinking they're the only ones in the world who have this "secret." I never had that. I was never alienated by my homosexuality. Just the opposite. The gays I knew at twelve and thirteen were all older and they took me in, doted on and cared for me. They gave me acceptance and even love. And not sex, by the way. That I got elsewhere—in train stations and in parks as well as on beaches.

Was religion a part of your childhood?

Lots of Roman Catholic horseshit. As a kid, every time I masturbated, I expected a bolt of lightning and the word of God to hit me. When it didn't, I figured he knew something the church didn't and said so long to any guilt. I also said so long to the church, although I remain deeply religious in my own way. I believe in God.

At what age did you begin having sex?

Nine, but it was mainly touchie/feelie rather than anything hardcore. I hung out in bad places, dangerous places, and I was lucky I didn't get my head bashed in. I was so small and so young. I look back on those years, the sex in parks and on beaches and in doorways, and wonder if perhaps I didn't want to get caught—if it wasn't just another way of trying to get someone's, *anyone's*, attention. Funny, 'cause I can't relate to that at all today. I'm very cautious and besides, hit-and-run sex holds just about no interest for me.

As a youngster, what did you want to be?

Nothing, which was about all I thought I was capable of being. Thank God for gay life. Again, it saved my ass. It taught me to dream, because all the gays I knew then had dreams. All were doing *something* with their lives. I was attracted to hairdressing because it allowed you to be creative *and* respected. It was also a good living, and since we were always one step out of the poorhouse when I was a kid, earning a good living was important to me. So, when I was thrown out of school, I . . .

Back up. You were thrown out of school?

Booted out. I had cut too many classes. I'd arrive at nine each morning, sign in and vanish. School was boring. It was all kids and at thirteen and fourteen I was hanging out with gay men of nineteen and twenty. That made it impossible for me to relate to people my own age. But getting expelled didn't exactly break my heart, you know. What did hurt was my mother's refusal to give me the $1,000 for beautician school. And she had it by then. So, to earn it, I became a delivery boy for Western Union. I not only earned my money over a year's time but had my first affair. Ray was nineteen to my fifteen, a very macho dude who had come to New York to be an actor. Despite my playing around all the years previous, I was still a virgin. In fact, I had never really experienced a sexual relationship.

What exactly do you mean?

All of my sex had been either standing up or half clothed. It was never in a bed. And it was always one-sided. Till Ray, I could never go down on a guy without getting sick.

Do you recall your "first time"?

You bet! It was beautiful. And in no way did I get sick. I think the difference was in my liking him and liking to please him and liking that I pleased him. It was a heady feeling, having someone dig you when you weren't sure that anyone ever would. I mean, I didn't know if I were lovable. But here was this really nice guy saying and doing all the right things.

How long did your affair last?

Not long. The city did him in and within months he returned to his parents' home in Rochester. But he left me a touch of something I had never had before—confidence. It must of changed me, because suddenly, on the street, in bars, men were approaching me.

Weren't you under age for admittance to a bar?

As long as I didn't drink the hard stuff nobody hassled me. So I stayed with my Coke and did all the places—the Silver Rail and the Terrace, Sixth Avenue joints. They were fun, but most gay bars were fun then. In the early '50s, the police didn't hassle the gay clubs. That began in '56 and '57 when they began pulling gays in as they closed up one place after another. It changed the atmosphere. Suddenly, everyone was paranoid. And for good reason. There was lots of entrapment in those days. Plainclothesmen would wait for you to come on with them and then haul you in. It was lousy.

Was there any mass protest?

Like the Stonewall? No. Gays didn't band together then, didn't fight. There was no unity or solidarity. Just panic. Everybody was afraid for his own life. As you can see, we've come a long way.

Prior to the raids, what was your experience in the clubs?

Fun. You never went alone but as part of a pack. Ten of you would get yourselves together and go in for a night of laughs. Even though you wanted to make out, you never did. No one could get through the crowd to get near you. But sex wasn't as important as hanging out with your friends, throwing nickels—right, nickels!—into the jukebox to hear Patti Page and Perry Como. In those years I cared much more about that kind of acceptance and companionship than I did about making out.

What else do you remember about the clubs in the early fifties?

That there were one or two dance bars, but they were considered the most dangerous, as men dancing together was still new to New York.

Those places opened and shut very quickly. Men-touching-men simply couldn't be tolerated by the police.

Funny, it seems like yesterday and yet, within those twenty years, amazing changes have occurred. There must be a dozen gay discos in New York today and almost as many back-room sex bars. And you never hear about police harassment any more.

Do you go to the back-room bars?

No. They wouldn't work for me. I need to see who I am having sex with. I also need to establish some kind of contact with that person apart from the physical. Which is why orgies don't work for me either. I can only relate to one person at a time sexually, and without some form of relating I can't enjoy the sex.

When I was a kid, I guess like most hot-pants young boys, I could trick without thinking or feeling. Not today. I have to like my partner. Each scene I do is an entire love-trip even if it only lasts thirty minutes. I make mini romances out of each encounter, which is why my sex life is very fulfilling. Not only do I get to meet a lot of guys but I become friendly with most.

Did you meet many men when you were a teenager?

Yes, but it was different. Although there is still a lot of role-playing today, most guys are pretty much themselves. In the '50s, guys were either butch or fem. In the bars it was almost like one team lined up on one side of the place, while the other held up the other wall. So although you met guys, you seldom got to know them because they were into this role-playing.

Could you explain further?

Sure. No man is strictly "butch," and I know few guys who are solely "fem" today. In other words, a lot of shit has slid on by. You don't define roles quite so much today. Most guys I know, when it comes to "bedtime," let whatever feels good at the time happen. They don't pretend to be anyone other than themselves.

You said before that your sex life is very fulfilling. Do you seek a particular kind of gratification today?

No. I can go on anybody's trip if he takes me there sensitively. Ideal sex for me is unrehearsed, spontaneous and whatever is right for the moment. I don't get involved in S&M. Many years ago I had a year in which I was active in that shit. And that's what it was, shit. I was beating up on people and enjoying it.

What made you stop?

It happened the night I realized that I was trembling not from sexual excitement but from rage. I wanted to kill. I looked down at this poor guy I was abusing and realized I wasn't angry at him, that he never did me any harm. So I stopped. Just like that. I was never able to pinpoint the anger. But what I did feel was its enormity. But it didn't belong in bed. It wasn't making me feel good to act it out on some guy who had a need to be punished. It was humiliating for both of us. And I don't believe in humiliating another person. It doesn't make me feel good about me.

Does it seem to you that more men are involved in S&M today than in the fifties?

Absolutely. But I don't understand it. Maybe a lot of that went on in the '50s and I didn't know it. I remember then, guys didn't speak about their sex lives that openly. You didn't admit you got fucked. As I said, everyone was hung-up in some kind of role. I was lucky. At seventeen I was not only living in what was to be a four-year affair with a lover, but was one of the youngest licensed hairdressers in New York. Furthermore, I was in charge of a small salon in the Village. As I said, I was lucky.

Twenty-three years ago, as you began your career, what were the attitudes reflected by straight and gay society toward hairdressers?

Nothing like today's. Then, it was a respected profession. Then, there was no stigma attached to being a hairdresser. Today, it is all fucked up. In the '50s, in my graduating class from beautician school, maybe 30 percent were gay. My first boss, the man who said of his shop in the Village, "It's a nut house. You run it. Don't call me about nothing or anything and I'll give you a raise every six months," he was straight. When I left him to go to Saks 34th Street, I was one of two gays among fifteen hairdressers. At Jay Thorpe I was the first gay the store employed in their salon. Over the years, I've worked the best places—the Plaza, Bendel's—and none were primarily gay.

In other words, the "Gay Hairdresser," the minty queen with a hair dryer who blow cuts, blow dries and blow jobs, is a myth. Sure he exists, but he is one out of every ten hairdressers. And of that ten, I would say six are straight.

Where do you think this image of the "gay hairdresser" stems from?

It's bizarre, peculiar and coincidental that the hairdressers who became internationally famous in the early '50s through their work in television and film were largely outrageous types. They did the hair of many of our top comediennes. They were on all the TV and film sets. But they were the tip of the iceberg. But certain vulgar comediennes and comics began doing cruel and tasteless hairdresser jokes. They got laughs, but I think it's pretty tacky to want a laugh at the expense of another person.

Did this affect you when you were young?

Not at all. I was making good money, doing good work and building up a following. And for three of the four years, I was enjoying a good relationship with my lover. The last year was hell for both of us and it ended shortly after my twenty-first birthday. But, basically, I was nurtured by both my relationship and my profession so that the negative vibes that were emerging about hairdressing weren't touching me.

Did the image projected by the media have an effect on the profession?

Yes. Far fewer gay men go into hairdressing today because the hairdresser is sneered at and suspect. The people who come to a hairdresser expect that he'll be an outrageous faggot and are surprised and even disappointed when he is not. And believe me, mainly he is not. The profession today is even more heterosexual than it was twenty years ago. The exact percentage of straight to gay I couldn't tell you because we, the hairdressers, don't count up. The great thing about the members of my profession, the men and the women, is that no one gives a fuck who you fuck. There is a total acceptance of life-styles and, I might add, of privacy. I can be as open or as closed as I wish to be, with gays and with straights. But then, the straight hairdresser has to be about the most together man I've met. He knows what is suspected of him but lets it roll off his back. The straight hairdressers I know are not closet cases but secure heterosexuals. The negative shit doesn't rock them. I admire them greatly.

You said before that people expect the hairdresser to be an "outrageous faggot" and are even disappointed when he is not.

That's true. And it's a bitch. Invariably, when a client asks—and many do—if I'm gay, when I say yes, she'll respond with an almost hostile, "But you don't look it!" Then she'll utter something equally offensive like "But you're so masculine. You don't look like a fag." And they're disappointed. It blows their prejudice to bits. They'd feel less threatened if I lisped, waved a wand and had wings.

Are there other such negative reactions to your declaration of sexuality?

There is always the woman who believes she's the one who can straighten me out, that all I need is a little nooky, *her* nooky, to see the light.

What do you do with such a woman?

Nothing. That gives them the message. You simply reject their advances with courtesy and humor. But before the wrong impression is given, let me state that the vast majority of women I meet, who do ask, then respond intelligently and even sensitively. Many are curious; few judgmental. Of course I meet an upper-middle-class or wealthy woman who has considerably more sophistication than, say, a suburban housewife. I don't know how that kind of woman would react, but I do suspect she, too, wouldn't care unless she has doubts about her husband.

Do you know who actually give me the worst time about being a hairdresser? Other gays. Many gay men, when they meet me at the baths or at a party, because of my looks, my body, expect me to be something else. Like a truck driver or a construction worker. Which is their fantasy trip. Really. Have you seen most truck drivers and construction workers? Beer-bellied messes. But many gays are tied up in fantasies. When I tell them I'm a hairdresser it kills whatever they have fantasized me into—which is usually some kind of masculine symbol. Some really freak when I tell them I do hair. They lose interest. Because they view the profession and the men who work in it as feminine, I become diminished in their eyes.

What effect has this on you?

I'm sorry, even ashamed, to admit that it *does* have an effect. Although I like my work, respect what I do and do not feel the least bit feminine because I comb and style hair, I find I seldom mention what I do for a living when in a cruising situation. In other words, I often deny that part of my existence. And I shouldn't. I have no hang-ups about my work or my masculinity so why should I let someone else's trip get to me? But I do because I don't want to be rejected. If I were totally together I'd never lie. But I rationalize and say "Hey, you're here for a night-of-love and not a long-term relationship" and cop out. In many ways, it's the better of two evils. I mean having a guy walk away from you after he's cruised you for an hour —walk away 'cause you've told him you're a hairdresser—that hurts. It's something I'm still learning to deal with.

Do your clients ever want to discuss your sex life?

Hardly. The women who are into discussing sex want to talk about their own sex lives. You'd be amazed by what a woman will talk about with her hairdresser. Almost *all* of my clients have "things" going on the side. Meaning: they cheat on their husbands. Which is fine if that's their thing. What isn't fine is that they feel I must be treated to every last detail of their last fuck when I don't give a shit.

Does any of this surprise you?

Not any more, but it sure did initially. I had no idea women were so into sex and that many are as size conscious as any gay. I never thought of women as being horny but my women sure are. And they're anxious to get into it. Years ago, when a woman would grope me from the chair—let her hand dangle against my dick as I cut her hair—it would get me uptight. No more. A little feel often means a big tip. On the job, despite my having on display a box for tips, many women prefer stuffing the money into my side pocket and slipping their hand in for a little grope. The first times that happened I was outraged. Now . . . shit, it's part of the job, part of the service. But I don't encourage it.

If you had to do it again, would you become a hairdresser?

Absolutely. It's a fine profession. Actually, there are very few things in my life I wouldn't do again, except relive my childhood and adolescence. They were bummers, times of great unhappiness when I felt ugly and alone. And as I've mentioned, some of the scars remain. Thank God for Michael. He changed my entire life.

Your mentioning Michael makes me realize there is a dimension to your life we have yet to touch upon.

It is more than a dimension. He, and the relationship, are the top priorities in my life. There is no one and nothing more important to me than Michael. There never has been and there never will be. In our eighteen years together, he has been mother, father, brother, teacher, friend and lover to me. It really is not an exaggeration when I say he changed my life.

How has he done this?

When I met Michael I was almost twenty-two, a street-wise kid who ran with other street-types and other "kids," some of whom were twice my age. The truth is I was all but illiterate when I met him. Other than my work, I knew nothing of what life can be. I had never even been to the theater!

Michael is Philadelphia Main Line society and I'm a Newark Nobody. Yet, he never treated me like a nobody. Actually, he treated me like a son, taking me under his wing and teaching me. He was understanding and he began my "informal education" by sharing his interests with me. When that piqued my interest, he began bringing home a book a week for me to read. And newspapers. And magazines. Then, instead of the rock 'n' roll I was drowning in, he would "suggest" I listen to some classics. In time, I began to like what I was hearing. Then, too, there were the visits to galleries and museums.

Michael was, and is, incredibly kind. He had this need to give and I had a need to take. Our first Christmas together, he tried to give me everything I had never received on a birthday or at Christmas. You might ask what could I give him in return. Only love. I don't believe anyone could have loved Michael more. I don't believe anyone could love him more. He opened the world to me. He made me see that there is a difference betwen being ignorant and being dumb. I was the former, and never the latter as I had thought. I had never learned because prior to Michael no one cared enough to teach me.

Why have you chosen not to have a monogamous relationship?

Chosen is not exactly the right word. For the first three years we were together it was monogamous. But sexually, it was not as intense or as abandoned as it should have been. I would allow—and that's the right word, allow—Michael to screw me but I never enjoyed it. It wasn't that I had a hang-up about being passive, it just wasn't physically enjoyable for me—then. So I would grit my teeth and get on with it which could not have been much fun for Michael. So, after a while, he went looking for sexual fulfillment elsewhere and so did I.

How did this initially affect the relationship?

Negatively. Initially, neither of us could be up-front about it. In other words, we were sneaking around, not admitting that we were having sex with others. That laid such a guilt trip on my head! For five years I slipped around on the side, as did Michael, without a word of discussion. And then one day we found ourselves confronting the issue and the situation. We set the ground rules. No tricking in our home. No tricking under one another's noses—meaning no carryings-on when we were together at a party or a disco. No discussion of what or who came and went, so to speak, ever. That's how it's been ever since and soon we will be celebrating our nineteenth anniversary.

In your usage of the word anniversary there is a sense of "marriage." Do you feel married?

Absolutely. Despite my not having had sex with Michael for ten years, he is still my lover. I am not looking for any other. I regret that we've lost the sexual side of our relationship, but I'm not unhappy about it. I often wonder if any long-married couples manage to maintain a sex life. Frankly, I don't know any, not among the men or the women of my acquaintance. So, sex doesn't work for us. But, everything else does. There is still such great affection and warmth between us. And love. There is still that. As I said, Michael is my whole life and sometimes that scares me. Did I say sometimes? Try often. Often that scares me.

Why?

I have this recurring nightmare. In it, Michael has died. I wake up in a panic. You see, Michael is eighteen years older than I. Although he is in great physical condition, he is approaching sixty. The likelihood is that he will die before me. The thought of his leaving me just destroys me. I wouldn't know what to do, how to go on. Oh, I know I would go on because man's instinct is to survive, but it will be very difficult for me.

Did I mention I have never lived alone? In the year before I met Michael, I lived with a roommate. In other words, I never discovered if I could fend for myself. Living with Michael has made me an emotional cripple. I've been dependent upon him for major decisions. He runs the home. We both contribute our salaries but Michael pays the bills, fights with the landlord and budgets our money. He has always taken care of everything as he has taken care of me. Before I knew I would be coming into a large inheritance, Michael made me open a savings account. Each week, from each paycheck, he saw to it that I prepared for the future.

From whom are you inheriting a large sum of money?

My mother. The old crone invested wisely over the years and is now worth about $300,000, which she is leaving to me.

Are you friendly with your mother today?

Cordial but not friendly. I still don't like her and refuse to pretend that I do. I see her twice a year at best. She makes a great fuss over our meetings but it is playacting. My mother has reached a stage in her life where she feels a mother should have affection for her son. I have never courted her for her money. I don't need it. What I needed from her, she couldn't give. She still can't. But, I allow her to think we have a mother/son relationship of some kind. I have no wish to hurt her. I am never rude to her, but she knows, without my having had to tell her, that my family begins and ends with Michael.

Has your relationship with Michael ever been threatened by your outside sexual interests?

Once. A wealthy producer fell in love with Michael. He convinced a film company to hire Michael as some kind of consultant—that was eight years ago and a film has yet to be made—and then offered to set Michael up as a production partner. Michael liked this man. It was hard not to. He was wealthy, good-looking and accomplished. I was pretty well shot while this was going on. There was a week or two when I was uncertain which way Michael would go. And then it was over. Months later, when I finally had the courage to ask why he had stayed, Michael simply shrugged and said, " 'Cause I love you"— not another word was said.

My outside interests never amount to anything because I don't allow them to. If I date a guy a second time I tell him about Michael. More than that, I tell him about *me*, where I am at with Michael. Then, if they still choose to see me—and many do—it is without subterfuge or tension. There are many men who prefer having a thing with a guy who is married. They feel safer, less threatened. Funny, but a lot of my women clients, the single ones, are constantly carrying on with married men for the same reason.

*Have you ever felt that your sex life has taken anything away
from your relationship with Michael?*

Quite the contrary. It's taken nothing away. I know where home base
is. I know where I want to be. The sex I engage in is very meaningful
at the moment but only at the moment. Also, it is a tension-reducer.
If my incomplete ego is fed, then I'm happier at home. I'm more
relaxed. Again, I want to state that I know the way I feed my incomplete ego is a false way of dealing with the problem. But it is the
only way that I know how to deal with it. And since it is hurting no
one, so be it.

Of course it would be wonderful, really wonderful, if by some
miracle the desire to have sex with Michael would return. To be able
to share sexually with someone you so much love must be where it is
really at. But, well . . . we have so much else. You know, we've
spoken of my sex life as if it occupies a major part of my life. It
doesn't. Maybe two nights a week at most I'll take off on my own.
But most nights I'm at home. We lead such a middle-class life that it
is almost laughable.

Why laughable?

I don't believe straights think of homosexuals or the life we live together as middle class. I think most see us as wildly decadent . . .
flighty . . . footloose about town.

That's such a laugh. Most nights Michael and I watch television.
Occasionally, we go to the theater or to a film. Frequently, we'll have
another couple to dinner. We don't drink and we don't smoke, except for a little pot and even that's a big event when we do it.

Even at *decadent, wild* Fire Island, where straights and gays are
carrying on wherever and whenever they wish, we live pretty much
the same way we do in town. We've become "simple folk" and you
know what? I like it, like it a lot. I have had and have an awfully good
life with Michael.

No regrets?

Only one. That we didn't adopt. We've spoken about it frequently,
but we could never find a way to work it out. Michael's job—he is
now a very successful entrepreneur—keeps him away eight to ten
hours a day. Until recently, I worked five days a week. Neither of us
could afford to stop working and neither of us believes in letting a
housekeeper or a "nanny" raise your kid. But God how I wanted a

child! How I wanted to give a kid everything I never got. To take him to the movies or even to a ball game, what a joy! It's still an idea I haven't quite given up, particularly now that I know of the inheritance. The truth is, I have this need to love a kid a lot.

Is that your only regret?

As God is my witness, yes. I am very contented but then I should be. Despite a rocky beginning in life, I became one of the lucky ones. I have work that I enjoy, that fulfills me, and I've made a "good marriage." The truth is, I'm that person that myth tells us does not exist —the happy homosexual. For that I thank God, Michael and me . . . in that order.

Howard Barbour

FIFTEEN YEARS AGO Howard Barbour * would have been another nice-looking young man, not particularly noticeable in a crowd. Today he is still a nice-looking man but with a difference: he is noticeable. He is the standout in a blue pin-stripe suit or one of gray flannel. His shoes are laced and black. His hair is cut short and worn with a side part. He appears to be outfitted by Brooks Brothers. He is best described by one word, "appropriate."

He is equally conservative in speech, seldom given to wild statements or gesticulations. He is every inch the corporate-Wall-Street lawyer. But occasionally, another person—one of great humor—darts in and then darts as quickly out of his conversation. He is a man concerned with credentials. He became a totally cooperative interviewee when assured that both publisher and writer did not wish to sensationalize, but to inform. Interestingly, despite his total candor—his ability to answer the most personal of questions with honesty, which was characteristic of the man—at no time did he allow the relationship to move from the professional to a personal or friendly one. That, obviously, would not have been "appropriate."

How would you introduce yourself to the reader?

As an intelligent, highly rational, fairly attractive, white Anglo-Saxon Protestant type male who practices law and homosexuality—in that order!

Since you say "in that order," is intelligence your most important personal aspect and homosexuality your least?

Exactly. I love the mind. I've been in school most of my life—and I'm forty-three—working toward . . . what? It's hard to explain but to learn is to grow is to be alive. There are all kinds of death. To me, the stagnation of the mind is a death of sorts.

I gather to be rational is very important to you.

Yes, I dislike disordered and illogical thinking. It produces ignorance,

* See Author's Note, page xii.

bias, prejudice. If you could just make everybody in the world "rational" . . . I think we'd reach Nirvana.

Rational as opposed to emotional?

Certainly, emotions frequently are invalid because they are seldom based in anything real or rational.

Is your homosexuality "real," "rational" or emotional?

Well, it is real, that's for sure. I'm a practicing homosexual. I suspect its causes are both emotional and rational in that they can be traced to very real and very disturbing events in childhood which created personality disorders.

Are you exclusively homosexual?

Yes. Although in the past I have experienced heterosexuality. A bust! I hold no secret desire to be bi or straight. I enjoy being single. I enjoy sex with men. And if someone offered me a magic potion that would turn me from gay to straight, I'd refuse it.

Why?

For several reasons. There are many advantages to being homosexual. You are responsible solely for yourself. If you earn a decent living you can live quite well and if you earn a mere existence, you can still live, as opposed to survive, which would be the case if one was married. The homosexual life is freer. The homosexual is more independent. Independence is the most attractive aspect of homosexuality. Is that selfish? Perhaps . . . but I think we have reached a point in time where many people can chose to live "selfishly" rather than by the old and expected norm of "sharing" your life with a family. I do not wish to be a breadwinner. Furthermore, I do not like to have people hanging on me: I am dependent on no one and I do not wish for anyone to be dependent on me.

Have there been or are there people dependent upon you?

There never were. Certainly my mother wasn't. She is a fiercely independent woman. She had a stroke a year ago that the doctors told us would impair her permanently, but she has come back from it by sheer will. She attends physical therapy classes daily with but one goal: to once more live alone rather than with my sister, upon whom she has been totally dependent over the past year. Yet, despite my mother's feistiness, I think of women as "clingers." And southern women are. The women I knew in Georgia where I was raised were cloying, clinging and dependent on their men for everything. I still think of them as typical of women. My dislike of women—and it is that, a dislike—is based on those women. Generally, women as I view them have a "gimmee" approach to life. They don't stand well or for long on their own two feet.

And men do?

Men have no choice. That's forced upon you from birth. That's the role of man. Every homosexual must learn to stand alone, on his feet, or perish. Society sure isn't going to carry him.

What are some of the other reasons why you would choose to be homosexual even if there were a "magic potion"?

Primarily, it is a question of identity. I have thought of myself as a homosexual for as long as I can remember. To change now would be to destroy my sense of self. At least a major part of my self. Being homosexual is part of my identity. And that includes all the positive and negative ramifications that color a homosexual's existence.

You have mentioned what constitute some of the positives. What are the negatives?

Social unacceptability. Society reeks its displeasure . . . its revulsion even. That feels lousy. It also heaps guilt upon you. Constantly you feel, or are made to feel, that you are sick and/or doing something wrong. Also, a homosexual has far more difficulty achieving the kind of security a heterosexual finds nestled in the bosom of the family. Even as the "head," the breadwinner, there is a safety. A sense of belonging, too. There is still very little positive sense of belonging in the gay community. Most gays hide their sexuality for partly that reason. You receive little support from your own, and to look to the straight world to approve, accept or condone your life-style is to look for rejection. Most homosexuals live with a fear of discovery.

Do you?

On the job, yes. Definitely. I am a lawyer within a very conservative, old-money corporation here in Manhattan. Often I think, wouldn't it be nice not to have to role-play, to even flaunt who and what I am . . . to drop the façade. But then I think, if I dropped *anything*, I'd be dropped from the job. And that is not homosexual paranoia speaking. I've been with this company many years and I'll be there many more and ten years more after that if I am clean. I'm sure most members of the board suspect I am gay. After all I am forty-three, single and living with the same roommate for fifteen years. But . . . they don't *really* know. Nor do some want to know or it would threaten their existences . . . present a problem for them. I am paid $40,000 a year to do a job. I do it quite well, but I tell you with certainty that if I were ever arrested on a morals charge, they would not only not stand by me but would help to push me out the door.

Is that a difficult realization to live with?

All homosexuals learn to live with that kind of nitty-gritty awareness very early in life. In school, whether it is high school or college, discovery can mean being ostracized. In the Navy, when I was stationed overseas and working as a lawyer, I watched horrified and helpless as the Navy conducted "fag raids." Any sailor caught with a cock in his mouth was prosecuted, given a dishonorable discharge and usually imprisoned. A sailor with his cock caught in someone else's mouth was just hustled out of service with what's known as an administrative discharge. It was so ugly. So many young boys suffered. Thank God I was never put in the position of having to try one of those cases. I don't know what I would have done. The Navy taught me to keep my dick in my pants along with my identity.

Were there lasting effects from your military experience?

Obviously. I mean I haven't kept my dick in my pants, but I have kept my identity covered. Mainly, the Navy taught me to be careful of straights. I mistrust them. Even those who are supposedly "understanding." But if there were other things that shaped or molded me after my experience in the service, they are lost to me. But even before the Navy, from the time I was a child, I was always in some kind of conflict sexually. My father used to suggest that perhaps I wasn't all boy.

Could you explain that?

I think my father suspected I would become homosexual. When I was just a child . . . and I mean, five or six, he would say things like "You'd be better off as a girl, boy." That was hard on me. Very hard. It made me feel hostile toward him. My father was very macho. Most southern men brought up in small towns are. He was very sensitive about and ashamed of what he considered to be my feminine traits. I didn't play baseball with the boys but played with the girls . . . when I played with anybody. Mainly, I was quiet, bookish and a loner. I seldom evinced interest in sports or most of the things other boys did. I never wanted to go hunting or fishing. I liked very private things.

> *When your father suggested you might be better off as a girl, do you recall feeling anything other than hostility?*

Yes, hurt! I'd go off somewhere alone and cry. I also recall being terribly confused—that maybe I was a girl instead of a boy.

> *How would you describe your relationship with your father?*

As no relationship, not until many years later, when I was an adult, living in New York and making quite a success in my own law firm. It was only then that he and I could converse. In fact, my decision to leave private practice and join this major company, although made solely on my own, was discussed with my father. But as a child, we were never close. How could we be? He was ashamed of me . . . resented me. He was certainly never affectionate or even friendly with me. But he never abused me. Not physically. And I always respected him in the sense of doing as I was told. I was never disobedient. But I never loved him. In fact, I often felt dislike for him. As I grew older—and I'm talking here of thirteen and fourteen— when I realized I was intellectually superior to my father, I used that to get back at him. I would dominate him with my knowledge and try to make him feel as small as he had made me. He was vulnerable as hell about his lack of education. I would zap him with that. I regret that today. My father was a lousy father but not a bad man. He always provided. I was never hungry. I was always clothed. I was just never loved by him.

> *Did you want him to love you?*

If so, I don't recall having had such feelings. I never fantasized about him or of being my "father's son"—if you know what I mean. He was never my ideal. I never thought of my father as the all-encompassing male. I did not look up to him or set him as an example. When he died, I went through a very strange metamorphosis. At first I felt nothing. I just flew to Georgia and made whatever arrangements that were necessary. But weeks later, I was sitting in my home when suddenly I felt very sad. I began thinking about the father/son relationship I had never experienced and which I assumed happened for others. I suddenly realized how I had missed not having had a father and I began crying at a loss that I had never admitted I had suffered. It was very strange. Before my father died, we had become friends of sorts. There was never love—not on my part—but there was something. I'm not certain what. When he died I felt sorry that a new relationship had ended abruptly, but I didn't grieve for a loved one. You know, I can only remember once in my life prior to my adulthood, winning my father's approval. And that was when I came home from the Navy on a pass with a case of the crabs. Although I picked them up in a gay bath in New York, he thought I had gotten them from a street whore. He was so damn proud you would have thought I had presented him with a grandchild.

How did your father happen to learn of your "condition"?

I was fairly ignorant about those kinds of things, so I had to ask someone and better him than my mother. I mean we were all pretty stupid about sex. Weeks later my mother said to me in a moment of confidence, "Your father once had crabs. He got them from a toilet seat." It was a very upsetting experience. One: I realized from what she said he told her of my "condition" as you put it. Two: I realized for the first time that my father had been unfaithful to my mother. Three: I realized how terribly naïve and trusting my mother was. Imagine him telling her one could get crabs from a toilet seat. And imagine her believing it!

Were your parents happy?

I always thought so. They really seemed to have a good, working marriage. They seldom quarreled and I grew up believing we were basically a happy family. I often think my father's resentment of me was partially due to my mother's open solicitousness toward me. I was always her favorite. She placed me ahead of my brother and sister and even ahead of my father. He resented that just as he must have resented the affection she lavished on me, as there was little open affection between them. And even less visible signs of sexuality. Although they did have sex. I used to hear them. I was twelve, maybe thirteen, when I would hear the bed bump for three or four minutes. I remember thinking that their sex life could not have been very stimulating, as it lasted for so short a time. I also recall thinking that it could not have been very stimulating for my mother, as I had read somewhere that it took a lot longer for a woman to get ready, to reach a climax, than a man.

Were there other feelings you might have had about hearing your parents at sex?

No. None.

What was and is your relationship to your mother?

Very loving. Always. There has never been any doubt in my mind that my mother truly loved me. I also felt she intuitively understood me. There was a very special rapport between us. She is very tuned in to me, although she does not know of my homosexuality.

Are you certain?

No. But my mother has lived her life fairly serenely because she neither looks for nor acknowledges problems that don't need to be examined. In fact, she will even avoid unpleasantness unless it is staring her in the face.

That does not sound very rational or realistic.

My mother is, after all, a very simple woman. Very simple. But she was the one person in my childhood that seemed to understand me. Yet . . . there is some confusion in my mind about that. I mean I was a good child but never a happy one. I had very few friends. I was never with the other boys either on the ball field or in the woods hunting. I preferred to be at home reading or doing the kind of busy work boys aren't supposed to do. I always felt I was different but I never knew in what way. But I knew I was not like other boys or even like other children. My parents were content, it would seem, that I was an achiever in school and obedient at home. I never gave them any visible cause for concern. But had they been more astute—had my mother not been blind to existing problems—she would have known that my behavior—my inability to relate to children my age— was cause for concern and required professional help. But parents then didn't or couldn't think that way. Besides, they had two other children and a home to run and appearances to keep up. The neighbors thought we were a "good" family.

What is the status of that "good" family today?

We communicate. My brothers are both younger, jocks, married and very much like my father—macho-uptight. My sister is a nice person. I am much closer to her than to my brothers, who treat me deferentially but without warmth. My mother is quite a marvel. A gutsy lady. When I first got news of her stroke I felt total despair—that I would be alone, without any kind of rock to cling to. But before her recovery, I went into a kind of acceptance period where I realized I could damn well take care of myself and, in fact, had always done exactly thus.

Even as a child?

My mother took care of my physical and to some extent my emotional needs. I was housed, fed, clothed and loved. But I took care of myself in that I was my only friend. I comforted me. No one else. When my father called me a "sissy," I tended to my wounds. When the town's kids picked it up from him, I tended to that wound too. It is tough growing up in a small southern town not being the all-American boy. I was never effeminate but I never went out for letters in track, football or any sport. There was not a day in my childhood when my environment didn't combine to make me feel inadequate. Particularly sexually. To survive, I had to deal with this myself.

And how did you do this?

I don't know. I suspect through schoolwork. Books . . . learning has always been a source of comfort to me.

Is that how you learned about sex?

Yes. My parents never discussed sex with me. They would do it in the other room—four minutes three times a week—but they wouldn't talk about it. My mother, when I was nine and had asked her some kind of sex question, suggested I read *Eugenics and Sex*. Which I did. It was a very simple book about the basics. You know what is amazing? Although they never spoke about sex, both parents talked about homosexuality. First there was my father hinting that I'd be better off as a girl. Then there is my mother—and this is weird—who, when I was four, cautioned me about being friendly with a neighboring five-year-old because he was rather feminine. That's staggering when you think about it! But worse, when I was maybe six, my mother told me the kind of story you just don't and shouldn't tell a child. It was about two men in a toilet and how one man wanted to put his thing through a hole in a partition so that the other man would take it in his mouth. But the other man didn't want to do that. The first man insisted and finally put his thing through the hole only to have the other man take a jackknife and hack his thing off. It was an awful story. Terrible. I still don't understand how my mother could have told me this—particularly at that age. Or why!

What effects did her story have on you?

Well, I've never put my thing through any hole in a john partition—that I can tell you! In fact, I have never been able to so much as even cruise a toilet.

Do you think there were psychological effects?

I don't know. I've never thought about it. Only recently have I wondered about that story and my not beginning to masturbate until I was twelve. I thought that was the usual age for boys to begin playing with themselves but it turns out many boys begin at six or seven. Did I begin late because that story frightened me in some way? I really don't know those answers. And frankly, they have never seemed very important to me. Like the night these men and I were talking about childhood masturbation. Some of the men recalled jerking off thinking about this movie star or that athlete. That was never true for me. I masturbated but I don't recall ever thinking about anyone when doing it. I only remember that it felt good. But there were no pictures in my mind when masturbating—certainly none that were homosexual in nature. If there were any fantasies, I'm sure they were heterosexual.

Why do you say that?

Because male/female sex was really all I knew about. Honestly, despite my mother's story, I never knew that men could have sex together. Certainly, it wasn't explained or illustrated in *Eugenics and Sex.*

Did you ever dream . . . day dream that is . . . of love . . . romance?

If I did, I don't remember having done so. My memory is very spotty. I have always avoided thinking about the past. My childhood was very painful. Maybe that's why I've forgotten it. What's the line from "The Way We Were"—"what's too painful to remember we simply choose to forget"—that's me. Till I was a college student, away from home, I was plagued by self-doubts . . . timidity. I had an overriding sense of inadequacy. I had only my intellect to use as a crutch.

What, if any, kind of social life did you have as a teenager?

I dated several girls. There were a few crushes . . . some feeling-up here and there. Even a petting session or two. But I never went "all the way." To the best of my knowledge, very few of the boys did at that place in time. But whatever sex play I had was with women. Yet, I remember now always admiring the bodies of the school athletes. I also remember admiring the size of one little guy's cock. But I don't remember wanting anything of him or his cock. But I sure as hell was impressed by its size.

My teenage years were not happy years. There were no happy years until I reached college. Then, everything changed. It was like starting anew. It was new. No one knew me. I didn't have any town reputation to live down. I was on my own. And unlike most kids of that age, college came easy to me. I was very self-disciplined so that study and self-learning were joys, not woes. But more important, people liked me. I blossomed. I came out of my shell. People sought me out because I was interesting to talk to. I was also attractive. College was the happiest time of my life. It was like awakening from a long and bad dream. Suddenly I didn't feel uncomfortable with people. I was accepted. I came alive. And that meant sexually, too. I was a sophomore when I had my first homosexual encounter. And up until the moment it happened, I swear I never had had any fantasies about men.

Was it a pleasant encounter?

Oh yes. I was very lucky that way. Nothing ugly or tawdry. He had returned from the service and was studying on the G.I. bill. His major, funnily enough, was abnormal psychology. We would have these long talks about sex. I guess without being aware of it, we'd get all revved up talking about sexual acts, deviations and such. Well, one night after we had talked sex for an hour he simply said he wanted to blow me and would I like that. I instantly said yes. He did and as soon as he went down on me I knew I wanted to do the same to him. And I did. For the next two years, we were having sex every chance we could get.

Were you lovers?

Oh no. There was only friendship. Strictly cock-sucking with no affection involved at all.

Why then did you have sex only with him? Weren't there other available partners?

The college I attended was full of gays but at that point I was afraid of discovery. I figured if I had sex with but one person, the chances of anyone ever finding out were minimal. I really didn't want to be known then as a homosexual. I really couldn't accept it for myself. It was a real love/hate thing initially. I loved the sex. But I hated my needing it. For a long time I kept hoping I'd awaken one day to find the desire gone. I kept hearing my father's voice . . . "You'd be better off as a girl, boy." It killed me. I felt he had been right. I *was* a girl.

What about today, do you feel male or female?

Male. I never really felt female. But in that first affair, I was so uncertain, unsteady, it just seemed to me that any man who liked another man was female. Now I know that isn't true. Also the guy I carried on with suddenly married his college sweetheart and produced four children in as many years. To the best of my knowledge—and we corresponded for many years—he just stopped sucking cock. So maleness to me is not about what or who you are sucking.

What happened afterward?

Do you mean sexually? Nothing! It wasn't until I was a freshman in law school that I really got involved. There, I met a guy my age —an altogether sexy guy whose body scent I can still remember— and I fell in love with him. He was very affectionate. He needed to touch and be touched. We became inseparable. We dated. That's what we did. There was always a tender affection between us but never any sex. Never any kissing on the lips. He didn't want that. Often we would sleep together all curled up in one ball. I would get an erection. He never did. Sex was never discussed and I never suggested it because I knew it was not his need. Yet, the bond between us was so great I remember my mother once saying, "It's a pity one of you isn't a girl so you could get married." We were *that* visibly fond of one another. But it all ended very badly. One night after a year of our being very close, we got very drunk and went to bed. And I came on with him. I kissed him on the mouth and he responded. I then moved my hand to his cock which was rigid. Within seconds, he came. I came immediately thereafter. We both then fell asleep. The next day he acted as though nothing had happened the night

before. He also acted as though nothing had happened the night before that and the night before that. In other words, he just withdrew
from the relationship until there was nothing at all. It damn near
killed me. I had never suffered so and I have never suffered like that
since. For a very long time I had no sexual contact at all. And then,
suddenly, one afternoon while sitting in the library brooding, it hit
me that it was over . . . finished . . . and that I was a damn fool
for not getting on with my life. After that I began making lots of
sexual contacts. It was then I really came out and began doing all
the gay bars in the area and most of the guys in them.

How would you describe this coming out period?

As fun. By this time I was ready and I had no trouble with the scene.
I was young, attractive and sexed up. Sex was easy and enjoyable.
Initially I was solely into oral sex, but later I got into everything. And
that's where I'm at today. Although there are specific acts I like to
do with specific people, I like everything! There have been, however,
some changes with age. When I was young, I could suck any cock
if I were horny. Today, I can't. I have to dig the guy, otherwise my
jaws ache and my throat closes. And that's strictly an emotional
reaction because if I dig a guy I can give Linda Lovelace a run for
her money. I had a good youth though. I mean, once I got going I
had a damn good time. I got into a lot of kooky scenes but that was
good. I find nothing wrong with experimentation. Like when I came
up North to attend college and work on yet another master's degree, I discovered the baths and multiple sex. I loved it. I remember
the first time I entered a dark room full of bodies. I remember being
fucked but not knowing by whom and that I was being blown but
again not knowing by whom. I thought that all great fun then and I
still do. I can still get into that scene. I don't look for any great
meaning in sex. Just that it be fun. I had a good time in my twenties
but never at my expense. Like I always knew my good looks wouldn't
last forever. I always knew sex was a toy. I never devoted my life
solely to the pursuit of sex. I worked hard at my schooling and later
at my profession. I have always had my priorities and sex, although
important, was never at the top.

Has your sex been exclusively homosexual?

Other than for one woman, yes. And she was a therapeutic experiment. A suggestion made by my psychiatrist.

Then you have been in therapy.

Very briefly. In 1957 I was very apprehensive about entering the Navy. I was worried about my homosexuality and a problem that I thought then was unique—an inability to piss in public. So I sought an analyst's help. He was a very nice man I'm sure, but he literally read the Scriptures to me. Not that he sat in judgment of me, but he insisted homosexuality was wrong. "You are sexually misdirected, son," he would say. "You have a pattern of sexual activity which is unproductive and unnatural. Change it or it will cause you grief." When he asked and discovered that I had never been with a woman, he was certain that was all that was needed for the cure. So I got me a woman. A very nice girl. God I was lucky! We had sex maybe four or five times in a two-week period but after my initial excitement— you know, a kind of look-everybody-I'm-a-man!—I had to accept that sex with her felt like nothing. Nothing at all. It was neither physically nor emotionally rewarding. But the doctor was satisfied. He pronounced me cured. I knew I wasn't but I couldn't tell him, as he was such a nice man and I was afraid of hurting his feelings. But I have held a very dim view of psychiatry and psychiatrists ever since. Yet, I am very grateful for the experience. Not for him! But for having been to bed with a woman. There is no doubt in my mind now that I am gay. As stated, I like having sex with men. It excites me. Sex with a woman did not.

What, in particular, excites you about sex with men?

I can only tell you why specific acts are pleasurable to me. But why these acts are only pleasurable when performed with a man, that is something I do not know nor do I feel it important to know. I do not have a "specialty" per se. Meaning . . . although I like to sixty-nine, it is not my thing. I like different acts with different types. With young boys, I like to fuck them. With big butch men, I like them to fuck me. Fantasy today plays a big part of my enjoyment.

Meaning your ability to fantasize during sex?

No . . . actually before. If I see a certain type, I fantasize him into whatever my sexual need is. Like if a man appears big, butch, I don't question that or explore it. I keep to the fantasy and try not to ruin it through conversation. I like the idea of being dominated sexually by a man who is physically bigger than I am. I like being fucked by a man who has a big cock. In other words, the big cock goes with the big man who is part of a big macho fantasy.

What is the significance of a big cock to you?

Rationally, it doesn't have any. Irrationally, however, I feel a man with a big cock is a big man, certainly bigger and more masculine than I am. So . . . a big cock means masculinity, which is bullshit, as there are lots of flighty queens out there with big cocks. But they are never the men in my fantasies. The man I fantasize about is big —at least six feet tall, dark and hung.

Does he have a face?

No, not really. He's just this amorphous being. No one I know or have ever known.

Was your father a big man?

That's a transparent question. Yes he was, but he was light . . . fair-skinned and blond. I'm certain the man in my fantasy is not my father.

Why?

I can't imagine wanting to fuck with my father. I never had any physical contact with him and to want any seems unnatural, as I really didn't care about or want anything from him.

What is it you feel when you're being passive?

That I am giving pleasure to someone. That they are enjoying me. Of course I enjoy it. I like the physical sensation of having a cock press on my prostate. I also like the idea of being filled up. And, as I said, I like being dominated by a certain type. And it has to be that type. Like when Robert—he is my whatever-you-would-call-it for fifteen years now—tried to fuck me, I couldn't do it. Robert doesn't turn me on that way. He never did. There is just no fantasy working with Robert. I need fantasy to be successfully screwed.

What about when you're being active sexually?

That's very different. I enjoy that greatly with the sweet, innocent type—or at least the young boy or young man who gives off that illusion. With him, I like to be very tender, affectionate, caring. I supply him with *my* strength. With him, I do the dominating.

Which role do you prefer?

I enjoy both equally. I really can't say I prefer one to another. I think that depends on what my needs are at any given point in time. Some nights I want to be passive; others I need to be active. And still others, all I want is to either get blown or to find a beautiful cock attached to some beautiful guy and suck on it.

What does sucking a cock mean to you?

It gives me great pleasure. Again, partly because I know I'm giving someone else pleasure. But for me, there is the tactile sensation in the mouth. I enjoy sucking. If I weren't sucking cock, I'd suck a breadstick or smoke more than I do. The sucking motion is a very pleasurable one to me. But sucking cock is not about "cum." That's the least of it for me. I'll take a guy—I can even swallow it—but it is not the payoff. Just the end. Do you follow my meaning? Some men suck cock to get the juice. Not me. I'm always sorry when the guy comes off. It means it is finished. That's one of the reasons I like gang-bangs. There I can suck a lot of dick or enough to satisfy me until the next time, which incidentally could be a month later. I'm not compulsive about sex. I'll go out nowadays maybe a few nights a month. I'll get it all out of—or all into, as the case may be—my system at the baths or at a gang-bang. And when I do that, I leave my head outside the door. I treat my sex life as a purely sexual experience. I don't look to have my emotional needs satisfied. Like when somebody is sucking my cock, I only care that it feels good. I don't give a damn what his politics are like or his ethics or his values. I do not try to make any contact with him or hims on any level other than sex.

But if I understood you correctly, your need for sex today never rules you or interferes with your life in any way.

Correct. My sex drive has diminished with age. Also, there is Robert who I've been with for fifteen fucked-up years but fifteen years nonetheless. We still have sex a couple times a week. But most important, my sexual drive has been channeled into work and into my continued schooling. Mainly I handle sex today with occasional visits to baths and bars; equally occasional threesomes with Robert which are generally disastrous. Sex is secondary by far to what I do professionally. Initially I became a lawyer to make money. Today, I do it for the excitement, the challenge. I'm a good lawyer and I'm going to be even better with age and education. Sex . . . listen, maybe I'm jaded but to really get it on with someone is unusual. A street encounter more often than not is like an appetizer but certainly not a full meal. Not usually anyway. So . . . there are better things to do than waste one's time cruising. But don't misunderstand, I love sex and when it is good, it is among life's great goodies.

Is there anything you wouldn't do sexually?

Yes, I find fist-fucking and dildos gross. Although I believe in having as many experiences in life as possible, I also believe there are many not worth having. Fist-fucking is one. All S&M activity is another.

How you experienced S&M activity?

Once and that was by accident. There was this very attractive man from the gym, big, dark . . . got the picture? I had known him for several years—had even attended some parties with him and had found him a really sweet—and that's the right word—guy. Suddenly, to my surprise and delight, we were in bed one Sunday afternoon but that delight turned to horror. After the most fleeting of embraces, he began slapping the shit out of me and ordering me simultaneously to perform certain sexual acts. There wasn't anything he wanted that I hadn't done in the past and enjoyed but his manner frightened me. I no longer recognized him as the man I had known. I have often thought he wanted me to slap him back but I couldn't. That really isn't me. Violence upsets me. He upset me! To the point where I turned over on my stomach and begged—only I was pretending—for him to fuck me. I knew if I could get him in me I could get him off and it would be over. And that's what happened. Except for one other oddity. As soon as he climaxed, he became his old self and was very contrite about what he had done and who he had become. But I was never able to feel good toward him again. Over the years I've met other men and boys who have wanted me to piss on them or who have wanted to drink piss or have me drink theirs—men who have wanted to be tied to a bed and fucked or who have wanted to tie me to a bed and fuck—and I have given them a wide berth. I truly don't understand these people. Nor do I consider their actions as sexual but as distortions of sex. I think they are sick and I say that with the full awareness that straights think all homosexuals are sick. I don't. When I say S&M is sick, I'm not singling out homosexual sado/masochist but all sado/masochists who, as we all now know, are legion in numbers. I guess each person draws their own line. But, no matter how I try to understand, I cannot categorize together sex and sado/masochism.

How do you feel about gang-bangs?

Well, I go to them, as you know, and they certainly don't disgust me.

What made you use the word "disgust"?

I don't know. It just came to me. Gang-bangs are something you do with your eyes closed, so to speak. Yet I like watching men have sex. I like to have sex watching men have sex.

Is there anything about gang-bangs you don't like?

I've never solved that I-don't-dig-you-so-don't-stick-your-cock-in-any-of-my-orifices dilemma. I always feel obligated to mix it up with the guests who want to mix it up with me. I don't much like that.

But you do it.

Sometimes. You must remember that if I go to one, maybe two, gang-bangs every three months I am able to go along with the scene without becoming emotionally involved or drained by the experience. I seldom, if ever, today fall into bed with someone with affection as my need. I look solely for sex when out cruising. When that boy I loved so much—the one who couldn't accept his homosexuality—rejected me, he put a frost on my ability to make an emotional commitment. I have never been in love since. And I don't think I have ever loved deeply since. I doubt if I have the capacity any longer. I deny myself affection but I don't seem to need it, so that the denial doesn't mean anything. For all the years I've been with Robert, I never think of myself as being deeply involved. I have never been in love with him although he was, and maintains he still is, in love with me. He is even affectionate . . . yet, still. I am not. Nor am I a warm person. I know that. I have almost no close—close in the sense of intimate—friends. And the older I get, the more withdrawn I become. Making out is no longer very important. Nor is maintaining my looks, although I work out regularly and watch my diet. I worry *somewhat* about age and about an eventual inability to drag anyone home to bed, but I don't worry very much about either. You know . . . after you've been around a lot, if you have any brains at all, after you've waded through a few thousand sexual encounters, you wake up one day and say, "Hey! What the fuck is this all about?" And a voice somewhere within you answers: "Not much!"

How fulfilling is your sex life?

Not very. Obviously so, as there is no longer much sex life to speak of. Even my sex with Robert is very one-sided. He sucks my cock and I fuck him. It is seldom exciting for me—although Robert is the best cock-sucker I've ever experienced—but it is always exciting for him. So why do I do it? Because he wants it and because it isn't distasteful to me. I do have a kind of affection for Robert after all these years. Most people can't stand the guy, as he comes on as a crusty old bear, but underneath that there's another person. Robert loves me. He loves me very much. Now there's no reason anyone should understand this 'cause I don't but . . . I am Robert's fantasy come to life. Fifteen years of knowing me and he claims to be as impassioned about me as ever. And I wish to God he weren't.

Why do you say that?

Because most of me doesn't want to stay with Robert and hasn't for many years.

Why do you stay?

You'd have to know Robert to understand. Shit! I met Robert in 1961 in a gay bar. I went home with him because he was kind of cute. He looked like Jack Lemmon. It was flattering as hell to be someone's passion. And he courted me. Literally. Presents and dinners and one year later an apartment that I moved into with him without thinking. I liked Robert and I enjoyed him. I still do. He has a great mind and can discuss most issues. He is a rather successful social worker. Intellectually, we are compatible. Sex is another story. Years ago I could go down on him because there was still some attraction. Today I gag, choke, but it doesn't bother him. After fifteen years Robert still goes on and on about love. I think his protestations are a crock of shit. I've even told him that but it doesn't stop him. And I had hoped that over the years we would turn into great friends who lived together—maybe even occasional buddy-fuckers but not lovers. It never happened. And it never will. Robert sees us as lovers. That's not what I want. I want the security of a friend . . . of a Robert, but I don't want to be tied down.

Is security then why you stay?

I stay because . . . well . . . he is my best friend and in some funny kind of way I love him, but it is not the kind of love he talks about. Actually, I should have left Robert years ago. And I tried, only then —that was years ago—he attempted suicide and I went back. When I left him, incidentally, I left with but two suitcases and the clothes on my back. He hired private investigators to find me, which, of course, was unnecessary as he was calling my office nine times a day, but he had no idea where I went to afterward. He spent $2,500 on detectives. When I got the call that he had o.d.'ed, I ran. I've been with him ever since.

Did the relationship alter when you returned?

Yes and no. He still threatened suicide if I left, but he did loosen the bonds. I was allowed out. He never liked it, but he permitted me freedom to cruise or just go to the movies alone. But, of course, there was a price. He became a drug addict—barbiturates to go to sleep; dope to get up; dope to stay up. He was so spaced so much of the time that he lost several positions because his employers at the time thought he was drunk. Once I came home from a night at the baths to find the firemen in our apartment. Robert had passed out while smoking and had set the mattress on fire. That shocked me into action. Till then, I knew that Robert was addicted but I wouldn't admit it. But when he nearly burned himself up, I had to face facts. I bargained with him. I would stay with him but *only* if he kicked the habit. Let me tell you if you haven't been with an addict when they've cold-turkeyed, you ain't seen life. I counted at least twelve seizures. The convulsions were horrible. It was *all* horrible. But, after a week—and I never left the apartment during that time—he kicked it. He's been clean ever since, although I suspect that if I strayed more than he felt I should, he'd begin the whole Demerol and Dexedrine scene again. But, it is so much better than it was. Robert has become very much more self-sufficient than I ever thought possible.

Do you realize you have described a relationship of dependency?

Yes. And that's what I hate.

But Robert is not a woman. You had stated earlier that what you like least about women is their clinging . . . cloying . . . that they don't stand on their own two feet . . . that they are dependent.

Yes.

Yet this is the type of person you have spent fifteen years with.

Yes . . . strange. I never thought of it that way. But . . . it has gone on for so long I just wouldn't know. . . . It would be like starting life all over again. That's very frightening. Yes, Robert is a lunatic. Yes, Robert limits my freedom. But, Robert is my security. He knows that now, which makes him considerably more secure than he ever was. That I guess is my weakness. I wouldn't want to be that alone again. To start over. . . . You see, I like much of my life with Robert. And he loves me. He truly loves me. He still courts me—

still invents admirers in the hope that I will treasure him more. Poor
Robert. Sometimes I have wished him dead but then I think . . .
what would I do if he did disappear! There would be such great
voids. There are sides to my life with Robert which are wonderful.
We have subscriptions to the opera and the Philharmonic. We both
like to attend certain political lectures. We are both issue-discussers.
Although he enjoys theater far more than I do, we frequently will see
what's available. That part of our life is stimulating . . . wonderful
actually. I would miss it. Without Robert, I'd have to fulfill myself.
I suppose that would be very constructive but . . . talking to myself
would not be as stimulating as talking to Robert.

Do you think of yourself as independent or married or both?

There is a trap in that question. Previously I said I was a very independent person. And I am. But what hit me as we were talking about
why I stay with Robert is that in some way that I don't understand,
I am very dependent on him. Otherwise . . . if I weren't, I could
leave. I would have left. I don't feel married to Robert but I suspect
I am. Actually, I feel tied, and the older we get the tighter the bonds
feel. I still think of leaving, still think of another and very different
kind of life, but if I did, the whole thing would start over again—his
insomnia, the pills he would take for it, the addiction, the suicide
threats. His lack of independence traps me. As does one other thing
—I see that now—*me!* I hold me where I am, with Robert, every bit
as much as Robert does. The question is why.

Do you worry about old age?

If you mean being old and infirm, yes and no. A long time ago I came
to the realization that I better take steps to insure my own life. I
have made provisions for myself. Should I require constant nursing
or a nursing home, I've amassed enough of an estate to provide for
these services. So I don't much concern myself with that kind of
worry. I will be cared for because I have taken care of that. I don't
much worry about being alone either. Or do I? All of my life I've
recognized that we are all alone almost always and certainly in death.
I have often thought maturation was recognizing and accepting that
fact. I have never believed in depending on others. I have tried to
depend on me. I guess in some way I do depend on Robert, but
mainly I depend on my brain. It has enabled me to work in a stimulating profession and to have earned excellent wages. My work is
my joy. My goal in life—the only one I am aware of having—is to

become the general counsel for my company. And that is now within the realm of possibility.

And is that all you dream?

Yes. Except perhaps to keep growing. This may sound pompous, but in all my life there has been one continuous search for the new experience. I have always felt that to stop learning would be to stop growing, which means to die. I have been a student all my life. Even today I attend school two nights a week working on yet another degree. I love ideas. I love books. I love the learning process. That moment when you feel your mind expanding—that's like a good orgasm. I do not dream of love. I do not hope to fall in love again. But I would not run from it if it happened. But the likelihood of its happening is near nil. I so seldom go to places where I might meet someone. And when I do go, I go with sex in mind and not romance. Frankly, I can't imagine falling in love again. Actually, what I would like is a real fucking-buddy, someone to play with, a live-in friend, one to fuck with when one felt like it, but a no-commitment relationship. Now I hear the question in my own head: Am I afraid of commitment? I'll let you know when I discover that answer. A part of me—that I've been unable to deal with as we were just talking of it —suspects that I am committed to Robert without having acknowledged that fact to him or to me. Anyway, love is not a priority. How could it be? I am hardly a romantic. And I certainly don't find gay life very romantic. When I was young I did, but it has changed. It, as well as me. Gay life has gotten kinky. The Fire Island scene is disgusting. Too many drugs, too many children fucking on beaches and anywhere else that two people can copulate. It's very alienated. I hate it. I am very conventional. Even conservative. I am a solid-citizen type. Very middle-class. I cannot understand or identify any longer with the many young gays who flit around the country crashing in crash pads with strangers, balling with anyone for poppers and pot. I like my home. Robert and I live in a luxurious high rise on the East Side. We have both worked hard to afford it. Nobody gave me the money. I earned it. I like that. I've also earned my place in my company. I like that too.

Are you saying therefore that you do not feel part of gay life and/or the gay community?

I live a homosexual life in that my sex contacts are all men and the people I know are all gay. I am uncomfortable with straights. But I do not feel a member of the gay community. I don't relate well to most gays. Most are inconsequential people who devote their lives to sex and the sillies—such as parties and pretty clothes and trivia and minutiae. That's not me. I think gay pride is a myth. Few gays have any pride at all. Obviously. Fist-fucking is a big rage today—more than just a cult thing. Well, if one has true pride in oneself, one doesn't let some spaced-out sadist shove his arm up your ass. Similarly, if one has true pride one doesn't cruise the truck stops and suck any cock that is available.

What is the difference between truck-stop cock-sucking and the baths?

There is a difference! A subtle one but a difference. At the baths everyone is gay. But at the truck stops, gays go there to suck straight men's cocks. There is a very subtle put-down of self involved. Similarly, sex at the baths, although it seems public and is, in that you can be watched and usually are, is not public in that you are not opening yourself up to public—in the sense of straights—criticism. But, when you start having sex in public places—like the sex bars that anyone can walk into—that's humiliating. There is no pride involved in allowing yourself to be seen as you are being degraded. I know it sounds like I'm into a double standard. But I'm not. Not really. Every gay reading this, whether he will admit it or not, knows what I am talking about.

Then you do not believe in the gay pride movement?

Quite the contrary. I not only believe in it but I wish there were such a thing. It won't happen until the world receives psychotherapy where homosexuality is concerned. As long as homosexuality is considered "sick" and perverted, gays will be sick and perverted. As I have stated, one of the prices gays pay is the galloping guilts inflicted upon them from birth by the heterosexual world. There will be gay pride when gays stand up not to proudly say that they are gay but to *act* with pride—when they care about their minds and bodies and refuse to allow others—including and perhaps mainly themselves—to put them down as *people*.

Have you ever been involved in the gay rights movement?

Only financially. I have anonymously sent money for several causes. I was deeply affected by the riots at the Stonewall when they happened. The gay pride parade each year moves me too. But it also upsets me. You see, I don't believe that the majority of people who march in those parades know what gay rights is about. Is it really about the freedom to suck cock? No! Sexual freedom should not be questioned. Of course it is. By everyone. What I find so atrocious is the inability of the governing agencies of this country to legislate bills that prevent descrimination based on sexual bias. Who one sleeps with should have no bearing on employment or housing opportunities.

Why have your contributions to gay rights been anonymous?

Because I have worked my ass off to attain a social and economic status. That is not worth risking for what is still a very confused cause. When those gay militants, those who are sincere in their political fights, get it together, maybe then I'll reevaluate my closet status. But now . . . no way. Not while I see gays thinking that sexual freedom is earning the right to suck cock anyplace, anytime. And not while I see gays leading destructive lives—lives predicated, it would seem to me, on self-dislike.

Do you like yourself?

I respect me . . . respect me greatly for what I have accomplished. I have had my own heartache in life—big deal, who hasn't?—but although I maybe fucked up—more than I even know—I haven't fucked up my life. I like my life. I like my place in it. I like the contribution I make in my work. I like what I have done with me.

Are you happy?

If happiness is euphoria, then no, I am not happy. But if happiness is feeling fulfilled and generally content, then yes, I am happy. Certainly I am not despairing. Only occasionally am I depressed. Most often . . . well, I said it . . . content. That's how I feel. I may even be more content than I have realized.

What do you mean?

Robert. It may just be that he . . . *us* . . . means more to me than I have been able to admit.

Tracy Roth

LIKE THE MAN, the apartment was in a state of change throughout the three weeks it took to complete the interviewing. Initially, Tracy * wore big, blousy shirts to hide—not successfully—his obesity. Tinted glasses also sought to hide—again not successfully—the man from the world. The apartment was in disrepair. He was renovating. The heavy browns and the even heavier antique furnishings were giving way to something new, but exactly what, he didn't yet know. The two cats did not care. They slept throughout the changes that took place. But not Misty, the dog, described by Tracy Roth in a quick, unguarded moment as "My life!" Misty was always up and about, protective of the man who often acted more his lover than his master.

Tracy was pushing forty "and, honey, it pushed right back and knocked the hell out of me!" He was "getting-it-together, changing-my-way-of-living-and-if-that-ain't-enough" was definitely agreeable to changing "the-way-I-strut-my-stuff." But it was no joke. The changes, even within the three weeks, were remarkable. The apartment became a light pearl gray with furnishings mainly of glass and steel. And Tracy, as another act of courage, wore his shirt *inside* his pants and heard his neighbors say, "My God, but you've lost weight!" But, as he noticed, no one said, "How wonderful you look!" and still no one rode to his Hell's Kitchen apartment on a white horse. So even as he felt better, he continued to feel sad. But he has his dreams.

You may use my real name. I'm ashamed of nothing. My parents are dead, although my mother continues to exist in Miami Beach somewhere. Dreadful woman! My sister, too, is alive-but-dead-and-living-in-New Jersey. Some town called Transylvania—I think. I haven't spoken to either of them in three years, which shows some kind of emotional growth on my part. They may be the only two women I *don't* like. Generally, I find women beautiful. I'm much more at ease with them than I am with men, who are much too competitive.

* See Author's Note, page xii.

Women are more sincere. But I hate fag-hags. I suspect a woman who only runs around with gay men. Am I rambling? I just realized I'm running off at the mouth and you, poor baby, haven't even asked a question yet. Go ahead. Ask.

Since you sought to be interviewed, is there something in particular you wish to say?

Yes. I want to thank all the little people who made this possible. And my director and . . . oh! Wrong speech. Sorry. Actually, I had thought that maybe my gruesome story might prevent some other person from hiding. . . .

Hiding?

From life . . . from behind a wall of flesh. Then, too, if I'm not X-rated out of this book, it'll be proof, to me, that I *do* exist.

Why the doubt?

Is this an interview of the beginning of a trilogy on My Rejected Life?

What would you like it to be?

Anything. Hang on to your buns, sweetheart, but . . . I want you to know it is absolutely wonderful to have someone listen to me. A unique experience! God that sounds self-pitying. But, it's the truth. I've been rather invisible my entire life. Other than the shrinks—and they were paid—no one has ever just listened to me.

Listen. Forget that! We're really off on the wrong foot. I'm usually very "up"—*très charmant*—witty. That's me.

Really?

What's with the *really* number. Yes, *really*. Those of us not born beautiful learn to be something other than what we are. Being "up" is never quite natural, but you have to do something when no one ever comes up to you and says, "I *have* to have you!" You become charming, witty, chic. It's all bullshit.

Why?

Because when people dig me the most I am play-acting, doing my "up" performance. I must "act" to get into a room filled with people. But, actually, all I want to do is walk in, sit down and be me.

Why don't you?

'Cause in a gay situation, no one will notice me. So I become this very gay creature—a laugh riot—the reverse of who I really am. You have no idea how hilarious I can be. Of course I never feel hilarious, only insecure, particularly among gay men. They're all so pretty. I never know what to talk to them about. They all have *fabulous*, hyperactive sex lives, which they love to discuss, while I have next to none. I feel like an outcast, but I am well aware that I have done most of the casting out.

How have you done this?

By keeping my face in the refrigerator. Would you believe I was once a svelte 145 pounds. That was thirteen years ago. Today I'm 200, down from 285, with a long way to go. But I'll get there. In becoming this obese "thing," I cast myself out of living. I went into hiding. No one can reach me and no one can hurt me behind this wall of fat. Why? Because no one wants to when you're gross. Isn't it amazing how the fattest people can go through life invisible—as though they are not there.

Was there a particular event that triggered your weight gain?

Honey, there has been a lifetime of events! And yes, there was a specific one. My first-and-only lover, Edward, took a walk on Valentine's Day 1964. I'm sure everyone has an Edward in their lives, the kind of lover you give everything over to who then turns out to be a shit. So you collapse in your bed and bore your friends with a nervous breakdown.

Well that was me and Edward. Now, you may ask, why did I love him. 'Cause I'm a mental masochist. I love to suffer and I have such wonderful practice at it, as it is all I've ever known. As the shrinks explain . . . if a child grows up feeling like a piece of shit because he has been treated like a piece of shit by the significant members of his family, then that child will attract shits who shit all over him. Worse, that child will love being shat upon because he feels he deserves no better. As I said, that was me . . . that was Edward.

After the *prince's* departure, I decided what I had sought in a man didn't exist and not knowing another way to get what I needed—which was love, m'love—I stopped looking. Actually, I stopped living. In not going out, in not cruising, I got gradually sloppy. It began with *only* ten pounds and then it was fifteen, twenty . . . one hundred and oh-my-God-how-did-that-happen! But I ignored it; rationalized that "the person who *I* want will want me for *me* regardless of size and shape." I was right. Anyone who might have dug me sure wouldn't have for my bod . . . unless he had a Santa Claus fetish and in this town anything's possible.

Was food always important to you?

Not at all. It was just something to eat. But after Edward, it became life itself. It filled the gap . . . the hole. It was a tranquilizer. It numbed the pain. But as food, it meant nothing. I hardly tasted what I was stuffing into me. And "stuffing" is the right word. There was this bottomless pit inside me and the more I ate the more it required to stay filled.

Then, about five years ago, when I had just turned thirty-three, I began the diets. My dear, I lost 3,227 pounds with Dr. Atkins, Dr. Stillman, monkey piss and God knows what else! Of course I put it all back on plus a few extra. None of it worked until I really wanted it to. About a year ago I walked my chubby little body through the doors of Overeaters Anonymous and here I am, a member in good standing. No crazy diets, just controlled eating. Best of all, there are lots of people to support you through an attack of the Munchies. I'm losing three to five pounds a week and I will never gain back what I've lost. But never! I'll go out a window first. Can you imagine, in a week or so I'll be a size thirty-eight! In another week, I'll be able to look down and see my knees. My very own knees. Tomorrow the world!

So physical appearance has once again become important?

Yes, thank God. It has taken me a long time to want to make the packaging better—thirteen years to be exact—but now I really want to be thin again. But for *me*. Not for "them" or *him* but for me. I want to wear nice clothes. I want to feel good about me. I want to think more of me. I want to live better and if I can walk past a mirror and say "Hi ya, gorgeous!" and mean it . . . I'll be living better.

Is there not the desire to be more attractive to others?

Listen kid, it wouldn't hurt. Sure. But if I'm just attractive and nothing else then I'm no better off than I already am. What I'm saying is that for the first time in my life I'm trying to like me, *all* of me.

That some terrific man might say "Tracy, you're a doll!" would be nice—oh would that be nice!—but it is incidental. I have to think I'm a doll and if I can do that, I'll be on the way to losing most of my neuroses. Which is at least a loss of another 112 pounds.

How do you feel when you are with attractive people?

Invisible, or like a shadow . . . that they don't see me. Just once before I die I'd like to join them. Just once I'd like to feel like a Beautiful Person, to be seen! Gays don't really see unattractive men. They don't look at us. Instant blindness. We're nasty, ugly, like someone who is deformed. You're there but you're *not* there. I've had a lifetime of that kind of rejection. Listen, this is going to be a very sad story, easily worth three and a half handkerchiefs.

If it is so sad, why are you making light of it?

Listen sweetheart, don't kill the laughs. The only thing I get out of gay life is the humor. Ever hear the expression, "Keep it gay"? But if it is straight up that you want, here goes.

I am thirty-eight years old, five-foot-ten and 221 pounds. I lied before when I said I was 200. My family is either dead or dead— we've been through that already. I don't hate them any more. Fifteen years on and off the couch has cured me of all but the bitterness. I don't even dislike them . . . well, maybe a little. Maybe even a lot! I was never a part of *their* family.

My father was an important executive for a greeting card company. He made good money. He was a verbally abusive man. He used to bat me around regularly too. Yet, he was not a virile man. My mother, the latent truck driver, ran the house and all our lives. She had been a medical assistant who gave it up to be a housewife and mother. She shouldn't have. She may have given a helluva enema but she sure didn't know from shit about mothering. Anyway, they were miserable together for fifty years. They were never anything but miserable. I think they were the most unhappy people I have ever known.

Yet, as a child, a state that may have ended about a year ago, I adored my mother. She was beautiful, intelligent, sophisticated in a bitchy Barbara Stanwyck type way. I was her Friday and Saturday night movie date until I was twenty-one. I was also her home-decorator, adviser and confidant. Everything but her son. I loved all my roles then. Now . . . she used me.

Strangely, despite his abusiveness, I loved my father and always hoped he would love me. God knows I tried and God knows I failed to win his love. He was emotionless. Once in his lifetime he was tender with me. Once in his lifetime—*once*—he touched me. When he was dying. He took my hand and squeezed it. Ten minutes later he was gone. I felt nothing at his passing. Nothing. Now, I feel sad for what might have been but wasn't.

I was a fucked-up kid. Other parents would have seen it. Mine preferred not to, although they did, at my pleading, send me to a psychologist from the age of twelve to seventeen. I had to. At school the kids were beating on me, calling me *fruit* and *fairy*. I never understood that. I was not yet out, although I knew at ten that I liked men. And I wasn't effeminate. I never was. I never wanted to be a girl. I liked being a boy. I am now trying to like being a man. But as a kid, it seemed no matter where I was, at home or at school, someone was beating me up. Of course I developed migraines and elephant hives. I was a mess. Now here's the pisser. Neither of my parents ever spoke to the psychologist. They ignored the entire mess. But then, how could they give anything when neither had anything to give. So you see, a "close" family relationship or any kind of positive relationship between family members is not in my experience. "Marcus Welby" and "All My Children" tell me they exist, but they are not in my experience. Thus, I do not miss my mother. She has made no attempt to reconcile. Nor will she unless I allow her to run my life. And even then I will have to beg forgiveness for not having lived my life as she saw fit. Not that she objected to my homosexuality. God, no! Now she could have me for her Saturday night date forever. Listen . . . are you bored yet? 'Cause if you're not, I am.

Would you like to stop?

No. I'm sorry. This just brings back unpleasant memories.

Do you recall your relationship with your psychologist?

Yes and no. I have successfully managed to forget almost everything of my first seventeen years. But I do remember he was a nice man. I liked him. He was somebody to talk to and he made me feel I existed. I also felt he cared. I would talk to him about my parents, wondering what I had done that they didn't love me. We also talked about my inability to make friends with kids my age. I didn't understand it then but now I do. I was never a little boy. And I was never a girl. I was neuter and the children couldn't relate to that.

That all added up to my feeling like Hitler . . . some unlovable ghoul. I felt ugly inside and out, which, incidentally, if I'm to believe the photographs, was not true. But *they* made me feel it was true.

Can you recall any happy times in your childhood?

No. I didn't know what happiness was until I joined the Navy at seventeen. But as a child? Nothing. There was nothing. No dreams. No goals. No love. That was a word on one of my father's greeting cards. Even today, it is hard for me to hope for love. A little voice within snarls, "If they couldn't, why should someone else?" Happily, within the past year, a more gentle voice has emerged who answers: "Because it was them and not me." My father's idea of loving was to buy me "things." The poor guy was a sad man. He did his miserable best. My mother did not. I was an embarrassment to her. She was only too happy to sign me over to the Navy at seventeen.

Considering the problems you experienced in relating to peers, wasn't it unusual that you would think to join the Navy?

No. I didn't think of "peers" or needing to relate to them. I saw the Navy as a home, a family, a place in which I might belong, be taken care of. It was my escape . . . a fantasy.

What about sex?

That, too, never crossed my mind. You must understand, I just wanted to belong somewhere. And at seventeen I didn't know there were men or boys my age who liked sex with men. I thought I was the only "strange one" in the world. I was sure the other boys I had balled as a teenager only did it for kicks, while I was in it because I *had* to be. I didn't know there was a gay world then.

In the Navy, I never fooled around with servicemen. I was a good sailor and I received numerous citations. The guys liked me, although they decided from the beginning that I was a banana from a different bunch. But they never bothered me. I had friends on the base. Off duty, in San Diego, I met many older men who were kind and generous to me. Although there was always sex involved, it was the last thing we did. Talk and more talk came first. I was popular. Of course I was young and I guess kind of cute in my Navy whites. Whatever, the Navy and my four years as a sailor were the happiest times of my life.

When did you begin having sex with men?

At fourteen. With a boy from the neighborhood. We explored one another. Then I blew him. I used to blow him regularly. Not that I enjoyed it, I didn't, but I did enjoy his wanting me. He would come over to the house frequently and I interpreted this as his wanting and needing me . . . liking me even. Of course what he wanted and needed and liked was being serviced, but I only knew then that there was another person who touched me and allowed me to touch him. And that was wonderful!

Do you know that to this day to be touched is still one of the two ultimate trips for me. The other is kissing. That is such beautiful intimacy. I've never cared very much about sex. It's always been love that I've chased and not the big basket. Pity. A big basket is so much easier to find.

Considering how happy you felt in the Navy, why didn't you become a career man?

Ah! The pursuit of love. But let me backtrack. I had thought initially of making the Navy my career. When I left my parents' home, I remember thinking to myself, "Don't look back and don't come back." And I wouldn't have had it not been for my father's letters. He began wooing me, writing such hitherto unspoken words like "We miss you" and "We love you." Always *we*; never *I*. But they were the magic words. The promise. Finally, he would love me.

I really was a banana. And I must have known it because as the plane approached New York I had an anxiety attack. I passed out and they had to carry me off the plane on a stretcher. Of course no one was there to meet me. When I reached their cozy little nest on the Grand Concourse in the Bronx the first words my mother said were: "You should never have come home. Your father will never change." She was right, the bitch. He didn't. Nor did she. Well, so much for the joys of childhood and adolescence. Any last questions before I close the door? I'm disappointed. You didn't shed *a* tear. God but I'm being bitchy. Well, I warned you I was still bitter. The remnants of that childhood are like slivers of glass under my skin— hard to remove but too painful not to. But I must. I can no longer live back there. I must get into today. And I'm doing it. Slowly. I recently converted to Buddhism and that has helped me enormously.

How did you come to Buddhism?

Well, I didn't go searching for it. I had no religion—although I was born Jewish—and could not have cared less until someone took me to a Buddhist church. It was incredible. Everyone had this glow. But what impressed me was the religion's stress on positives. It said I could be and should be happy. It said God loves me and wants me to be happy. And if being happy means loving another man, that's okay and not a sin. So I converted about two years ago and I really do believe *my* God wants me to find peace and contentment. It was shortly after my conversion, incidentally, that I began thinking of Overeaters Anonymous. And as I began redoing me, I began redoing my apartment. It was like wanting to change everything that had been and start over again. I'm excited about life now. I see possibilities I did not see before. I'm working hard on putting me back together. No more walls. I don't wish to be divided from life. Some days I feel like Susan Hayward in *I'll Cry Tomorrow.* As if I'm coming back from a long drunk—getting back into life. Only it is not Susan Hayward. It's me. I often feel that everything that passed before was an exercise to prepare me for a better life. That's a very Buddhist philosophy, by the way.

   What would that "better life" be?

Well, I wouldn't be straight 'cause that doesn't interest me. If I went to bed with one hundred women—what a depressing thought!—I don't believe I would feel any happier or more fulfilled. I'm no longer ashamed of being gay. I used to be. That changed with the Stonewall riots. It woke me up. I would never at that point have stood up and fought as a homosexual. But afterwards, after those boys and men stood up and did *my* fighting, there was nothing to hide from any more. I was so damn proud. I owe all those guys. I breathe easier today because of them. I have never felt outside my homosexuality since then, although I still feel outside the gay world. I can't say I find any joy within that world. Not for me anyway. It's a helluva life, sweetheart. If society doesn't kill you, the homosexual life-style can. I find the latter repulsive. Most gay men, with their rampant sexual behavior, alienate themselves from the world and vice versa.

   What, as you see it, is the homosexual life-style?

A bunch of guys sitting around dishing about the trick they had the night before . . . running to the baths and the bars, the trucks and the bushes. Fucking at Fire Island. The ultimate dream and goal in gay society is sex. You ain't doing it, baby, unless you're doing it. And, if you don't look like Mark Spitz or Robert Redford and make it with guys who look like Mark Spitz and Robert Redford, you ain't nowhere. I am here to tell you, my love, for men like me who look like Jackie Gleason, it's hell. The accent in gay life is on the physical. But definitely! If I should be so lucky as to begin dating a handsome man, gay society will think one of three things: that I'm keeping him; that he's a masochist; that he is blind.

Do you have much contact with "gay society"?

No. I did when I was younger. After the Navy I worked as a waiter in a gay restaurant and then, when I got into design and display, I worked for *that* famous department store on the East Side and hung out with the gay men in its employ, a little mini-society within the store. But today, I give gay society a wide berth. I have to. I can't be a victim of sexual homicide.

Would you explain what you mean by that?

I cannot be *that* rejected. I cannot be around gays. They're merciless. They make me nervous. They are all generally attractive men . . . so much better looking than I am, although they are not nicer. But life, my dear, works better for the Beautiful Persons. As Bette Davis once said—and if it wasn't Davis, it should've been—"Nice guys finish last." Additionally, my values are so much different from most. I'd never ignore someone just because he wasn't pretty. Gay men would rather be desired, I think, than be successful. And yet, the most desirable, the Drop Dead Beauties, seem to be searching. I look at their faces and gorgeous bodies and think . . . for what? What are they looking for that they cannot find? It seems to me that if I were a D.D.B. I'd want to share it with one other person—present it as a gift—but these people seem to spread it around. That would be okay if their promiscuity brought them happiness. But it doesn't. Now why is that? Why can't the Chosen People be happy?

How do you feel toward these "chosen people"?

Mostly angry. Sometimes hatred. They abuse their beauty and they abuse others with it. They take, take and take some more and give back precious little. They need constant reassurance, but I don't know of what they want to be assured. They're "chosen," golden, what more can they possibly want? But I've seen some of these beauties, watched them as they turn down coldly those who don't measure up to what they feel befits them. They assume the right to disdain. They also assume everyone has a choice like they do. Well . . . not everyone does. Not everyone can walk into a bar and say "You! I'll take you!" and succeed. Just once I'd like these guys to walk into a bar and feel that no one wants them. What a sobering and humbling experience that would be. Imagine finding that some do not choose to be alone but are because no one wants them.

Is it possible you are jealous somewhat of these beautiful people?

I don't know. Maybe. Then again, I'm bored with men who think of sex as the cherry on top of life.

Would you say that if the "cherries" were readily available to you?

That's cruel. You're assuming they're not. Well . . . you're right. They aren't. They never were, but even less so today, ever since I took myself out of the rat race. I haven't been to a gay bar in ten years.

Where do you go to find sex?

I don't.

What do you do about sex then?

Fantasize and masturbate when necessary. And if I really need sex, which is not often the case, I'll buy it. I'll pick up the phone and order a piece-of-meat-and-love from my neighborhood madam. There is great safety in buying by phone. One, you don't have to leave your home, thus avoiding the possibility of muggers, and two, no one can look at you in a bar and say, "Get a load of the Fat Lady!" Yes, a hustler removes all possibility of rejection. He isn't about to say, "Sorry, I'm waiting for someone." A hustler doesn't have to like me. He doesn't have to ask for my phone number . . . and then not call. He doesn't have to come back. Not ever. He's wonderful because he doesn't make me feel like chopped meat, all ground up to feed the dogs. Yes, and another wonderful thing about hustlers. You can romanticize them into anyone you like. I treat all hustlers like they're the best money can buy. Funny about that choice of words. What I mean is, I treat them beautifully, as if they were potential lovers. Why not? It's my fantasy and my money. Why shouldn't I get what I'm paying for?

Do you ever seek to meet partners on a non-paying basis?

Well, of course I did prior to Edward, and I did well enough. But now . . . no. I can't. I just can't. I may be strange but I'm not crazy. I know no one is going to want me as I am so why put myself in the position of being hurt. And baby, it hurts! Like hell. You can't know what it feels like to have people walk away from you, or look past you, as though you were nothing, just because you are too much. No, I will not subject myself to that kind of pain. Besides, I've already told you, sex is not that important to me. I'm much more of a romantic homosexual than a physical one. I may be the only "Let's Love" instead of "Let's Fuck" freak in this town.

If the "let's fuck" was available to you, would that still be true?

You really are merciless. I don't know—which is not the answer you want. You'd love me to say yes. But I really don't know. I do everything to repress my sex feelings. I mean . . . I so seldom feel sexual and the thought of feeling sexual embarrasses me. I think if I admitted to feelings of sexuality I'd feel even more rejected than I do. It would also make me vulnerable to admit I need something that I'm not getting. But it is also possible I have a minimal sex drive. But, maybe I don't. Maybe I'm just full of shit . . . afraid.

What makes you say that?

Because I suddenly realized I go around mentally photographing beautiful men. I store them in my mind's eye. Then, when I need a masturbatory fantasy, I conjure them up. I'm wondering now, this second, if I don't want to attack them on the spot. But it's easier to keep them as fantasies . . . easier to romanticize them into whatever I need.

But do you get what you need from a fantasy?

You've got a big mouth, you know that? No, I don't. I'm lonely. But I'm too afraid to approach someone. When I'm thinner. . . . Really. Then I'll approach the world, but now I have to hold on to me. Besides, there is another element to all this. I'm a lousy lay. I don't know how to just fuck. I never did. Even when it was available to me, I went into sex for love, which is like going to Russia for freedom.

You cannot seek love in sex. Sex is a part of love but love as a part of sex is for the very young. When I was a cute, young sailor, I was in love in every sex encounter. And I got hurt each time as only the young can. I never just . . . slept around. I was never gay in that sense. Actually, I was never gay in any sense. There was always this heaviness, and I'm not talking about weight. When I was discharged and returned to New York, I discovered gay life in the Village. It was very "up." I wasn't. I was already a psychiatric outpatient at Jacobi Hospital in the Bronx. I found I could not accept my homosexuality because it was one more strike against me. It confirmed my worst doubts: that I was different and in a very negative way, and even more on the outside looking in than I had realized.

But what I was going through was largely growing pains that most young men go through when they find their sexuality doesn't match the norm. Of course mine didn't even match the *abnorm*. But I survived, and let me tell you, darling, for a homosexual to do that in this crazy society is a sign of enormous strength. I really believe homosexuals may be the strongest people in the world. The blacks thought they had it bad? It was all shortnin' bread in comparison. Blacks survived through their music, gays through their humor. We may be bitchy as hell, *evil*, but we *are* funny. We are also outfront with our evilness, which straights are not. We are very cruel but there is an honesty in our cruelty.

Can you support what you just said?

Let's take my weight. Nooo, *you* take my weight; I'm tired of it. Anyway, straights would look at me when I was at my heaviest and not say anything. Not a word. As though I wasn't a double for the Goodyear blimp. I would waddle into my various free-lance jobs, doing my lighting-and-display work, and the various folk would say, "My, don't you look wonderful!" or some such social bullshit. But behind my back they were saying other things. Ugly things. Gays say ugly things, disguised as humor of course, right to your face. I prefer that. When some guy greets you with "How are you, Totie?"—meaning Totie Fields when she was fat-fat—you get the message. It's cruel but outfront.

Has anyone ever been blatantly "outfront" in rejecting you because of your weight?

No one has ever said, "Ugh! Go away you fat thing!" but I have often felt as if they had. There have been times when I've lured a man home only to have him excuse himself when I've removed my raincoat. Worse is when you've stripped down and the person suddenly develops this headache and walks out. That experience is the other side of dying, only dying would have been preferable.

What do you do when that happens?

What do you do? What *can* you do? You swallow your pride and about 147 chocolate fudge Keebler cookies with it and you go on. Of course today that doesn't happen because I won't allow it to. I don't try to put-myself-together to go out to a party to meet someone. I can't, as others do, just throw something on me, any ole thing—unless it's a tent—and look wonderful. I have to work at just looking passable so that people won't laugh. And I'm really sick of that. I don't want to work at looking good any more. I just want to look good, period. And all that charm and wit I possess? You can stuff it up an ant's ass. Just once in my life I'd like someone to desire me physically. Just once I'd like to know what it is like to have someone hot for me 'cause they groove on the exterior. And don't start talking to me about inconsistencies or contradictions. You've made me so crazy with your questions I don't know what I'm saying. All these dirty little repressed thoughts coming out of me . . . it's wonderful! All these years I haven't needed a shrink but an exorcist.

Ah me. The truth is there is no one truth. Yes, I would like to be wanted for purely lustful reasons. But it is also true that *that* in itself is not where I am at. A cock, as a cock, means very little to me unless it is attached to someone I care for. Although I can masturbate to strangers because I can fantasy them into loving partners, I can't really function with them in real situations. Without intimacy, I can't get fully erect. That's why going without much physical contact has not been all that difficult. But going without intimacy, without a person to touch and be touched by, that has been very bad. That's where Overeaters Anonymous has helped. It is the first place I've been able to admit my loneliness, not just to others but to myself. And in admitting it, I felt the pain of being alone. And in *feeling* the pain, I no longer had to cover it up with tons of food. Now, I see what I must eventually do.

> *Are you saying that part of your motivation for losing weight is to be attractive to another person?*

I don't want to say yes to that. It hurts too much. It makes me vulnerable. God, suppose I get thin and nothing happens? So I deny that. I'm getting thin for me . . . so that I can feel good about me. I don't want to be a clown, a fat clown whose only means for attention is to make people laugh. What I want . . . oh shit! Here comes the answer you wanted . . . is to be with *a* man rather than *any* man. I want a very different kind of sex than what I've known in recent years. No more "Hello, I'm your friendly service station." No more of I-am-worth-nothing-and-you-are-worth-everything. I want out of my fantasies. I want to move toward attractive people rather than away from them. And I don't want any more people to move away from me.

I almost forgot to mention that, darling. So, just a little more about what it is like to be gay and fat, which is a contradiction in terms. Do you know most gay men avoid me—even those with whom no sex is involved. Why? Because I don't complement them in appearance. I do not complement the image they carry of themselves. Pretty people only want to be seen with pretty people. It's understandable. Of course it is. If your pretty feet are covered in Gucci and your body in Cardin or Blass, then all else surrounding you should also be handsome.

You make it sound as if all people are like that.

Would you like me to qualify it with "some" or "a few"? Well, I won't! People really don't try to know the real person. People rarely get to know me.

Do you give them the opportunity?

. . . I don't think I like you. . . . No, I don't. I'm afraid. I'm just so afraid. I cannot handle any more rejection. It is so much safer to stay angry and be bitter. It doesn't hurt as much. There is only one other thing I fear more than rejection and that is my never knowing again the comfort that can exist in a relationship between two people. I will admit to you what I so very rarely admit to me: that I hope for another, one who hopes for me and the comfort we can bring one another. And I know, before you can ask another one of your sadistic questions, that in order to live, in order to obtain what I need for my life, that I will have to risk rejection . . . will have to approach some man I like and say . . . what? For chrissake, what do I say? Something terrifically clever like "Got a match . . . the time?" . . . "Come here often?" . . . "Wanna get married?" And oh my God what if he says yes. What do I do? I have nothing to wear. Nothing fits. I wonder if I can get away with wearing white . . . again.

Erik Edwards

THE YMCA in New York City. The gymnasium floor is filled this Saturday afternoon with young and old men of assorted sizes, shapes and sexualities. The attention of many is riveted on the daring young man on the flying rings. Except for his red shorts, he is bare, and his slight yet muscular body flies through the air with the greatest of ease from one end of the gymnasium floor to the other. He handstands, holds his body in a near-perfect line before dropping to twist and arc to yet another acrobatic position. It is a breathtaking and beautiful display of physical ability.

He is Erik Edwards,* a physical therapist/masseur who is, at twenty-four, a perfect physical specimen—the Body Beautiful. His face is handsome, the moustache upon it barely hiding its boyishness. His eyes are bright blue—very bright indeed.

That was quite a display.

Yes, I enjoyed it.

What made it enjoyable?

Partly the attention I received but mainly that incredible sense of freedom, of feeling your body soaring . . . flying. That was *me* in control of my body. That was *me* making a picture.

Your body is very important to you.

Yes. Everyone should feel their body is important. One of the things about tripping when you're exercising . . .

Tripping?

I took some nutmeg an hour ago. It's a lot like mescaline. Everything comes into much clearer focus. Up there, I could not only feel my body but I could see its muscles and organs working. Tripping gives me a total awareness of the body. I need that. As I had started to explain, we all need to know our bodies. We live in them. We should

* See Author's Note, page xii.

therefore communicate with them. If we don't value our physical being, we often don't value ourselves. You can't disregard the physical part of your life and live fully.

Is that what you teach?

Yes. I call it body awareness, which is not a new term. But you would be amazed at how few people know what it means. Most who come to me are dead from the neck down. All cerebral. Even weight-lifter types are pretty dead. Lots of big muscles but very little use of them. The idea is to make full use of your body—to understand what it can do and what it can be. To be able to move . . . to soar . . . even to fly.

Then body awareness is not just a narcissistic "trip"?

Not for me it isn't, although I do love my body. What I love equally is that I can make it work for me. I am seldom tired or enervated and that's because I know which buttons to push to revitalize my system.

Were you always physically oriented?

Not at all. For many years I denied my physical being. In fact, during my childhood and adolescence, I ignored it because it was a source of embarrassment to me. I was always short and slight. As a kid, I didn't fit the mold of what a young boy should look like or be. Because of my size, I avoided athletics.

But many short children take part in street and school athletics.

But I was very sensitive. If anyone commented on my size, I'd feel small. And I never understood that kind of competition. I found street games cruel . . . barbaric. Sports were played to win. The fun was secondary. And if you couldn't help in the winning, you were pushed aside. I hated that, so I denied everything that was physical. Pretty ironic, isn't it, considering how my living is made today by my physical being?

How do you feel about your childhood?

As though it happened to someone else. I don't much think about those years. They were too painful. I was very unhappy. In fact, I cannot remember ever being happy as a kid. Even in those supposedly "happy times" caught by a Kodak Instamatic, underneath the smile was depression.

Do you have any memory as to why you were depressed?

Oh yeah. On the top there was school, which I hated. I couldn't deal with the competitive society there so I rejected it. They, in turn, rejected me. By high school, I was so depressed, I seldom spoke to anyone.

Was psychological help ever suggested?

By who? My parents didn't see the same child my teachers saw. I was much happier at home. But even there, I was always somewhat off-center. From the age of five, I felt different. I was already then a homosexual. I began masturbating at that age and would jerk off thinking about older boys. And at that age I was terrified of what I was feeling and afraid of punishment. Isn't that incredible! How does a little kid get to be guilty about something he knows nothing about?

Was homosexuality your problem in school?

Yes and no. Yes in that the guilt always played on my nerves, but no in that I never was discovered acting it out. It was the environment at school that I hated. The only way I got through it was stoned.

On what?

Name it and I took it. I began with grass and moved to speed, mesc, cocaine and acid. I was the school hippie. Long hair and spacy eyes. That wasn't exactly "in" in suburban Connecticut. That's one place that's very upper middle class, uptight and straight. I was always getting my ass thrown out of school for being spaced.

Why were you taking drugs?

As I said, to get through. I needed something, I was so damn depressed. Drugs allowed me to escape. They put an excitement into my life. And . . . they gave me an identity. They were my statement and people heard it. At last, I was being noticed.

I was a very wild and rebellious kid. I ran with a bunch of hoody guys—all older than me—and we would steal cars and drive them as we were flying on coke or speed. It was all very macho, very straight. Only now do I realize that the tension that existed between most of us was sexual. I also realize it's a miracle we didn't kill ourselves.

Do you think that may have been an unconscious intent?

Maybe. As I said, I remember little to nothing of my youth except that I was unhappy. And let me explain something right here, at the top. I don't see that it matters. Sure there may be great meaning to my not remembering . . . great clues as to why I am as I am today, but all that was *then* and my life is about today. I take full responsibility for my life. Whatever was, was. There is no blame. If my life doesn't work today, it's because I choose not to make it work. And before you ask, no, I have not been in EST training. One doesn't need to spend $250 and seventy-two miserable hours to discover the responsibility for one's own happiness or unhappiness is in one's own hands. I find all introspection interesting and necessary. But the psychological sifting through the past is not for me. Today, right now, I feel a gifted and happy person. I feel positive about my life. And I have a very positive relationship with my parents. We are very close.

Was it always so?

There was a great deal of love in the house, although it took me many years to understand my father's kind of love.

Could you explain?

He was always very busy at his factory. He had hard times for a while. So he was away a lot and thus became a somewhat distant figure. Then, too, he is a man who deals mainly on an intellectual level. He does not show his feelings.

Did you feel he loved you?

Sometimes. But only sometimes. He never related on a one-to-one basis. Whatever we did was as a family. I never had time alone with him. He was not the father I would have liked.

What would you have liked in a father?

Do you remember "The Donna Reed Show" and the man who played her husband . . . Carl Betz? The kind of father he portrayed—one who was a buddy to his son—that's the kind of father I would have liked. I wanted my father to be a friend. I resented that he wasn't.

Did your mother fit the Donna Reed mold?

Sort of. I was very close to her in my early years as she was a very warm and affectionate woman. But when my father's business went bad—I was about nine—she went bad. She became very nervous, high strung . . . even bitchy. I used to hate coming home from school, a place I already hated, because I never knew what kind of a mood my mother would be in. For four years that mood was seldom good. It was like some stranger had moved in to replace the mother who had given me so much and for whom I had felt so much.

Who was there for you?

My brother. He was such a great guy and I idolized him as a kid. But pretty much, I was alone . . . a kid who felt separate. I couldn't escape feeling different because of my homosexual thoughts and actions.

Actions?

I was six when a neighborhood friend jerked me off. I liked it. It felt good. Then, it would feel bad. Very bad. This cloud would come over me and I'd start to shake. But it didn't stop me. By ten, I was having sex regularly with my brother. And I don't mean adolescent mutual masturbation. I mean sucking and fucking. I lived for it, despite the fact that immediately after orgasm I'd fall apart. Breathing would be difficult because I'd become so anxious and depressed. Yet, I had sex with my brother until he went off to college. Then, he changed. He became vehemently heterosexual.

During your adolescence, did you have sex only with your brother?

No. There were several guys in Connecticut with whom I had sex. All of them, like my brother, grew up to be heterosexual—at least in current day activity. With all, I would be flying until orgasm. Then, I would crash. I had no understanding then of my needs and even less acceptance of the way in which I was fulfilling them. But I do remember feeling as though I were carrying this enormous weight which each day was pushing me farther into the ground.

What had you heard about homosexuality at that point in your life?

Just about nothing. I didn't know there was a gay community, and even if I had, I would not have been able—despite my having sex with boys—to admit to myself that I was gay.

But why?

Because somehow, without ever having heard the word gay or knowing a homosexual, I felt it had to be a terrible thing to be. When I was twelve I overheard my mother saying to my father, "But face it, George, Erik is effeminate." Her tone and his reaction left little doubt that effeminacy was something awful. It killed me. There could be nothing worse said about me because I knew that I was not by the standards I saw around me all "male." In the movies I went to, the leading men made love to the leading ladies. But why, I wondered, when I wanted to make love with them. Everything around me in this town led me to believe men slept only with women and to do otherwise was "strange." I, therefore, was "strange." I suspected there was something terribly wrong with me. Why else was I always so terribly depressed? Hearing my mother speak of me as she did confirmed my worst fears. I was a boy who loved boys and that was shameful!

Were there ever sexual encounters with women?

With women, no, but with girls in high school yes. Each time I felt forced . . . pressured. It also confused me because I was not turned on. What does a hard-on mean when emotionally you feel nothing? I functioned but so what? So does a machine.

Look! All of this is basically horseshit. As far as I am concerned I was born and life began the day I came out.

When was that?

August 15, 1970. I remember the exact moment because it changed my life. I was with my friend Joe, who was admittedly gay. Previously, I had toured the gay joints with him but as his straight friend. I remember thinking as I watched boys and men dancing together that at last I had found a world where I might fit in—where I might be popular—where I might have something that was wanted.

Later that night I came out. I simply said to Joe, "I am gay." He stared at me. I said it again, only louder, more to make me hear it than him. I am not exaggerating when I say that from that moment that enormous weight that I had been carrying dropped off my back. For all I know it still lies there on the floor of the Dew Come Inn, somewhere off the Connecticut Turnpike.

Was it that simple?

Simple? You call nearly eighteen years of denial and agony simple? It was anything but, up until the time I said it. But once I declared myself, my life has never been the same. I remember I was leaving the next day for the West to get settled at the one college that had accepted me before the actual semester started. On route to the airport,

I dropped acid. As the plane took off, so did I. Somewhere over Philadelphia I began crying and I cried all the way to school. They were tears of joy . . . of happiness. At last I knew who and what I was. At last I accepted me. I was a man who loved men and I could hardly wait to begin the loving.

Do you know that from that moment of admittance I have never had another bad orgasm. Prior to coming out, I'd sort of come, stopping myself midway, never fully realizing a total climax. Now, with the shame gone, I was exploding all over the place—with joy.

Was college then a happy time?

No. I should not have been there. Why was I? Because if one is middle-class, one goes to college, just as one breathes. I hated everything about college. From the computer cards to the dorm without privacy where I had to listen to these cunt-crazy jocks rapping out that macho shit. I couldn't deal with it. There wasn't one fellow happy homosexual to relate to. By midyear I was so lonely that I attended a campus marathon for gays just to see who else was in the same sexual situation as me. What a disaster! One of the psychology profs was running it and the idea was to make somebody cry. If in twenty-four hours you could cause pain—make another feel it—the marathon was considered a success. I thought it horseshit and left.

Were those in attendance there because of problems with their sexuality?

Not that I could see. They had the same problems we all have— loneliness, alienation and lousy relationships. Most were nice kids. I made friends with several, which allowed me to get through the year but not very successfully. And when I returned home, I didn't get through that year very successfully either.

Why?

'Cause I was eighteen, cute and horny. Nightly I was running to the bars and my parents were hassled by my coming home with the morning's light. You can be very popular at eighteen. Particularly when you are one of Perdue's best—meaning I was an A No. 1 chicken with a high, firm ass that got a lot of people crazy 'cause I didn't use it. Some pig had once hurt me, so I had wrongfully decided getting fucked was not for me. But everything else was, so . . . I was keeping pretty late hours. My parents were on my back a lot, which is what caused me late one night to say to Joe on the telephone, "I think I'll have to tell my parents that I'm gay." At that very moment my father had picked up the phone to make a call. He heard my words and flipped out. He was screaming as he came for me and continued to scream as he dragged me into their bedroom. My mother was also screaming.

Were you frightened by their reaction?

Do you know I was more angry than I was scared. My mother kept saying, "We'll get you the best psychiatrist money can buy," and I kept saying, "But I'm happy. I don't want one." My mother then slashed me with "Well, if you want to live your life as a girl . . . ."

It got worse. I eventually went to a shrink, not for me, but to ac-climate them to my being gay. The third session was a horror. We were all together. My father was saying things like "If the word homosexual is used I'll throw up." My mother was mouthing "Some parents have polio or palsy to contend with in their child. We have this." It was horrible. *I* was horrible. At one point, when I was hurt-ing, I turned and pointed at them and said: "I am what I am because of you." A day later I split for Texas where I stayed with a friend. During that time my mother entered therapy. When I returned home, my father blamed my "condition" for causing my mother's near breakdown. He turned to me and said: "I wish you were dead and so does your mother."

That's pretty heavy stuff for anyone to handle.

Well, I ran as far as I could from it—to a slum apartment in the Bronx—but those words never leave your mind. When your parents wish you dead, call you a pervert, sick, a disgrace, there's really no place to run. I felt very bad but I never felt "sick" or a "pervert." But I did soon feel angry. Actually, rageful is closer to it. As far as I was concerned, they could rot in hell before I would ever come near their bigotry and ignorance again.

But you eventually did reconcile?

Yes, they called and acted as though nothing had ever happened. We were resuming cordial relations when I fell in love and moved in with my lover. One night, when they phoned to ask where I had been keeping myself, I told them about Cary. My mother began screaming: "There are areas of your life we never want to hear about." I yelled back: "Why am I not allowed to be in love and loved?" They hung up. A few days later I received a beautiful letter of apology. It ended with: "And we would like to meet your friend. If you love him, then he must be special." Since then, my parents and I have been very close. My dad still has trouble discussing gay issues but he tries. My mother has discussed *everything* with me. She is now perfectly at ease with my homosexuality. I truly love and respect them both. I admire them. They came the full distance with me and I understand, given their backgrounds, that it wasn't easy. I admire one other thing about them: their marriage. They are one of very few happy couples I have ever seen.

Had your parents not accepted your homosexuality, would you have remained separate?

Yes. Had they continued to put labels on me and not seen me as a person, I would have had no choice. But I always knew, somehow, some way, they would come around. My parents are quite unique. Very strong and under all the shit they had to dump all over me . . . very loving. I may not have made this clear before but . . . even as a child, I always felt loved. Even in those times when I did feel neglect, I also felt they cared about me. I have always known love of some kind all my life and it has given me a strength that many years ago I didn't know I had. Like the relationship with my brother. It was about love because even today, minus the sex, he is one of the people I love the most. He is my friend as well as my brother.

Are you with a lover now?

No.

Does that bother you?

No.

Would you like another love relationship?

I hope to have many other love relationships. I've had three in four years. The first was meaningless—someone upon whom I hung my fantasies of love. We played at it without ever feeling it. Cary, thirteen years older than I, was love. But I had to leave him. He was famous, successful, and I was neither. After a while I felt engulfed by his presence. I'm not much for being kept. I have to make my own way. Cliff, my most recent, was my age. We just grew apart. We still love each other but not as lovers.

Does it bother you that your relationships have not been long-lasting?

No. I want my relationships to last only as long as they are good for both people. I'm a mover. I come together with people for a time and then I move on. Not because I'm fickle but because there's an endless amount of exploring to do in this world and if the person I am with is not a fellow explorer, I have to push on. It may sound like a crock of shit but . . . my real lover is life and I'm trying to know this lover by every means possible. I feel life has given me gifts which I must maximize. There is a place, or perhaps even places, for me in life that I've yet to find. I sometimes think I may even have greatness. I paint. I write and I teach body awareness. I want to be a success. Money is only meaningful because freedom costs money. I've done my slum-time. I prefer penthouses. People often tell me—and not happily—that I'm very gutsy, ambitious and secure, as though it were wrong to be all those things. What they don't see is that in addition to having those qualities they ascribe to me, I am also frightened.

Can you define your fear?

Sure. I don't think it is any different than anybody else's. Loneliness. I would not like to go through life without a hand to hold. But, don't make this into that stupid stereotype of the lonely old faggot because that's bullshit. Anyone can be lonely, straight or gay.

Do you have other fears?

Yes, I don't ever want to lose my hair. My body will never go but my hair might.

What makes you certain that your body will "never go"? Have you discovered a prevention for the aging process?

I will always have a beautiful body. Even at sixty . . . seventy, it will have its own life. It will be the beautiful body of an older man. That will be the only difference. I will always work *at* and work my body. That is the secret. Funny how most people continue to use their minds but not their bodies.

When did the body, as a means of expression, become important to you?

At nineteen, after the initial blowup with my parents, I returned to the Southwest to study ballet with an eccentric, destructive genius who ran his troupe through negative reinforcement. He never praised but only criticized. But I loved ballet. When I was a child, I wanted to be a trapeze artist. Ballet, with its leaps and spins, made me feel I was one. Ballet also tuned me into my body. It was an instrument that could either support or fail me and which of the two it did was my choice.

Did you actually dance?

Yes, and I was good, very good, only I didn't believe it because my instructor's method of working was to tell me I wasn't. Which was just as well. I quit partly from discouragement but mainly because I knew I had started too late to be a really great dancer. Better to know that early than at thirty-five and still a member of the corps. When I returned to New York, although I hadn't any idea of what I wanted to do professionally, my body demanded to be worked. It was then I joined the Y and began with the rings and the bars.

How did you begin teaching body awareness?

When I left Cary, I was broke. I had met him immediately upon my return from the West and left him eighteen months later with a series of nonfulfilling jobs behind me. I needed money, so I posed for one of those meat magazines. It paid me $200 and I didn't have to do anything but pose bare-ass. Then I began posing at the Art Students' League, where I met a very well-known masseur who taught me all there is to know about massage. I never sought licensing because I knew it wasn't anything I would choose to do the rest of my life. But again, it taught me still more about the body and today I get a great deal of pleasure in the administration of it. And let me make that "pleasure" very clear. It is nonsexual. I was trained to believe massage is an art and it is. There was no fucking around in my trainer's work and there is no fucking around in mine. If a client wants to get laid, he goes elsewhere. When you come to me for massage, that's what you pay for and that's what you get.

But isn't massage a very sexual experience for both parties?

It is more sensual than sexual, although it certainly can be both, just as it can be neither. For me, it is often spiritual. I am not a doctor. I have no medical knowledge and yet . . . some men come to me limping or doubled up in pain. They leave an hour later free of whatever it was that ailed them. There is a theory about the "laying-on-of-hands" and how some people have the touch that cures. I may be one, which is why I say my work is often spiritual.

Is that what you find satisfying as a masseur?

What is satisfying is that in some way you are helping people. Usually, it is about easing their tensions, giving them the relaxation their bodies crave. But often, it is about touching. So many older men come to me in desperate—and that's the word—need to be touched. They are lonely people who have difficulty in finding someone to be gentle with their bodies . . . to fondle them. Again, I am talking strictly of a nonsexual occurrence. It is about nurturance and not sex. So you massage them gently and feel good that you are helping them to live.

Do any of the clients come on with you?

Initially a few do. I think they're confused by the mixed signals I give off. When I open the door, they see a spectacular body poured into tight pants and a torso T-shirt. I don't do this as a sexual turn-on but to instantly establish physical mastery. In other words, they must see my body as a perfect instrument if they are to respect and thus allow me to treat their own. The guys who get horny and come on with me verbally, I respond to in very clinical language. I sound like a fucking textbook, which cools their passion very quickly.

Do you ever get turned on?

Sometimes, but the moment my hands hit the body—make contact on a professional level—my hot turns to cold. I care about my work. I keep my cock in my pants when on the job. If I do find someone attractive, I will ask to see them at another time and at another location.

Looking at you, it would seem to be a safe assumption that you never lack for partners.

A very safe assumption.

Do you see yourself as a sex object?

Yes, particularly when walking down the street. I get cruised a lot. I like that.

Do you encourage it?

I know what I'm doing when I pour myself into a pair of jeans and a tight T-shirt. I've got the body and I don't believe in hiding it. I get off on being admired . . . wanted.

Do you see yourself as a beautiful person?

Yes, but here's the bummer . . . not always. When you are physically attractive, it's a many-headed dragon, one which needs constant feeding. I try not to be dependent on reaction to my body, but some days I am.

Are those good or bad days?

Bad if I don't get the feedback I need. Usually, at those times, I'm feeling unbeautiful and need to be reassured that I am. That's why I like being objectified. When someone, or many someones, cruise me, it helps. It's a reinforcement. It assures me that I am beautiful.

Then you are not secure in your "beauty"?

I don't know one beautiful person who is. In fact, the most beautiful seem to be the most insecure. Like I know I'm attractive but I don't always feel it.

Funny, so many people think if only they were beautiful, their lives would be beautiful. It just isn't so. Those of us considered beautiful are slaves to the maintenance and support of that beauty—and that support can only come from others. That's one of the worst of the dragon's heads. He expects certain responses and if he doesn't get them . . . crash!

What's the solution?

Hopefully, maturity. Hopefully a gradual believing internally that I am beautiful. I still often feel like that short, skinny kid from Connecticut that nobody wanted. I've only recently become a physical ideal. It's still not totally comfortable wearing that mantle. I wake up sometimes fearing that my old self in my old body has returned. You see, in my wildest dreams I never thought I would one day be a beauty sought after by other beauties.

In general, how do you feel about your beauty?

I love it and hate it. I don't know any truly beautiful people who are happy. Frankly, it embarrasses me that I'm hung up on my own. It's one dependency I'd like to eliminate. Yet . . . my physicality works for me. I know that and use it accordingly. Every affair I have ever had has begun with the attraction to my looks. That's the joy and that's the pain. Your beauty attracts and your beauty kills.

Who does your beauty kill?

Mainly me. Why? Because I am never certain who wants me for *me* and who wants me for the possession—the consumption—of the beauty. There are those who want to fuck with the beauty—not the person—and end up fucking over both. If you allow it, you can sometimes feel as if you are nothing more than an apparition—a beautiful one but, like all apparitions, doomed to fade and disappear.

Do you worry about your own "disappearance"?

No more. I've pretty well learned to avoid those who seek to add a notch to their cock-size by bedding down the beautiful image rather than the person. I will no longer be used, abused and discarded. I don't allow me to get lost any more. Years ago, when I first became attractive, I got into sex with many people who would have wanted my body despite my having been deaf, dumb and blind. These same people exist today but the boy I was does not. Unless I am relating to someone and they are relating to me, I go with no one. I am not just another pretty boy, but a man with a mind and feelings. I avoid those people who do not wish to recognize that. It's very seldom today that I just fall into bed with anybody. When I came out, I did. I got off on all those beautiful people wanting me. I spread it around pretty good back then. But today, I cannot relate to anonymous sex. No back rooms, no bushes or meat racks.

How do you meet people?

At the gym, the opera, ballet, on the street, at parties. Everywhere. But I never go home with a stranger any more. You want to have sex with me, you have to know me first, like me; and I have to like you. I just don't get off on indiscriminate sex. It doesn't give me what I need—the contact other than what is just sexual. And I don't mean love or romance but that something that lets me know I'm a person and not just a "thing."

And yet you admit you often dress like a "thing."

Yes. I throw out certain signals and I have no one but myself to blame if they are misinterpreted. But what I'm saying is . . . once someone approaches and speaks with me, if they don't see and feel that I am more than the object, I'm not interested. The sex we would have—if we had it—would be meaningless.

Then sex today must have a meaning for you.

Yes, although the meaning differs with each person. Sex is like a conversation. Some can be exciting dialogues, impassioned and heated; while others can be chitchat . . . pleasant but not memorable. Frankly, sex is best for me today when it is an expression of liking or caring. Sex has to do certain things for me. It must either put me in touch with me or it must make me transcend myself. But it must not take me away from me. In other words, I never use sex as an escape from what I am feeling. Sex as an escape from reality also doesn't interest me. When sex is best for me, I forget my name, my age, the time, the place . . . everything but the experience itself as it is happening.

You stated "sex as an escape from reality doesn't interest me." Is fantasy then not a part of your sexual repertoire?

Right. It is not. I don't fantasize about truck drivers or construction workers or sailors. Those kinds of images mean nothing to me. My fantasy is starkly simple. It's about two beautiful men making love and their lovemaking has no particular script. Even when I masturbate thinking about that fantasy I have no prescribed ending-with-orgasm. In other words, I can get off on anything. I cannot say I have any sexual preferences. I can say that I do prefer sex. In fact, I love it. I am very animal.

How would you define "animal"?

As something all of us are if we allow it. I sort of touched on it before . . . that rising out of and above yourself . . . leaving your mind and your "shoulds" and "shouldn'ts" out of the bedroom. To me, it is animal when it is free from fantasy and just is—when the rhythm is right—when you roll with what you feel rather than prohibit or inhibit the feeling. It is animal when two bodies communicate without words.

What is it you like about sex with men?

The feel of body-to-body contact, of muscle-to-muscle. I like well-developed men. I enjoy beautiful bodies. I am very visual sexually. I can come off just looking at someone's anatomy or by touching a particularly beautifully defined line of the body.

Does penis size have an importance in your enjoyment?

Yes. Although I am not limited to having sex with men who are well hung, I prefer to. There is something very exciting, visually, about a big cock. And although I know it is bullshit, it does represent masculinity to me. The cock is, after all, the male organ. The fallacy is . . . many a non-masculine man has a big dong. Most gay men I know, if given the choice, would rather make it with a guy who is hung than with one who is not. I am very glad I've got a big joint. It gives me a sense of prowess. I like to fuck with it. That sounds very macho and I don't mean it to because I get as much enjoyment from being fucked as I do from fucking. But I seldom get screwed, maybe because I'm so aggressive in bed that I just take over. But I do like the physical sensation of having a man inside me. Also, in any relationship I might have, there can be no primarily active or passive partner because whatever is acted out in bed is then carried over out of it. If I'm to have a relationship, it must be of equals.

> *You mentioned you liked the "physical sensation" of having a man inside you. What, if anything, do you feel emotionally when in a passive role?*

Nothing that I am aware of. . . . Let me think a minute. . . . It depends. Sometimes I feel very vulnerable. I will not let just anyone fuck me.

> *Why vulnerable?*

Cause you are. When someone is in you, you're defenseless. You can be hurt and . . ."

> *And what?*

I just saw something about myself and I don't like what I saw. The truth is I don't allow myself to get fucked as often as I would like to because I feel my masculinity is at stake. I have to feel a man respects me as a man before I can relax and let go. Goddamn! What bullshit! I'm depriving me of something I want because I'm worried what someone else might think. Goddamn!

> *What else is distressing you?*

Oh c'mon. It's obvious. I mean if I really respected myself . . . didn't in some way put a negative judgment on getting fucked, I'd be doing it. Shit! When it comes to my sexual needs, it should begin and end with what I think of me . . . what I want for me.

I'm really kind of surprised because I don't feel one negative thing about my homosexuality. Certainly there is no guilt. I am gay. I say it loud and I said it proud. I would not choose to be anything else. I love men. I always have.

Which, by the way, is another reason why I'm against S&M. It's a put-down. I choose to love, not abuse, ridicule or hurt. That's one of the reasons I now stay away from fist-fucking. Something tells me there is a power-trip involved—that, and humiliation.

But you've done it?

Yes, with my last lover. Visually, I found it very exciting. And while I was doing it, I felt he was giving me all his love by allowing me to be that deeply inside him. It was never violent or ugly but there is just this nagging suspicion about it that gnaws at me. Maybe it has to do with the extremes so many people are into today. Particularly my peers. Everything sexual has to be larger-than-life. Drugs help make everything bigger. When you're stoned you're capable of doing things you might normally never do. It seems to me very few of my age group are satisfied any more by simple sucking-and-fucking. They're into more esoteric pleasures. They tell me I'm repressed, but frankly I think they are enslaved to what they think is sexual liberation.

How would you define sexual liberation?

As finding out what you like sexually and then doing it. And that is a lifetime quest, as I believe our likes and dislikes continue to change from person to person and from year to year. Sexual liberation has a helluva lot more to do with attitude than with specific acts, as far as I can see.

How do you see your peers' definition of sexual lib?

As anything and everything. They fuck like rabbits, singly and collectively, and the younger the rabbit, the greater the thrill-seeking. There is more fist-fucking and semi S&M stuff among the eighteen- and nineteen-year-olds than there is in the over-thirty group. They can't seem to have sex unless they've got a popper up their nose or a dildo up their ass.

Do you really see that as being representative of your peer group?

It's a generalization but it is true of a great many. And although this many is still a minority, it's a noisy minority. They're the ones defining "liberation" for others and I think they are going to pay a heavy

price. Pretty soon these kids won't have to leave their homes to relate
to another person. They won't want to. There are so many gadgets
available, they can fuck themselves. And even when they go out,
they find real live gadgets to play with. There is very little relating
going on today. It's crazy. It's ass-backwards—no pun intended. People get down right away, get it on, and then as soon as they get it off,
they find they have nothing to say to the other person. The price for
this is alienation—from self and from others. All this "liberated" fucking is resulting in the inability of people to become truly intimate.

My generation has thrown away all the old values, the old ethics,
which is fine, only they haven't replaced them with anything else. At
the moment we are amoral. In fact, morality has become a dirty word.
Talk about it and you're looked at as a freak. That's another thing
about this supposed "liberation." If you don't conform, you're ostracized.

Are your friends mainly older men?

Not necessarily. Firstly, that would be limiting. Secondly, what I was
saying about my own age group is true for many but not for most.
Unfortunately, the most are the silent majority. I have many friends
among them. These people have made the choice to be better than
mediocre—they wish to be able to relate to others . . . to eventually
become close, intimate, with another person.

Is this your goal?

Of course. But I've already said or implied that.

*Have you an idea of the kind of relationship, or person, you
would like?*

Yes. I don't want to be anyone's mother, father or crutch, and I don't
want anyone to be that to me. I'll handle my own life and let my
lover handle his. I'm all for supporting and being supported, emotionally that is, but I'm nothing at all for turning over the responsibility
for one's life to another.

I don't know how I feel about a monogamous relationship. I've
never done it but I think I'm moving toward it, only because I've
tried the other and despite all the rationalizations, it's never worked.
Sharing intimacies with a stranger has always seemed to take a certain intimacy away from me and my lover.

Another thing: This sounds so simple and yet . . . I'd like my
lover to be my friend. I've never known that before. I don't know

why sex has always stood in the way of *that* kind of intimacy. I'd also like my lover to share my excitement about life . . . about his personhood. Of course that means he must be secure in his sexuality. He must be able to hold my hand in public and tell all those who give us attitude to fuck off.

You are talking about "gay pride"?

Yes.

Do you see it growing or diminishing?

Growing, despite the insanities I spoke of before. There are many young men who will no longer wear the oppression straight society tries to suit us up in. I marched with some of these guys at the Democratic Convention. Their heads were together.

What was your reason for marching?

My rage and hatred of straight society, which treats me the way it once treated "niggers." Like shit. Gays are an oppressed minority. I am denied my rights as a citizen. Had my number been called in the lottery, I would have refused to enter the military. I will not defend a country that does not defend me. I will not defend a country that makes me hate the people who have repressed me, who have treated me like a second-class citizen, who would stop me from loving. As it was said: In this country, you get a medal for killing men and dishonored for loving them. Well, fuck that thinking. I choose to love men and if that messes with some people's minds, good! Maybe if they really stop to think about it, they'll realize love can never be wrong.

Do you expect to be active within the "Gay Movement"?

Always. As I am, as I live, as I love, is an activity. I am a declared homosexual. The only reason my real name is not used in this book is to protect my family from those small-minded bigots who might hassle them. In truth, I wish my real name was used. To deny who and what I am is to deny me and my life. And me and my life are too important to be denied. I have known sorrow and now I know joy. I don't pretend to know all the answers—not even most. But, what I do know is that there isn't anything or anyone who is going to stop me from trying to find them.

My name is Erik. I am a person. I am a homosexual. You don't like that, mister? Go fuck yourself!

Johnny Doe

"Y OU ARE YOUR own miracle!" insists one of the hanging signs. "Gay Is Good!" proclaims another. "This Is the Friendliest Place in Town" announces still one more. And they are but a handful of the messages that greet the eighty participants—all men— who crowd the room within the West Side seminary where the chapter for alcholics who are homosexual meets each Friday night. There, boys and men discuss both their homosexuality and their alcoholism. The atmosphere in which they do so is certainly among the friendliest in this town or any other. And, if one is to believe their stories —and there is no reason not to—these men are their own miracles. One in particular, Johnny Doe,* never hesitated when asked to be a contributor to this book. His answer was an immediate and enthusiastic yes.

A small but compactly built man whose impish good looks speak more of thirty than forty, which is his age, Johnny doesn't walk but bounces into a room. At our initial meeting at the seminary, he was more a social director than a participant (in truth, he was both), knowing most of the men in attendance on a first-name basis. In subsequent weeks he continued to bounce through a series of interviews in which he attacked the questions with the same gusto that he attacked the food placed before him. If one word were to describe this man it would be . . . alive!

You asked to be immediately established as an alcoholic. Why?

Because I *am* an alcoholic. An understanding of me begins and ends with that knowledge. I have a disease that is physical, mental and spiritual, a disease for which there is no cure. I face that because I choose to face reality today—which is a change. In other words, I choose to live.

As opposed to die?

Exactly! And there was that choice. At twenty-nine, I began drinking steadily. At thirty-two, a little voice which I ignored whispered "alco-

* See Author's Note, page xii.

240

holic." At thirty-four, I knew it and was terrified. But, I reasoned, everyone has to die of something. A year later I was unemployed, drinking two quarts of vodka per day, and desperate. I could not pay the rent. I could not buy food. I could not get companionship. I could not get sober. I could not get the snakes off my walls. I would lie in bed, watching them slither as I shivered. I wanted to die. That was only five years ago. I don't ever want to forget it. Remembering keeps me sober. Remembering also keeps me alive.

Are you a member of Alcoholics Anonymous?

Yes. If I were not, I would allow you the usage of my real name. But, as an active member of A.A., I cannot do that. Anonymity is a law of the organization.

How did you become a member?

I tried to hit on a former drinking buddy for a loan, not knowing she had sobered up. When she heard, and then saw, the condition I was in, she persuaded me to attend an A.A. meeting. When *they* heard, and saw, the condition I was in, they advised a hospital. Had I cold-turkeyed on my own, I might have convulsed and died.

By the way, going to A.A. was the first time in my life I had ever asked for help and found it given without strings.

I just realized there is another reason why I introduce myself here —but not in life-situations—as an alcoholic. When I sobered up, the first five months felt like one big float on a big cloud. Pure euphoria! Perhaps it is hard for you to realize what it feels like to be free after years of being hooked. But after the euphoria came the reality: life, and in particular, *my* life. I couldn't deal with it. I became severely depressed, remaining in bed eighteen hours a day. I got up only to buy necessities and to attend A.A. meetings. I was a zombie. I couldn't be helped and I couldn't be hurt. I was on nothing and yet I was drugged . . . on my past. I cannot in words describe the pain of that year. Cannot! Thus, when I say "I am an alcoholic," it is because, one, I don't want to forget from whence I came and, two, perhaps others who need help will see themselves in me and be able to make the same admittance to themselves.

Can you delineate the depression?

I felt my life had no meaning and that it never would. I felt I had no meaning, that I didn't matter and I never would. Not the real me anyway. And what was the real me? I had worn so many masks that I had forgotten. Now, sober, I was too tired to wear them and A.A. told me I not only shouldn't but *couldn't*, if I intended to remain sober.

What ended the depression?

I was very lucky. I was in A.A. counseling with a woman psychologist who cared. She had great skills, not the least of which was her own humanity. She pulled me through. I saw her twice a week and attended her group once weekly. When the depression reached such proportions where I was thinking of killing myself, I asked her to have me locked up. She did not say no. She simply said that if I went to an institution they would put me on drugs and did I want to be hooked again. She left the choice to me. She helped me to believe I could make it. She helped me to fight. She set me on the road to self-acceptance. A.A. doesn't suggest that you be comfortable with yourself, it demands it. If you can't wear your own skin, you are going to drink.

What did becoming "comfortable with yourself" entail?

For me it meant giving up the American Dream. Achievement! Be Something! I gave all that up to Be Me. My depression was about many things, of which one was how I *should* be all that I wasn't and could never be. It was about everyone telling me what I *should* do and never listening to what I wanted to do. It was about not being what and who I really am. Breaking through that depression meant accepting me just as I am. And when I did that, I found the world wasn't half so bad a place to live in and that I had a right to live in it just as I was and not as society said I should be. When I reached that place, I found a passion for living that is unending.

Does your homosexuality enter into your being what you are rather than what others dictate?

Absolutely. As we say in A.A., it is the loneliness of the secret that kills. My secret was being gay. I viewed that as an awful secret— thirty-five and still so frightened of discovery. And guilty. That, too, thanks to my parochial upbringing. I was positive that public discovery of my sexuality would bring penalization and rejection. God knows my experiences in the straight world fostered this belief! I worked in public relations for a man who once refused to attend a social function because "there will be too many fags there and I hate being around those sick people." It killed me when he said that. And

I couldn't respond because he held my purse strings. He had power over my life. I felt like he had stomped on my guts. But I couldn't stand up for me. Today, I could.

The guilt about homosexuality stems back to childhood when my mother threw the word "sissy" at any male behavior that didn't measure up to her standards of masculinity. She also warned me about "fairies." By the way, a thought: I am not an alcoholic because I am gay. Being gay was my secret but my alcoholism has nothing to do with my sexuality. My father was straight and he was an alcoholic. My mother's father, also straight, was the town drunk. There are many reasons I became an alcoholic but my homosexuality is not one of them.

You stated that when you went to A.A. it marked the first time you ever asked for help that it was given without strings. Can you amplify that?

No one in my family knew how to give. There was a price paid for anything one received. I can remember at seven, wanting to be free of them. In fact, at ten, I was nearly financially free because of my paper route and a daily job setting up pins at a bowling alley.

I was four when my father hanged himself in the attic. My mother, despite my having been in the house, my having seen the undertakers take him down, denied the truth to me. She never told me he was dead. I was not supposed to know. A week after the funeral I was not allowed to attend, my mother lined her three youngest in a row— we were still babies—and explained how there was just not enough of her to go around and that we would have to choose other mothers from our elder sisters, who were in their late twenties. I remember as though it were yesterday wanting to scream at her, "Don't you know I'm frightened. Don't leave!" But you couldn't be frightened in that house. You couldn't show any emotion.

I have hated my mother from that day. I learned then never to ask for anything because she wouldn't give it. I chose my sister Lillian to be my mother. She *gave* me everything in return for possession. In Lillian's mind, she owned me. Anyway, in one week I was not only abandoned by my father but kicked out by my mother. Oh, I continued to live in the same house, but all of us acted as separate divisions of a large corporation of which my mother was chairman of the board. We never shared a holiday or a birthday. I never knew what a real family was. Nor did I ever view real relationships. My mother and father screamed at each other and occasionally fought physically.

That is about all I remember about my father—that he was drunk a lot and yelling. I recall nothing positive about him or our relationship or any kind of yearning for a father/son relationship.

Did Lillian actually function as your mother?

Totally. I was her baby. She loved her mother role and I quickly learned to manipulate her to my advantage. It was Lillian who paid for my piano lessons as a child and it was Lillian who paid my college tuition. Lillian was the family's "Good Girl," a martyr type who gave up any chance for her own life to be a daughter to my mother and a mother to her brother. Lillian is still a foggy and threatening figure. There was something incestuous about our relationship. She bathed me till my early teens—long after a boy should be bathed by any woman. Since I was uncircumsized, she would peel me down ostensibly to show me how to keep clean. I think I once got an erection, but if I did and what happened, I don't know.

Had you begun masturbating as a child?

No. That would have been a sin. You see, as soon as my father died, my mother returned to the Catholic church. She washed us all away in the confessional booth. I was taken from public school and placed in a Catholic institution. And good Catholic boys don't touch themselves or have sinful thoughts. I don't remember all that clearly the exact teachings of the church on sex and homosexuality but I do remember that sex—no matter with whom—did not exist unless you were married, and even then only for procreation.

How did you feel about this new "family" in your life?

At first I hated the church, but then, when I excelled in school, I began to love it because of the attention and safety it gave me. I was an altar boy who later trained altar boys. I was considered the best. And I learned, when you're the best, when you excel, people leave you alone. No one touches a winner. And that's what I wanted . . . not to be touched . . . to be alone. I was already an isolate, which is often the mark of an alcoholic.

There were very positive aspects of being a Catholic. I was, they said, in the hands of God. And he cared about me. That's a nice fantasy.

You say you were an isolate. Had you no friends?

Just the two girls downstairs. Which is interesting. From an early age, the only friends I ever made were females. Even today, my best friends are women. I feel safer with them because I know which buttons to push. When you grow up in a house with one mother and three older sisters, you learn that. But I was very much the sissy as a child, only no one ever called me that. I was beyond name-calling. I was an honors student, an altar boy and a pianist, giving recitals throughout the state. That, too, I loved. Being up on that stage . . . alone. That's really been my theme song through life: If They Would Just Leave Me Alone.

Why do you say you were very much the sissy?

Because I was. I had no male interests, per se. I knew I was different as a child. It was then I began to wear a mask to avoid discovery. There was one boy in the neighborhood who was very effeminate. He was terribly abused by his peers and even ridiculed by adults. By watching him, I learned to hide my own effeminacy. I made sure how *not* to stand or wave my hands. I adopted "butch" mannerisms. I wore the mask. That's why coming out was so difficult. From childhood, I didn't want to be that awful "thing" my mother said about others . . . a sissy. I didn't want to be humiliated. I have always lived in fear. For that, I thank the church. Yes, I loved being in God's hands, but the church and its teachings terrified me. They made me feel God was about fire and brimstone . . . hell. Daily, I thought to be punished for my "mortal sins." What possible "mortal sins" can a ten-year-old or a child of any age have? It makes me furious to think about it. I remember itinerant priests coming to talk to us boys and saying how those of us with a true "calling" to the priesthood who denied that "calling" would rot in purgatory. My life belonged to God, they insisted. I felt they were speaking of me and that I would pay for my sin of omission. Not that I felt a "calling." I just enjoyed the pomp and pageantry. I most certainly did not want to be a priest.

What did you want to be?

A pianist. That is all I have ever wanted to be. I won several state competitions but did not pursue a career because it would have meant asking for a scholarship, and by seventeen I couldn't ask for anything of anyone. I lost me when I gave up the piano. It was the one thing in life for which I had a passion. One year later I gave up playing totally to get away from my mother and Lillian. I left Des Moines to come to Los Angeles, where another sister awaited to take care of me. Lillian consented to pay my tuition at U.C.L.A. I cannot tell you how relieved I was to leave. By then, I was feeling gay and I was terrified some of my encounters with sex might become known to them.

When did you begin having sex?

At twelve. An older boy who had been having experiences for several years seduced me by talking of them. It got me turned on. I remember nothing about the first time—it's wiped clean from my memory. But I remember our other encounters. It was oral, on both our parts, and I enjoyed all of it. Except the guilt. That made me feel in constant jeopardy. God's wrath was sure to strike me down.

Had you experienced any sex feelings prior to this encounter?

None. Which isn't strange if you are a good Catholic boy.

Did you confess to your "sin"?

Yes, but the priest dismissed it as adolescent activity. He told me to repent, change my ways and *sin* no more. But of course, I continued to "sin." And throughout my teenage years I walked guilty and frightened. I was constantly depressed. At fourteen, I would some weekends get blind drunk. The sex that I had, although exciting, was always tainted by its furtiveness. Lots of hidden away and ugly places. That felt awful. I felt awful. *Sinful.*

A little irony here. I was leaving Des Moines to get away from this downpour of guilt. Yet, as my sister in Los Angeles drove me from the airport to her home she pointed out an effeminate man and told me about "perverts," how sick they were and how they preyed on young boys. Later, she gave me this horrendous article from *Reader's Digest* that actually suggested that all homosexuals were dirty old men. I should have stayed in Des Moines.

As you can see, everything I had ever heard about homosexuality was negative. No wonder one goes into a closet and is afraid to come out. My first four years in L.A. I was so afraid of discovery that I had no sex. This, despite my having severed with the church the day I severed with Des Moines.

Was that a difficult decision?

Not in the least. It was "Hello, L.A." and "Good-bye church." Had my sister in L.A. been a churchgoer, I probably would have gone along for the ride. Which is interesting. I have always seen me as a leader, when in truth I am a follower. But then, alcoholics tend to have rather distorted views of themselves. In fact, distortion is one of the main marks of an alcoholic.

Would you clarify that?

Alcoholics feel special and we wonder why the world is blind to our specialness. As a child I had this recurring dream. In it, I am sitting in the back seat of a long, gleaming-gold limousine. Up front, two men in livery drive me through beautiful golden clouds until we reach huge golden gates which guard the end of the world. But the gates immediately are thrown open upon my arrival. We drive on through and fall off the earth through billowy, golden clouds that gently ease me down, down, down. We do not crash. I cannot crash. I am golden . . . I am unique.

The dream always made me feel very special as a child. I loved it. It also made me feel very privileged. That is an alcoholic's feeling: one which is not based in reality. In truth, from childhood, I had such a desperate need to be unique—to be *something* rather than the nothing they made me feel—that I had to be special, set apart from everyone. How else could I live? That is still part of my disease . . . to be unique, apart from others . . . self-sufficient . . . not in need of another person.

When I crashed, at the hospital they would ask me why I thought this had happened. I responded: "Because they will not leave me alone." I always felt people . . . my mother . . . Lillian . . . the church, wanted something from me that I couldn't give—that I had to be all kinds of things that I wasn't in order to be accepted. And why couldn't they realize I was unique—special? When they didn't, I wore masks to be pleasing.

So there is the inconsistency. Golden in dreams but in reality . . . gray, empty . . . incomplete. Carl Jung once said that alcoholics use alcohol to attain a feeling of wholeness. That's true for me. When I drank I felt wonderful . . . complete . . . whole. I felt a part of the universe, a fellow man. Which is all so strange. Feeling special on one hand and yet needing to drink because I am afraid to live. But, incongruity and inconsistency are two very frequent companions of the alcoholic.

But much of what you say could be describing the average normal neurotic. What makes alcoholics different?

We drink! We don't go through the experience that causes pain. We narcotize ourselves from feeling. Thus we learn nothing. When and if we get sober, we must go back and retrace what happened and then, hopefully, grow. It is not easy. In fact, it is damn painful to wake up and discover you have coped with nothing most of your life but have instead swept it all under the carpet. So painful that one of the reasons why many do not stay in A.A. is because treatment requires cleaning out every last particle swept under that rug. Not only sweeping it out into the open but examining every last piece. You discover all kinds of ugly little things. In my own case I saw my need to control—how I like to write my own script for life and then direct as I also star in my little dramas. Alcoholics generally want total control. When people don't behave as we would wish them to, we get very disturbed.

Why?

When you have no control as a child—when everything is taken from you, decided for you—the need to control, to not be so powerless, becomes overwhelming. I have enormous fear, still, of being at the mercy of others . . . a little boy *being told* he must choose another mother.

How did you adjust to Los Angeles living?

I was a "good" boy. I attended U.C.L.A. and dated a very nice girl who suggested sex but which I declined. I had no feeling then, or now, for women. I wanted very much to have sex with boys, but I didn't know how to go about it. I still could not distinguish who-was-and-who-wasn't. I stayed to myself until I was picked up by a boy my age—also a senior in college—and we went to bed. A real bed. The first I had ever had sex in.

We really should have a choir of angels here but. . . . With this boy in bed I had the most beautiful and fulfilling experience of my life. It was an awakening. I think I really severed with the church —not the guilt, however—then and there. In making love, I remember thinking that nothing so beautiful, so loving, can be against God's will. I still feel that. Unfortunately, five months later I fell out of love with my first affair and in love with someone else. This upset me. In my M-G-M mind, one fell in love once, settled down and lived happily ever after. That has never happened. I fell in and out of love with every new moon. And why not? Once introduced to the Hollywood gay scene, I discovered homosexuals were not dirty old men or perverts, so screw you *Reader's Digest!*

Was it a happy time?

Now that's what's strange. It was and it wasn't. With all my sexual success I felt lonely. I could never understand that until recently.

Gay life wasn't fulfilling then or ever because *life* wasn't fulfilling. I was happy because finally I was attractive and accepted. But inwardly I felt a lack. I had always felt that lack. The incompleteness. There was something missing in me, and my fellow gays then didn't notice because there was something missing in them. We all wore masks. You see it today in both straight and gay bars—the pretenses, the playing at who you are not. In gay joints, there is what I call the costume drama—guys all emulating the masculinity of a Mark Spitz or Burt Reynolds, men who feel so insecure about themselves that they wear the Macho Mask. Christ! If we would all just rip off the masks and say "Hey! Here I am and I'm frightened too," we probably would have the first generation of happy homosexuals. Instead, we hide. Afraid to stand naked, we preen and pose in costumes and behind images. It's sad. Sad that because you have been treated like a piece of shit . . . because your feelings have been ignored or mocked . . . you must wear a mask or be vulnerable again to that kind of pain. And who wants to be that hurt again. So we mask what we think are our flaws and inadequacies.

Of course I am also speaking of me, particularly years ago when I first came to New York. I was fresh out of U.C.L.A., armed with a degree in music composition and a few dozen masks for all occasions. Again, socially and sexually, I was a great success. Or so I thought. But professionally I couldn't get it together. I was too special for a regular nine-to-five job so I took a series of temporary positions—like seven years worth of temporaries—where I could say "So-long-and-good-luck" whenever I felt like it. During that time there were lots of short affairs and several short drunken periods. The worst was before and after receiving my draft notice.

Military service was still compulsory in those days. I had gotten a student deferment while at college, but now there was no recourse other than to be inducted unless I declared myself. Which is what I did. It is not something a closet-case does easily. I drank myself into the decision—arriving hung over for the medical exam—and drank myself into oblivion afterward. I was very ashamed. But the idea of being confined with men—men/men—was too terrifying for me to deal with. I could not relate to straight males. I feared them. I had heard of fag-hunts in the Army. I knew if anyone was to point a finger at me I'd fall apart. Rather than risk that humiliation, I declared myself.

That made me fall apart in quite another way. I was raised on God-and-country. I believed in both. I truly felt it was my duty to serve. I felt ashamed. I felt I had emasculated myself. But, I took a few drinks and swept those feelings, along with all the others, under the carpet. I then drifted from one job to another. Ditto lovers. The boys I chose were never themselves but whatever I made them into. Fantasy figures . . . larger than life and not at all real. Of course they did the same with me. We were intimate strangers.

Were you drinking during this time?

I was always drinking, but I could put a cork on it for weeks on end. It wasn't till I turned twenty-nine and became career conscious that things began coming to a head. Suddenly I felt this frantic urge to amount to something. That produced anxiety attacks, the likes of which sent me to a shrink who decided he would not charge me if I would consent to try something experimental. I agreed. It was a good experiment. He asked for open-ended hours rather than the formal fifty minutes. In other words, I'd arrive at 8 P.M. and often not leave till 4 A.M. A lot of ground was covered. Unfortunately, the good doctor served beer throughout. After four months of treatment I had a lot of insights and no anxiety. I was cured. Except for one thing: I was drinking. If beer eased the anxiety then imagine what vodka could do!

Then . . . a miracle. A job as a reporter for a music trade paper. There, my drinking was not only accepted but approved of. From that position, I went into show business public relations. The jobs kept getting bigger and better. The drinking? Just bigger. It culminated a few years later with my waking up in Memphis but not knowing why I was there and which client I was to service. It was then I knew I was a drunk. I could not get out of bed mornings to shave without first taking a drink. I drank throughout the workday and yet I never appeared drunk. From 10 A.M. till 10 P.M. I did the straight world's "thing." Then I would run to a gay bar where I would do my serious drinking. I would usually close the place at 4 A.M. A gay bar was the only place where I felt any sense of comfort.

Why was that?

During the day I led a double life and hated it. I took orders from people I loathed and I *acted* straight because discovery might have cost me my job. I ended each day feeling dishonest, guilty, like a piece of shit. Drinking calmed all that. In gay bars I was safe. They would take me as I was. No need to pretend. I could drink, share my feelings, act up a storm if I chose to and it was all all right. In the straight world I felt unloved. In the gay world I could be me. And no one at 2 A.M. in a gay bar criticizes you for having one-too-many. At that hour, mainly what's left are the alcoholics or the soon-to-bes.

And another thing. I never had trouble picking up bed partners. I was always wanted. But I would delay for as long as I could. Not because I couldn't function—I could do that even up to the crash —but because I enjoyed knowing someone desired me and I wanted to bask in that as long as possible. I would tell him my life story, if he would let me.

You stated you knew you were a drunk. Did the thought to seek help cross your mind prior to your "crash," as you call it?

No. Because although I knew, I never really accepted it. No alcoholic ever does. He denies there is a real problem. No alcoholic is ever an alcoholic in his mind. No . . . I drank because it made me feel wonderful. And we all die sooner or later anyway. I drank until there was nothing else I wanted to do but drink. Lovers got in the way. Besides, who needed a lover when I had booze? What more predictable and satisfying love is there? Besides, by then, after so many disastrous affairs, I had decided love didn't exist among homosexuals so why chase after rainbows? Instead, I chased after snakes and rats and other things that crept up the walls and hung from the ceiling. I lost my job and never left the house. I just drank and hallucinated until I called that drinking buddy I previously mentioned who then brought me to A.A.

Does Alcoholics Anonymous work differently with homosexuals than with heterosexuals?

Not at all. Alcoholics are treated as alcoholics. The only difference for homosexuals within A.A. is that they are accepted. At the meetings, when people strip to their guts, we all learn that straight, gay or in-between, all people have the same feelings. Hurt, rage, revenge —those emotions are not the province of any particular sexuality. Nobody at A.A. makes a judgment about which side of the bed you sleep on.

Does the homosexual alcoholic have special problems in belonging to two denigrated minority groups?

There can be a dual guilt and, if one wants to continue carrying it, a dual stigma. But once in A.A. alcoholics drop the guilts and the stigmas. What we see is straight or gay, alcoholics have sexual hang-ups. There is really very little difference that I can see between the straight and the gay alcoholic. The problem and the solution are the same. You drink . . . and then you must *not* drink.

Yet there are special groups for homosexuals?

Yes, just as there are special groups for doctors, lawyers, etc. Many gay alcoholics arrive at A.A. feeling so isolated from the world that they can only open up before other gays. They truly believe straights will not understand or, worse, will humiliate them. These particular men are not ready for a heterogeneous group.

Do you attend these special groups for homosexuals?

Occasionally. They are not very useful for me anymore. A.A. brought me out. Or I brought me out. Anyway, I don't need the closet any more. I have ambivalent feelings about the gay groups. I see their usefulness in making alienated gays feel comfortable, but they are bad for me because they once again set me apart. I've been isolated for too much of my life. The Gay A.A., if I solely attended those meetings, would remove me from the mainstream I am trying to enter. But, I repeat, for the new A.A. member who is uptight about his homosexuality, the gay groups are great. He comes to grips with himself and his homosexuality first within this group and is then able to take it elsewhere.

There is another reason why I continue to attend the gay groups. They make me proud to be gay. The men discuss both their alcoholism and their homosexuality. And let me tell you, there ain't no bullshit. But none. Nobody gets into a My-cock-is-bigger-than-yours or a You-should-have-seen-what-I-had-last-night number. No way. These men get into their feelings and express them as I have never heard men do before. And I attend the straight men's group as well. That's a sad group because many are still playing jock—still wearing the mask before their peers, still messing up with macho shit. But the gays are beautiful. Just beautiful. I am very proud of what they, of what *we*, accomplish.

Are the groups for homosexuals a meeting ground of sorts—
a place where you might meet a potential lover?

Yes, but that is not their intent. I have had sex with a few of the men and one brief relationship with another. But none of the alcoholics who attend these groups do so to meet a bed partner. We go because we share a special interest—our homosexuality. We go because we are alcoholics—sick people, and yes, I still view myself as sick. Despite the fact I have not had a drink in five years, I know there are no "cured" alcoholics. Just recovered ones. And even then we all know of those who have fallen after twenty or thirty years of sobriety. It is not just gays who might pair off with one another. Generally, alcoholics tend to pair off with alcoholics. Prior to joining A.A., a drinker must associate with those who approve of his drinking. Upon joining A.A., he must associate with those who do not. Thus, alcoholics tend to look to one another for comforts, particularly those which are found within oneself. Which makes me realize that I *do* look for a possible lover within A.A. because all alcoholics within the organization are committed to one thing: change.

Can you evaluate the changes you have made since joining A.A.?

I can cry now. That may not sound like much, but for someone who could only *feel* his emotions when drunk, it's a helluva change. Then, too, I learned that I am all the things that I dislike in another. I, too, manipulate, seek to control and wear the mask. Only I am trying to change this—trying to live less defensively. I can relate better to people today because I respect them more. I don't have to see their pain to know they have it. All people have pain. It is a relief *not* to judge others so harshly any more, but it even more of a relief not to judge me so harshly.

Regarding your last statement, can you be more specific?

I no longer have religious guilt—just the bitterness. All that pain because of archaic religious attitudes about sex! I still have bitterness toward those straights who continue to put gays down because they cannot deal with their own sexual fears.

How were you relieved of this religious guilt?

I just lifted it off my shoulders and let it float off. As we say in A.A., I turned it over . . . gave it away. I saw that if I were to survive, I couldn't harbor irrational guilts or angers or resentments of any kind. I couldn't carry any dead baggage. I had to sweep everything out . . . look at it and then throw it away. Otherwise . . . it's self-destruct time again. And I'm through with all that. I'm committed to life.

Do you retain a belief in God?

More than ever, but my God is not the God of Catholicism. My God is Supreme Intelligence. He is a positive force who is nourishing, supportive, all loving and only cares that people find and give love—

not about with whom. My God is not vengeful. Why should God need to punish or humiliate? Man needs to do those things. Not God. With my God, for the first time, I do feel cared for and loved. He is like a huge electrical current which I can either plug into or not. Obviously, my choice is to plug in.

How do you feel about yourself today?

If you mean do I still feel special, the answer is yes, very. Special and privileged but not *better* than other people. I am not on an ego trip. My specialness is about being alive, being sober and being free to live in a special way, which is *my* way. There is also something very special about having fifty to one hundred people in your life to turn to for help for which there would be no price.

What of your fear of being in the control of others, particularly authority figures. Have you solved this professionally?

Yes. I no longer work in a competitive environment. I cannot let just anyone be an authority figure in my life, as my hatred from the past prevents me from giving up that power. I cannot wear a mask of obedience any more. Nor can I sell out to succeed. I had a choice— which is what it is all about—to either pursue the American Dream and be uncomfortable or to be comfortable and live successfully by my standards. I chose the latter mainly because I had to.

I no longer work in public relations. I take no job that makes me dependent. No one holds my purse strings. Years ago I earned $25,000 a year and spent $30,000. I *had* to hold that job. Today, since my life is not about trips to Europe and foreign cars and houses-for-the-summer at the Island, I take any job where I can own me. I work today as a secretary for a charitable foundation. I have been there several years but I could leave tomorrow should the situation suddenly become intolerable. I only earn $200 per week, but because I only earn that sum I am free. Nothing holds me. I can make that amount of money anywhere. Thus, no axe hangs over my head. I control my own life. By most people's standards, I'm a failure, but by mine, I'm a success. I have self-esteem, which is a damn sight better than having money. I don't dread going to work any more. I no longer kill myself to survive in a business world that kills me.

How do people react when you tell them you work as a secretary?

Mainly, they are surprised. Something in their attitude toward me invariably shifts. Status is the name-of-the-game with most people and particularly with gays. Yes, I do believe gays are more concerned with achievement and Being Something than straights. I think gays often put on a mask with status. It reduces the anxiety they feel about *not* Being Something in society's eyes.

Most gay men I meet are polite when they learn of my work but many do not come back. They feel I am not impressive enough. Because I understand where they are coming from, that no longer bothers me. But they do not turn off when I tell them I'm an alcoholic. I think first they disbelieve me because I don't look like a bowery bum and then, too, an alcoholic in their minds is Ray Milland and Susan Hayward and both won Oscars. Very glamorous. But most people can't understand what it means when someone admits he is an alcoholic. Unless you've been there, there is no way to understand. I accept that, too. What another person understands or accepts is not important to me. Not any more. That, too, I've given up. The only person whose respect I must earn is me! And I have to earn it daily. I'm still working out erratic patterns of behavior. For example: I choose rotten potential lovers. Always someone younger than myself who has a young, attractive body. In other words, I cruise, still, on a physical level. Whoever I meet, I then hope the personality will be there to support the physical. So I begin with a shaky foundation. Add to that the generation gap—usually about ten years—and I'm really begging for it. Usually after sex with this "child," there is nothing to talk about. Their heroes are not mine. Okay. There's the destructive pattern. I recognize it and I am trying to change it. Alcoholics must do this constantly. We must evaluate our behavior in order to grow—to not walk down rocky roads that lead nowhere.

Previously you mentioned "it is the secret that kills" and that your secret was your homosexuality. Is that true today?

No. Being gay no longer poses that problem for me. I am no longer paranoid about discovery. I no longer fear being crucified—now that's an interesting choice of words!—for it. I approve of my sexuality. It is a part of me that I accept. I do believe, however, that homosexuality is an illness which occurs in childhood that perverts the sex drive. I believe nature intended for sex to be performed by man with woman. But, because I believe homosexuality is a neurosis formed in childhood does not mean that I believe it cannot be a rewarding and fulfilling way of life. You can be heterosexual and be perverted in how you seek sex. I truly believe sex and relationships are what you make them. Every gay knows two men can love each other deeply and beautifully. Love between the same sex members, although *unnatural* as defined by what nature intended, can nonetheless be immensely rewarding. As can be the sex for sex's sake. I do the baths and the bars. What I don't do are some of the sex trips I see today which I think are negative. I admit to myself that the negative part of me finds them exciting, but I choose not to travel that road. I don't wish to be either the abused or the abuser. I choose to stay with the positive experiences.

I am very much in sympathy with the various gay activist groups. They are raising consciousness throughout this country. Positive changes are being effected. I think in recent years a lot of straights have begun wondering about what is so wrong with *loving* a member of your own sex. My only quarrel with most gay groups is that they tend to be isolationist. Most gays are already alienated from the mainstream. I think they need to feel part of rather than apart from it.

Do you think of yourself as sexually liberated?

Yes but no. I am still blocked with women, so obviously I'm not totally liberated. Only once have I had sex with a female and that was to prove to her that I could do it. So I did it. Big deal. I think she had about 112 orgasms but I was bored. I think it would be nice to feel juicy toward both sexes. With men, I think I'm liberated but others would say I am not. Those trips I judge negative, a lot of guys enjoy. They would say I am not liberated. But truly, I find S&M drag ludicrous. All those masks to cover up feelings of masculine inadequacy! I find their acting-out of the rage more sad than anything else. How much happier they would be if they could locate and define their anger.

I am into very old-fashioned sexual pleasures. I prefer being active in all roles but I do not say that as a macho thing. Actually, it's a hang-up. I have to carry the ball game in bed. I cannot just lie back and let someone else take over. I cannot lie back and enjoy someone giving me pleasure. I must take charge, must control everyone's orgasm. I am very resistant to receiving love. I like to give it. I think of real health as being able to both give and receive. I'm not there yet. I am trying very hard to understand why I cannot just relax and allow someone to love me. I think it may have to do with Lillian and my fear of her overwhelming me. Love, as given by Lillian, felt like I was being used. That terrifies me still.

Have you felt used in your past relationships?

Only recently have I seen that I've been both the used and the user. My relationships have invariably been about me supplying the ingredient that makes the other person happy . . . complete. . . .

what I can do and be for them. What I really have wanted is to be that other person's drug—to make him totally dependent on me. Why? If he needs me enough, he will not leave me. But I never want this from someone else. God no! That would put me in their control, leave me vulnerable. Back to Lillian again, right?

I am going to be free of that shit! Why shouldn't I receive comfort, nurturance, love. Let me tell you, there's a little virgin within me just waiting to be brought out amongst the living—a little virgin who can receive as well as give. I and that virgin know we are afraid of being intimate with people. The whys and wherefores are almost unimportant. What does matter is that I want to change.

Previously you stated that at a certain point in your life you stopped believing in the possibility of relationships between men. Do you still think that not possible?

No. I think it is possible but very difficult because of the masks. There is often too much fantasy and not enough reality in gay cruising. There is only one Burt Reynolds and I bet even he is afraid sometimes. What I mean is . . . until the masks are removed, real relationships are very difficult to form. What good is it if gays come out of the closet if they don't come out from behind the masks. Straight people wear them too but gays wear a particular kind. It's to enhance their sense of manliness, which in most cases is weak. But a lot of gay men are breaking through to be themselves. These men have stopped worrying if their slips are showing. And the only thing these men ask of the men they meet is that they be themselves too. So . . . there is hope. I have hope. I would like to share my life with someone, but I no longer expect that someone to be a Magic Man who will help me to live. I look to one person for that—me. And I suppose the kind of man I will now be attracted to will have come through some kind of therapy to find himself. He, too, will not ask of himself to be anything other than what he is. Nor will he ask me to be anything other than what I am.

But I am not searching for someone. Wrong. I am. But that someone is me. I am still not totally secure. I still fear being in another person's "clutches." I still fear that others—the Supreme Court, the state courts, politicians—have the authority to control my life . . . to pass judgment on my sexuality.

Would it therefore be more comfortable to be straight?

Funny, I've thought about that recently. I've even allowed myself a few good fantasies involving women, but the answer is no. I am not

interested. I think my fear of having the courts decide what can be
and what cannot be done sexually is a valid, rather than a neurotic,
fear. My being "comfortable" is not about being straight or gay. It
is about intimacy—learning to be comfortable with it with another
person. So why wage a battle—and that is what it would be to become
straight—when the war is about something else? Frankly, I wouldn't
want to change my life-style today. Why invest energy at this stage
of my life to learn a new one? I would much rather learn to be a
comfortable homosexual. If it be love and intimacy that I need, why
not from a man?

What is your life-style?

Obviously, A.A. is an enormous part of my life. That, by the way,
poses enormous problems for any man with whom I get involved
who is not in A.A. Those of us in the organization enjoy a special
fellowship most people will never know. Because we have seen, and
felt, one another's guts, we love each other. No matter who I meet,
he finds it difficult to compete with the love I receive from my A.A.
family. In truth, I get all the love I will ever want or need, which is
why I don't hound the bars or the discos looking for a lover.

Yet, there are certain needs not met at A.A. A lover "loves" in a
very special way. No embellishment needed, right? Thus, if one
should emerge in my life, it would just enlarge the picture.

I am not afraid of growing old because I've already been that. Nor
am I afraid of dying because I've done that, too. I will never be alone
unless I choose to be. There will always be "the family."

But have you a life apart from A.A.?

I do not *live* with alcoholics but alone in a very pleasant apartment
with a dog and two cats. I am very involved in Yoga and meditation.
I know a great many people, although I see no one frequently but
everyone from time to time. Occasionally, I go to the opera or the
ballet and when I do, I totally enjoy it. Before, I went constantly
because it was the thing to do—an almost competitive one-upman-
ship type of thing. I also go to the theater and some Saturday nights
I'll do a Fred Astaire number at one of the gay discos.

In truth, I pretty much live my life today without plan. I do what
I want to do when I want to do it. If that means the baths next Tues-
day, then I'll go. And I'll have a terrific time because I'll really want
to go rather than have to. My sex life today is really terrific because

that's what it is: a sex life. I no longer romanticize it into anything else.

My life is fun because it is spontaneous today. Truly I don't think about the future. Alcoholics must stay centered in the present. I don't need the regrets of the past or the fears for tomorrow. Perhaps to some it will read as an unexciting existence when actually there isn't a day that goes by when I don't feel excited about life . . . about being *in* it. Just to be *in* the world rather than *out*—how much more excitement can one need? All the pain I experienced was worth having to reach this place in life. Many people go to their graves without having lived and without having known what life meant. That can never be me. Not any more. I know. And I thank *my* God for that knowledge daily. I also thank him for *my* life.

Tony D'Agio

I<small>T WAS A</small> birthday party to which Tony D'Agio * had invited his "closest friends," men of assorted size, shape, color and age. The ten candles on the birthday cake exuded more warmth than the men did collectively. "Happy Birthday" was dutifully sung. At its conclusion, no one rose to embrace the birthday boy or to offer a toast. Nothing was offered, least of all a feeling.

But Tony D'Agio, a "gorgeous Guinea" with black wavy hair, beaming black eyes and a boyish manner which is at odds with his mature and muscular body, was oblivious. He was caught up in the drama, in being center stage, on this, his fortieth birthday. A big red ribbon tied about his neck floated to the floor. He looked "adorable," which again was at odds with his handsome-but-mature face.

An actor with several Broadway credits, Tony D'Agio is nonetheless struggling. He is far beyond "ingénue" and, yet, he is not quite leading man. "But he could be," confides one of the guests, his drama teacher, "if he ever comes out of the closet . . . as a *human being*." Tony is indeed skillful at hiding. It took him many weeks before he would say yes or no to participating in this book.

I have a lot of ambivalence about being included. Suppose it's not good enough.

It? What's "it"?

Me . . . my life. Maybe it's just not . . . well, enough. Why are you writing that? Leave it out. It's not important. You're writing about homosexuality, aren't you?

I'm writing about people.

Well, there is very little to write about me. Will you be changing all the names and places?

Yes, your identity will be preserved.

Say I was born in Cleveland. There's a big Italian population there.

* See Author's Note, page xii.

Okay, you were born in Cleveland. How do you feel about turning forty?

It was a nice party, didn't you think?

What did you think?

I had a good time. Those are my best friends, people I can talk with, be with. One of the guys, Bob, I go back with seventeen years. It's nice to spend birthdays with friends.

Do you feel this birthday is a landmark?

I haven't thought about it as such. I mean . . . most guys still think I'm thirty, thirty-two or thirty-three, at the most.

That pleases you?

Well, it is flattering. And I don't know what *feeling forty* is supposed to feel like. Am I supposed to feel old?

How do you feel?

Excited! Like a big kid. As though my family has given me a big birthday party.

Was that usually the case when you were a child?

Yes. I was the baby of a large family. My mother was closer to fifty than forty when she had me. My eldest sister was twenty-three. She was like a mother to me. In fact, all my sisters—bless them all—were like mothers to me.

Were they any good at it?

That's a funny question. It makes me think how mad I would get when they would up and marry and leave. It seems the women in my house were always leaving.

Did your mother work?

No. She was around . . . there . . . you know, someone to run to when you scraped your knee. But not someone to talk to. She was an old-fashioned Italian woman. Wore black and was just a bit frightening. Not that she wasn't good to me. But I never felt she was open or emotional. I never felt any love from her and I can't say I loved her. I guess when you've already had many children, there isn't much love left to give.

Did you feel similarly toward your father?

The truth is I felt abandoned by both my parents—as though neither was there. But I didn't know I felt that way then. You see, they were ritualistically "good" parents. I was always cared for. There was just never a sense of companionship or compassion. Or, for that matter, a feeling of unconditional love. I got what my mother could give—which were the essentials.

And from your father?

The best money could buy. But he was never there. He operated a big restaurant in downtown Cincinnati . . .

You mean Cleveland.

Oh, right. Cleveland. Anyway, he only was able to come home weekends. Then, he would arrive at our big house in the country loaded down with foods and gifts. He was a great giver of things, my father was. And I took. But he never gave me what I needed.

Which was?

Well, all the other kids went fishing or played ball with their fathers. I had none of that. In fact, I have no recollection of him as a person —just this man who would give me, give me, give me.

Perhaps that was his way of showing love?

Perhaps, but his love was not the kind I needed. I wanted a daddy to be with. As the baby, there was never anyone in the house to talk to. I was treated like a doll, dressed up and paraded—to be admired by the neighbors. I looked forward to those Friday nights when he would drive up to the house in his big Oldsmobile but I don't know why. We never did anything together. He never knew me. But then, when I think back, no one knew me until I turned twenty-seven.

What happened at that age?

I had sex. For the first time. Listen, don't write that. It's too embarrassing. People will laugh. A twenty-seven-year-old male virgin. Don't write it, I'm telling you.

What makes you think people will laugh?

No man reaches that age without having had sex.

But you did!

Yes, and I'm still so goddamn angry at those stupid nuns and all their religious teachings that I could punch holes through the walls.

A strict Catholic upbringing?

About as Roman Catholic as you can get. Altar boy . . . mass every day and hell next week.

Why hell?

'Cause at seven, I was this awful sinner.

Why? Were you lusting after your neighbor's wife?

I was touching myself.

Masturbating?

Right. Constantly. And according to the nuns, I was a sinner . . . going to hell for my wanton lusts.

Wasn't there sex education from any other source?

The family doctor. I was about nine and he was giving me a thorough work-up when I got worked up—got an erection. He looked at it and said: "Son, do you know what that is for?" And I said, "No, sir." And he said: "For making babies when you are married and not for anything else."

What about your family?

Sex was never discussed. Everyone hid from one another. Not even the boys walked around naked or showered together. One of my few recollections of childhood is of people clutching towels or robes to their bodies so that I wouldn't see their nakedness.

Yet you masturbated at that age.

At that age and at all others.

Do you recall your fantasies?

There weren't any.

Do you really remember not thinking of anyone, male or female, while masturbating?

I remember nothing other than masturbating but not to orgasm.

Why not to orgasm?

In my mind, it was less of a sin if I stopped before that exquisite point. To feel that climax was to risk purgatory. It seems to me I spent most of my childhood in the confessional seeking absolution for my sins.

What sins?

There was a doll in the house. My sister's. And I used to lift the doll's dress to see if there was a hole. Don't write that!

Don't write what?

Hole—it sounds so ugly.

Would you feel more comfortable if I wrote about a doll's vagina?

Don't make fun of me. This may be a joke to you but not to me. You see, I confessed for weeks that I looked for a "hole." And when I went to Scout camp and saw my bunkmate jerking off, I confessed for weeks, but I never knew why. I just felt frightened . . . dirty. I have always felt that. As a kid, I had very few friends. Maybe one best friend at a time. But as soon as he or the kids would talk about sex, I'd run home. Once they had some dirty pictures and they made me look and I threw up. So I'm telling you, I grew up asexual.

Tony, a child who masturbates is not asexual.

Well, then I grew up without sexual feelings. I felt no sexual interest in girls or boys. None. I did well in school, was reasonably happy and that's that!

You say it with great finality, as though there was nothing more to your childhood.

This will surprise you, but I remember little to nothing more.

Well, what did you want to be?

Nothing. I never thought about that. Somehow it just seemed I would grow up, get married and have babies. That was all that was required of me. I don't remember having other dreams.

Not even of acting?

Not until college and that was discouraged by the nuns. Too risky. I'd starve to death. So, initially, I thought to become a teacher. I came within a year of obtaining my degree at Catholic University when I quit. Don't ask me how or why because I don't remember but . . . I decided to become an actor. Despite what anyone said or advised, I came to New York. It may have been the first thing I ever did for myself in my life. But I don't know.

Tony, do you really not remember feelings attached to all of this or is it that you would prefer not to speak of it?

Both. I would prefer not to speak about it because I'm beginning to feel rotten—like the pukey, frightened child I was. All this makes me feel . . . small, insignificant. But the truth is I don't remember how I felt or if I felt. It's like someone else went through my childhood and adolescence. Like where was I when other kids my age were parking in cars and necking? I was home hiding. Even in college, I was so repressed, so cut off from any sex feelings, that I didn't feel deprived. I never even thought it unusual that I didn't have a girl. I knew people my age were sleeping together—but only sort of. I just denied sex from consciousness.

Do you have feelings about that today?

You're damn right I do. It makes me madder than hell. All that guilt. For what? All those years of being chaste, pure, and yet why? All those years I lost . . . my youth. All the fun I could and should have had. All kids are interested in sex. They should be, dammit. Why was I convinced it was wrong. Why was I made to believe it was a sin when at its best it is so beautiful. Why couldn't there have been one person in my life—just one—to tell me about sex as a form of joyous communication? And you ask me today if I have any feelings about all this? I am one great big bleeding puddle of feelings. They all started leaking out when I went through EST. And now I can't stop the blood from flowing. Now I'm halfway between nowhere and somewhere. Feelings, you ask. Well I *feel* every one of the goddamn nuns, priests, the doctor—all those bastards—they're the ones who should rot in hell for the crimes they committed against me.

What were the crimes?

They killed me—me, the sexual person. He died and didn't resurrect until he was twenty-seven. And if you want to know how I feel about turning forty—which you asked sometime back—I hate it because I want my adolescence. I want my youth!

Three months have passed between meetings. A summer has elapsed. Tony D'Agio had "turned forty" by playing on the sands of Fire Island. Unlike his childhood, which he recalls as being without "playmates," such is not the case now. There are many "playmates." Yet, he admits, he is not happy. He sits, looking broodingly beautiful, in his one-room, with loftbed, studio in Greenwich Village and talks about his summer.

I was also at the Hamptons quite a bit. The island for me is both moth-and-flame. All that sex, I love it and hate it. The Hamptons depressed me. My hosts were guys my age. All either owned places or were capable of spending a few thou to rent for the summer. And here I am, past forty, without more than a pot to pee in. I realized during my summer of '42 I should be further along.

Where is it so written?

On my forehead. Thou shalt be further along at forty. I'm filled with these "shoulds." I feel trapped by them. Like, I *should be* established as an actor, *should be* living in a more opulent apartment, *should have* money in the bank, *should have* a stable relationship—a million voices all telling me what I should be.

But whose voices?

Well, I could say my father and my mother, but EST made me realize they are really my own.

When and why did you seek out EST?

About eight months ago I started turning funny again.

"Turning funny" again?

When I first came to New York I went to a Gestalt therapist seemingly because I had difficulty auditioning for jobs—I'd freeze from fright—but in reality—I went because I was following men home. And not just following them but imagining them to be my lovers. It was all very terrifying. But it passed. I stayed with Gestalt for a year and we worked on little else but my inability to audition.

And then life settled in. I began to work and I began to meet men and life wasn't bad. I thought it was pretty okay actually until one day you wake up and say "Hey, I'm going to be forty and where the fuck am I?" Don't write that!

Don't write what?

"Fuck." It's unimportant.

Agreed! Fuck is unimportant, but your reasons for entering EST are not.

I was unhappy. An actor's life is always unstable, but I had begun to feel particularly vulnerable. I also realized that I was cut off from emotions. Drama coaches would scream at me to *feel* this or *feel* that and I couldn't. Worse, I couldn't relate to anyone's pain or joy because I couldn't relate to my own. In short: nothing in my life was working. I knew I had to make changes or I'd starve to death—literally and emotionally. Well, EST opened the door. Suddenly, I'm assailed by feelings. Suddenly I'm overwhelmed by feelings of hurt or despair. Only I don't know why? Despite my continued participation in their evening workshops I have no greater understanding of me. Just some. And I accept their philosophy that I am responsible for my own life. I accept it but I don't like it.

Why?

I want my daddy!

Literally?

Yes. Goddammit! I want a father. Do you know in each of my past relationships I made every one of those men into my ole man. And guess what? Each one was a fuck-up. None of those men delivered.

What should they have "delivered"?

They should have protected me . . . loved me . . . given me what I needed. Like the man who brought me out. He cheated me. Oh Christ did he cheat me! He never told me he was only in New York on assignment, that he'd be leaving and that he had a lover stashed away in Omaha. That stinks! That really stinks. And here I am thirteen years later and still pissed. I'm forty years old and still looking for a daddy to take care of me. I *should be* taking care of myself.

Aren't you?

Yes. But resenting it. However, I think I'm coming to grips with it. I'm thinking of entering analysis . . . thinking but not doing anything about it. That's part of my problem. I can't seem to work up to do anything. And I must. I *am* past forty.

So the age factor has caught up with you since we last spoke?

Yes. At the island. I played all summer in the sand castles with lots of other little boys. Only I'm not a little boy. I'm forty. That is a fact. And suddenly it frightens me. What have I got other than talent and a great body? Nothing. Once I thought I had close friends. Now I realize I haven't permitted that. I've kept a wall up between me and people.

Do you know why?

No. Only that it is protective. Occasionally I feel someone might try to take away my "youth"—the one I never allowed myself and which I am now experiencing. I *like* being in the sandbox, playing with the children. I like not having responsibilities. And yet, I hate not having money. And yet, suddenly, I also hate not feeling adult.

What were the men like that you met this summer?

All kinds. No particular mold. I did a lot of threesomes. I like that— like being the center of attention. And that's interesting. Here a part of me thinks I would like to be some man's lover, while another part purposely picks people who are attached. I often wonder if on an unconscious level I didn't know that my first affair was also "married."

How did you meet him?

At a mixed party. There are always a lot of those in New York among the acting set. I was about to be twenty-seven and still pretty much believing in *saving myself* for marriage. In other words: no conscious homosexual thoughts. Anyway, Fred—that's what we'll call him—was very attentive to me at the party. So were about a dozen other people, men and women, but I was oblivious to the come-ons as only I could be. But Fred was persistent. He literally courted me. There were daily phone calls, dinner dates, presents. Yet, I never acknowledged to myself what was happening. I kept pretending that it was all . . . what? Friendship. Of course. I needed him to manipulate the situation and he did. On my birthday we got just a little drunk and ended up where I guess I wanted to be.

Was it an "awakening," so to speak?

It was more like a Sominex. A big nothing. Mutual masturbation. That I could have done myself. But in truth, I was so damn uptight, how could it be any good. I could never release the passion inside me because the guilt blocked it. He could have helped me but he didn't. He could have taught me—not about fucking and sucking—Christ! Don't write that! Say sex—he could have taught me about sex. But he didn't. He seemed totally satisfied with our arrangement.

But you weren't?

No. I wanted so much for him to take my life in his hands and to take care of it and me. I wanted so much for him to love me. I wanted so much, period. After all those years of starvation, I wanted nourishment. Do you know that prior to having sex with him—when on an unconscious level I must have known where we were heading—I began experiencing a nervous esophagus—I couldn't swallow—and hives. Big brutal hives. Then, after the sex, I lost those symptoms and suffered anxiety attacks instead. This fear would clutch at my throat and I was sure I was dying. It was all guilt.

Did you experience any happiness with this man?

Yes. After the insomnia and insanity passed, I was happy. For a week! Then he was transferred, told me of his lover and left.

And your reaction?

I started sleeping around with anything and everyone. I quickly got over my sexual reserve but I never got over the guilt.

That's interesting . . . never got over the guilt. Even today?

I suspect so. I don't go to church—haven't in many years. I'm too angry and resentful. But I'm also a guilty Catholic. I may have severed with the church but never with God.

Is it your homosexuality that keeps you guilty?

Do you know up until EST I would have said yes. Now . . . no. It is my sexuality that keeps me guilty. I shouldn't be sexual—shouldn't have sex. A part of me—despite what I thought was my joyful participation at the baths, the bushes, the tearooms and the orgies—continues to think of sex as dirty. Not just homosexual sex but any sex that is without the sanctity of union.

How do you feel about your homosexuality?

I deal with it. I exist in it . . . perform. I cope with it.

Why do you choose the word "cope"? Does it take coping?

Shit! Listen, I shouldn't have done this chapter with you. I realize that now. A little voice inside me keeps saying, "I don't want to be homosexual. I never have wanted to be homosexual. I don't belong. I have never belonged. And it has cheated me. I have not gotten one thing I've wanted from my homosexuality."

Are we talking about a father again?

Yes. I guess so. I subtly seduce my men and put them into positions they can't possibly fulfill. I fuck up in the fucking. But . . . I know that now. That's one of the things EST has helped me to see. I really feel changed by that experience. That even shows in my work. I'm able to touch more deeply into the soul of the character I'm portraying.

And of your own soul?

I'm still six characters in search of an analyst. Only I don't search too hard because I also know I want my analyst to be my lover—a father again, a man to make decisions, take charge, dominate.

Is that carried into the bedroom?

Now that's something I have no understanding of at all. No, it isn't. Sexually, my relationships are always balanced. I am more inclined to be active—much more inclined—but I can be passive. Initially, I could not get fucked—don't write that for Chrissake. It sounds awful! —just say initially I couldn't be passive.

Tony, what the fuck is wrong with the fucking word fuck?

It's gross; it's disgusting; it's vulgar . . . dirty. Okay? Clear? Fucking is dirty. Now let's get the *fuck* on with it. Initially I couldn't get *fucked*—couldn't give that much of me to any man. But today I see it as a receiving and I like it. I even feel nourished by the orgasm of the man inside me. It's like his semen feeds me in some way. And I enjoy having sex with a man who likes to *fuck*. Actually, I can be led into anything if it is with a careful, gentle partner.

Clarify "anything" please.

Well, I'm not into a freak scene but this summer I did try some light S&M.

What constitutes "light" S&M?

I did a slave/master thing with a boy of twenty-six. But I was very gentle with him. I mean . . . he would have done *anything* to please me if I would only tell him I was pleased. But I didn't do *anything*.

My sensibilities wouldn't allow me to misuse or abuse him. I just *fucked* him and made him blow me and used him in other exotic and erotic ways. All of which was his need. But I also gave him affection and approval. And the kid came apart! That upset me. You see, in that slave/master role-playing, I could feel my own need to be a slave to some man if only he would accept, approve and perhaps even *dare* to love me. And that, other than for a onetime shot at fist-fucking, has been my S&M activity.

What were your reactions to that?

Well, I had been tripping and there was suddenly this fantasy of total union with another person. I actually felt a part of that man. It's really weird being that deep into someone. I felt trusted . . . valuable. I liked it.

Would you like it done to you?

No! Absolutely no! I wouldn't want anyone becoming that much a part of me.

Why do you suddenly look so shocked?

Did you *hear* what I just said? I can't believe that fell out of my mouth—that I wouldn't want anyone to be that much a part of me. Maybe that explains why I've never had a lover. Maybe I don't want to be that close to another person.

Or have another person be that close to you?

Yes, there is that difference. Like I don't mind being the pursuer but I hate being the pursued. I like being in control.

Why do you think that is?

Christ! I never had any. The youngest is always told what to do at home, in school, in church. My worst fear, my most recurring nightmare, is of my being penniless and needing to return to my parents' home to live. God, when I visit today I'm bananas for weeks afterwards! The sisters that didn't marry, and those that did but divorced, live together. And I'm still treated like the baby. I feel totally smothered out there. And my mother—near ninety—she climbs up to sit on my lap! I feel consumed . . . like a living character in an Ingmar Bergman film. I can't wait to get back to my own little home and my little life. Which isn't so little when I view it realistically. I work, sporadically, but I do work; and I have a few acting students of

my own and my evenings are spent truly contentedly at the opera or
the ballet. I have fun with that part of my life. The wondrous thing
about New York is its vitality. What a life you can live if only you're
alive to live it!

That's a very interesting statement. Go a little with it.

I was dead most of my life, right? No feelings, sexual or otherwise.
What did I enjoy? Nothing. What did I hate? Nothing. But when you
come alive, even if it is only at first to feel pain, at least you are living
—part of some kind of human experience. I want that now—the pain
and the joy. And I would like to be in love. Adolescent love I might
add. I'd like to be lost, drowned in another person's being. I refuse to
give up that concept of loving, of knowing a completeness with someone else. Now, to achieve this, all I must give up is the fantasy.
Daddy is dead. All my life—well, since twenty-seven, which seems
like all my life—I've searched for the storybook relationship. The
Prince and the Pauper. Guess who I play? But that, despite the feeling of *still* wanting that kind of man, is impossible. There are only
people and I must learn to see each clearly for who and what he is.
Unfortunately, I also have a tendency to choose from the physical
first and the emotional and intellectual last. Often, I try to force them
together, which is akin to the square peg in the round hole.

Is your sex life fulfilling?

It sounds like you ought to add an "at least" to that question. Well
. . . through most of this summer I would have thought yes but
now . . . something very strange and upsetting is happening to me.
It's not impotence but it is a loss of feeling in the head of my penis
and a diminishing of fireworks at orgasm. It's no longer the Big Pop.
I've seen a doctor and he greatly doubts it is male menopause at my
age but thinks it very likely to be emotional.

What do you think?

That I'm fucked out . . . and fucked up. But I'm not nuts from
it. At EST, some women spoke about "drying up"—not being able to
get wet like they used to. Funny, when we spoke about it, it was almost as if our emotions had withered . . . dried, first, and then the
sexual part of us followed.

Can you explain that more fully?

I guess 'cause I came out late sexually, I tried to make up for lost
time. Initially, because sex-without-love was too much of a guilt trip

to bear, I was in love every third night. I would fantasize love when there was nothing. Only I really believed otherwise. That's why when this "Prince" would leave me, I'd be devastated. Here I had "given me" and then had it thrown back in my face. That hurt but I didn't know it then. How many times can you throw yourself out there, have someone pick it up, use it and then throw it back, before you stop throwing out anything but sex? Today, I can go out to a bar, pick up a guy and make it, but I don't put me on the line. It's strictly sex. The problem, as my body now seems to be telling me, is that I'm having sex with too many men who I really don't want to be with.

Then why do it?

This will be the dumbest answer in the world . . . because it is expected. You go to a bar for the evening, talk to some guy, dig him . . . know that he digs you . . . you just don't shake hands at the end of the evening, you suck cock. Don't write that, for Chrissake! Can't you just write, "you have sex"?

Anyway, it seems like you never really know who you are sharing yourself with. I often wonder why do I do this. Why do I share myself with so many people I may not even like once I know them? Why? For what?

You tell me "why" . . . "for what."

I am forty years old and still trying to shake down the apples from the tree of my youth . . . apples that just went rotten from misuse. I want my adolescence!

Does that mean you still want an older man as your lover?

If I found anyone much older than me, he'd be wrapped in mothballs or some kind of preservative. No . . . I now want a guy my age, or thereabouts, a guy who could be my friend, my father and my lover.

Could you be that to him?

I honestly don't know. That's what I'm looking at. Daddy gave, gave and gave. And I took, took, took. That pattern has stayed with me all my life. It's tough to change but now that I see why I have acted as I have, why my needs have been unfulfilled, change is no longer impossible. It can't be. I really want a grown-up life with a grown-up person. I'd like that kind of stability and security. I would hate to grow old without having experienced that kind of give-and-take relationship.

The damnedest thing is, had you asked me this six months ago, I wouldn't have dealt with it. Turning forty puts you through incredible changes. The simple fact is, no matter how good you look or feel, you are in your declining years. And each passing year narrows the chances of meeting someone.

What makes you think that?

Remember the song, "They're either too young or too old. They're either too gray or too grassy green." That's true. Most men my age are either settled down or settled into some kind of middle-aged rut that I find maddening. The pool of possibilities narrows. Ask anyone past thirty-five and I'm willing to bet he or she has thought about life-at-sixty without someone at his or her side.

Does that thought scare you?

That, too, is not easy to answer. It's another of those questions for which I have more than one answer. Yes, the thought of being alone at sixty is upsetting, as the thought of never experiencing The Great Love Affair is upsetting. Yet, I sometimes think I have set it up to be alone . . . that being alone may be what I really want. But don't ask me to explain that because I can't . . . *yet.*

I caught the accent on "yet." What are you implying?

That I will find the answer. You see, I've lived most of my life with my head up my ass. Don't . . .

. . . write that. I know.

I've lived in a vacuum, totally cut off from myself. That's changing. You ask me certain questions and I can't give you answers *yet* because I've never thought about these things. Like this summer at Fire Island, I would have to fast for five days to keep the Body Beautiful. But all those young, beautiful blonds, they had to do nothing but be young, beautiful and blond. But in fifteen or twenty or ten years, they'll be where I'm at today. There will always be a new batch of beautiful blue-eyed blonds. Always. But there is only one me and he gets older each year. To compete on a physical basis is foolhardy. So what then? Friendships. A deepening of relationships. And I'm trying. You know why I don't fear being alone in my old age so much? Because I've always been alone. By choice! Now, I can make the choice not to be alone if that's my real choice. I can have very real and deep relationships today if I just *give* rather than take.

Tony, since you have never had a lover, do you believe in homosexual love?

Very definitely. I've had glimpses of it. It was gorgeous.

But do you think life might have been easier for you had you been heterosexual?

I've always suspected that it would have been, yes. I've never been a happy homosexual. I am still paranoid about discovery. I still expect society to think the worst about faggots. I have a dread of anyone in my family or anyone who knows my family finding out about me.

But why?

People would say awful things. They would!

But why should you care?

You're right. Why should I care? But I do. I'm ashamed. I'm afraid they might reject me.

You used the word "faggot" before. Is that how you think of yourself . . . as a "faggot"?

That's how the world thinks of all gay men. We're not people. We're faggots . . . something less then men.

Tony, are you something less than a man?

How can I answer that? I have no yardstick . . . no way of knowing. Before I die, if once I could have sex with a woman, I might feel more like a man. It bothers me greatly that my sexuality—my sexual feelings toward women—was turned off and never turned on again.

Am I a closet straight? I haven't the vaguest idea. But let me tell you, usually, at forty, when you're straight, you're married, with family, a good job and a home. Security . . . permanency. That I'd like. And it makes me fucking mad—don't write fucking, just say mad— that all that was denied me because a bunch of idiots deciphered God and sin to suit themselves and the needs of a system.

I said before I have never been a happy homosexual. And I'm not going to take that back because it's true. But, I don't regret being one. You see, I left one thing out: As I sat on that beach this summer and thought about me, my life, or my lack of a life, I realized that my unhappiness is not about sex and men but about me. I have never come to grips with Tony D'Agio, adult male, who has a right to be who and what he is.

The truth is, all those shit questions before about being alone and finding someone and relationships . . . what does it all mean if you don't know who you are and where you're coming from. Do I want to live with someone ultimately? You bet your ass I do! I want to live with me! But I want my happiness to be dependent not on another person in my life but upon having *me* in my life. And if that reads to some like a crock of shit from one of those "How to Be Your Own Best Lover" handbooks, they can go fuck themselves! And *that* you can write down.

In the fall of 1976 Tony D'Agio entered analysis. Initially, after each session, he was quitting.

It was too painful.

And now?

It is even more painful. But something is happening. I feel lousy most of the time but it's a different lousy. I'm doing something with my life. I see it's not just about my childhood but about my present life. I fuck up. A lot. I want from people, and I take, but I'm afraid to give . . . afraid it won't be enough, or good enough.

Like your being afraid initially to be part of this book.

Right. I don't understand yet why I think so little of myself or why I have so little confidence, but there is something encouraging about hanging in there to find out. Shit! As soon as I hit that couch I start talking and go nonstop for fifty minutes. I figure, why not, it's my time and my money. At first I kept waiting for El Shrinko to say something really terrific that would change my life. Forget it. Occasionally he asks a question that spins my whole head around. It's good, even though it feels bad. I think it's going to feel bad for a long, long time.

Does that bother you?

Of course. Pain sucks! Feeling like a fucky little child half the time sucks! But now, on better days, I'm beginning to feel like . . . well, like a man.

And how does feeling "like a man" feel?

That's what is so terrific. It feels like *me!* You know, there just might be some truth to that old adage. Life may begin at forty-one.

That's "life begins at forty," Tony.

Who asked you to open your *fucking* mouth!

George Schuvaloff

FOR SECURITY REASONS, George Schuvaloff * cannot be described. Although he is in the United States legally, it is under false pretenses. And even that cannot be explained, as it could possibly jeopardize his position. He fled Russia a year ago and under his pen name, George Schuvaloff, he has been quite vocal in his criticism of the Soviet Union and, in particular, their treatment of homosexuals. Thus, if his identity became known, the family he left behind could be subject to unpleasant pressures by the Soviet authorities.

In his mid-thirties, George is far less concerned for his safety than are his friends, mainly Russian expatriates. Although he is not impulsive, he is quite precise and states exactly, after due consideration, what he thinks. A philosopher, social critic and poet, George, after a year's exploration of the United States, has settled in New York City, where he is currently working on his first book for an American publisher.

Known to American intellectuals through his writings prior to leaving the U.S.S.R., George is currently enjoying his fame and the ability to speak out on the social injustices within Russia.

Were you a threat to the Soviet Union when living in Russia?

Yes. My political views had become known.

Why then did Russian authorities permit you to leave?

To be rid of me. I knew too many foreign journalists, had much access to foreign information and was not at all ill-disposed to disseminating such information.

Why did they not confine you?

But I was not a criminal. True, they could have created charges against me, had me imprisoned, but it would have had far-reaching repercussions. It would have been . . . how do you say here . . . very bad public relations for them to have had me jailed. So, it was

* See Author's Note, page xii.

actually advantageous for them that I leave. Actually, they allow many of the intelligentsia, the opinion-makers, the potentially dangerous, to leave.

Was leaving that simple?

Nothing in Russia is simple. It took me a year to get my visa. There was that much—pardon the pun—"red tape" to get through.

Did your homosexuality have much to do with your leaving?

It had a great deal to do with my leaving. In Russia, gay people are not supposed to exist. When they do, they are detested in an especially virulent way. In the one-dimensional vision of the Soviet authorities, homosexuality appears as an outrageous example of something totally alien to the normal state of things.

Is there a history for such an attitude?

But of course. In the 1930s Stalin began his total extermination of all people who seemed "suspicious," who revealed the slightest signs of rebellion or of being different. The Great Terror occurred between 1935 and '36. During that time, to make all of Russia subservient to him, Stalin murdered millions of people. *Millions.* He demanded, and got, absolute power. Not for Russia but for his own maniacal ego. Some of the most productive and brilliant died by the maniac's decree. Anyone counter to Stalin's thinking was killed.

Initially, the laws he established against homosexuals were the means to jail certain otherwise untouchable freethinkers. In January of '33, artists, writers and musicians were accused of homosexual orgies and sentenced to prison or exile in Siberia. The panic that ensued caused a rash of suicides in the Red Army. A federal statute which forbade homosexual acts under threat of imprisonment up to eight years was introduced in 1934. During Stalin's reign of terror, being homosexual was tantamount to being condemned to death.

Are there other factors which allowed Stalin to so freely persecute the homosexual?

Yes. The centuries-old puritanical religiosity of Russia caused homosexuality to be seen as a sin . . . something that was totally taboo.

And today?

Overt sexuality of any kind is almost nonexistent. In Russia, straights and gays grow up without any understanding of their sexuality.

Freud's name is known to few, his work to almost none. Thinkers such as Adler, Fromm and Kinsey are totally unknown even to the most educated of persons. Such ignorance, combined with the conservative, even conformist tendencies characteristic of Russian culture over the centuries, has proven fertile ground for the growth of negative attitudes toward homosexuals. They are considered freaks . . . savages . . . something completely hostile to the norms of the community—people to be punished or educated into conformity.

To the bureaucratic leaders, gay people seem totally bizarre, beyond understanding. Worse, they are viewed as threats to the system. Why? Because homosexuality is considered a sign of one's instrinsic freedom and that, of course, is dangerous.

Let me make more clear what I mean. To sleep with someone of your own sex in a country where that is politically and socially prohibited and persecuted—where you can reach the age of twenty-one without knowing there are such persons as homosexuals for all the evidence your environment gives of such a "phenomenon"—shows a great degree of inner freedom, the same inner freedom that characterizes dissenters. As a result, homosexuality and political dissent tend to become equated in Russia. In short, if you are gay, you are a potential disturber of the bureaucratic peace.

And the ramifications of being such a potential disturber?

Are so vast you would not believe. You run the risk of losing your job. After all, if your sex habits are that much out of line, there is no telling what you might do next. So, it is better to get rid of you, the homosexual, before you cause your employer any trouble. Americans cannot conceive of how horrendous it is to be fired in Russia because of "social unreliability." Almost no one will give you a job again. You either change cities and professions or you starve.

But certainly there exists some form of homosexual life?

True. But no one discusses it. In Russia, the paranoia is so complete that one does not even casually mention the word "homosexual." Translations of Shakespeare's sonnets always substitute "she" for "he" where "he" is intended.

Has none of the so-called sexual revolution of the sixties reached or affected Russia?

Russians have only a vague idea of sexual life in other countries. Publications like *Playboy* or *Playgirl* are prohibited. The same is true of pornography. In fact, an American friend, before I left Russia, sent me *Sex in the Movies*, but the authorities confiscated it.

Has Russia no radical young?

Not in the strict sense of the word "radical." There are many young people who react most negatively to this puritanical code but their "radicalism" is not encouraged.

Six to eight years ago, it was somewhat . . . how you say . . . "in" to be bisexual or gay. Now, it has become very difficult. But the majority of the young intelligentsia in Russia no longer wish to marry. Life is more simple when single. But, people do marry because the government demands it. Sex without marriage threatens the family structure and therefore threatens "Mother Russia."

Is there then no gay movement in Russia?

But surely you jest. No? Or are you too naïve? How can you even suggest such a thing? There are no protests of any kind in Russia. Once in my lifetime I remember four people congregating to protest against the Russian invasion into Czechoslovakia in 1968 and within a minute they were hauled off by the KGB, the secret police.

Before, you did say some form of homosexual life does exist in Russia. Where and how?

Men met on the street or in parks. Every major city in Russia has a known cruising area. Often, sex takes place outdoors, as there usually is no place for two men to go. Always there is the danger. The KGB haunts homosexual hangouts. They entrap beautiful young boys and then blackmail them into service. There are homosexuals used by the KGB throughout the world as informers. The Russians feel they must have many such informers in order to obtain information about everybody. Since most gays travel within the intelligentsia, what better way to obtain information on possible dissenters than to place a spy—a gay spy—within that environment.

It is very easy to intimidate gay people in Russia. There is no recourse if the authorities decide to imprison you. No lawyer will represent you. There is no Civil Liberties Union. You are considered a dead person. Risking repetition, let me reiterate: The Russian government hates homosexuals. We are "out of order"—out of the mold. And in Russia, all people must be alike. Differences are not tolerated.

To answer more fully your question, what gay life exists does so very privately and very cautiously. There are "salons" where gay men can meet. Orgies do occur, but rarely, as the most "liberated" at an orgy can be a KGB informer. The punishment for group sex, by the way, is eight years of confinement, three more than the "crime" of sodomy between consenting adults.

And prison for homosexuals is beyond your worst nightmare. A living hell. Gays are put with the most depraved of criminals . . . intentionally, knowing that when word leaks—and it always does— that they are homosexual, they will be sexually abused and perhaps even murdered. I have one friend who was nearly sodomized to death in prison. In one night, sixty men used him and the authorities did nothing. They allowed the murderers an outlet for their pent-up furies. My friend survived—he lived—but to this day, and it is many years later, he is still incapable of having sex. He is . . . how you say . . . yes, traumatized. Thus, when I say to be gay in Russia is to be doomed and damned, I exaggerate not. Blackmail is a fact of life, as is suicide among gays. Many try to defect. Still others arrange marriages with foreigners in order to leave.

It is amazing, given what you say, that any two men would risk sexual liaison in Russia.

Ah, but the need to love conquers all fear. That certainly was true for me. Besides, to live in Russia is to live with fear. It is a given, a constant and, thus, not always a deterrent. In my own case, my father was arrested in '47 when I was but a child. It occurred during what is now called Stalin's "Second Wave." Without having committed any crime, my father spent eight years in a labor camp. One year after his arrest my mother was taken, and only because she had protested too loudly my father's innocence. I did not see either of my parents again until 1954, after the death of Stalin, and when a general amnesty was declared. By then, I was an adolescent, one who knew that fear was a permanent condition of Russian life.

Did the war greatly affect you?

No. I was raised by my grandmother, an aunt and two governesses, behind the lines, away from the guns and bombs. My father had been very "noble" and we were not destitute. In fact, I was treated like a little prince . . . spoiled and shielded. My father had been an influential party leader and my mother a successful architect. Thus, I saw very little of them, which is not uncommon in Russia. So, I was not very affected by my parents' arrest. Since they were both professionals, working, and away from home frequently, I remember no feelings of

affection or love from either. All that I received from my grandmother and aunt. Basically, I was raised without a male influence on
my life and whether this played any part in my becoming a homosexual I do not know.

During your childhood, were you in contact with your parents?

At first, they wrote from jail, but when taken to the labor camps,
all communication ceased. It was like they had never existed. Then,
after eight years, they were again "existing," a part of my life. I became very close to my mother but not to my father who was, and is,
a cold and aloof man.

In retrospect, how do you view your childhood?

As a most happy one. I was doted on by the women in the house. I
was an eager student and was greatly appreciated by my teachers at
school. I got along well with boys my age. I wanted for nothing.

Do you recall sexual fantasies as a child?

No. A few flirtations with girls I remember but never was there any
feeling toward boys or men. But then, a Russian child knows nothing
of such things as homosexuality. There is never a discussion about sex
in school or at home. Sex, of any kind, has no place within the Soviet
system except as a means of communication and propagation between husband and wife.

Do you remember any fantasies as a child?

Oh yes. When very young, I wanted to be a ballerina, which I think
now was an early manifestation of suppressed homosexual emotion.
Later, I wanted to be a pianist and then a figure skater. When I
reached the university, I was already enthralled with philosophy and
wanted to both write and teach.

Is there dating among the young in Russia?

When I was a teenager, we socialized in groups. For a young boy
and girl to have sex then was unheard of. Today, although not common, it is not so rare either. So, in answer to your question of before,
I see that sexual liberation has come to Russia. But I was the excep-
tional teenager. At fifteen I had a mistress. She was thirty and our
affair was very glamorous, exciting and grand. Sexually, it was quite
stimulating, although it did not contain the passion I was later to
learn could exist.

You are speaking of sex with men?

Yes, although I repeat, I knew of no such thing when I was fifteen. I had no such fantasies and had heard of no such encounters. Oh, once one of my friends pointed to a man and said: "He's a pederast." I was mildly curious, the way I would be if someone pointed out a Polynesian or a Martian. It simply held no interest for me. Even when I met Alyosha in an art supply store—he was an artist—I was unaware of sexual interest. I was unaware that he was rather taken with me. But then, I was unaware that any man could be taken with a well-shaped and rather handsome young man—which at eighteen, I was. When I began talking to Alyosha about his work, when I promised to visit him in his studio, I was unaware that he had . . . how you say . . . designs. I was even unaware that he was a handsome man.

When did you become "aware"?

The morning after. I awoke naked in the same bed with Alyosha—and, although nothing had happened, as we had both gotten too drunk, I felt it strange that we should be sleeping together when there were other beds in the house. It all made me feel . . . how shall I say . . . peculiar, as though there was something unnatural in his feelings toward me.

How did you react to this?

With semi-outrage. I left his studio determined not to see him again. But, he called and he courted me. Despite my repeatedly sending him away, he would always return with gifts of books and records. He quite literally laid siege.

How did you feel about his attentions? Were you gradually aware of what it was he wanted?

The relationship embarrassed me, but I cannot say I was either appalled or interested. I liked him . . . as a friend. Anything further did not intrigue me. I had no idea of sex between men—no conception of what two men might do together. It was very strange . . . very conflicting. I did not want to be involved with Alyosha and yet, I distinctly remember my not wanting to lose him.

After a month of this, when I was sure I had successfully reduced him from my life, I attended a party with my mistress, got quite drunk and heard myself asking, to everyone's astonishment: "How many homosexuals are there in Russia!" To which someone replied: "Why? Are you thinking of becoming one?" Everyone laughed and their laughter loosened their tongues. Suddenly, everyone was talking about how so-and-so secretly was a homosexual. Some of the most famous Russian names were being bandied about. It was quite a revelation.

Suddenly, I felt very sick of my mistress. I behaved abominably by insulting her and then leaving. In the street, leaning against his car, waiting for me, was Alyosha. I still to this day do not know what he was doing there. I remember in my drunkenness being both furious and very pleased. We drove to his place where he proceeded to make love to me and by morning I felt this incredible relief sweep over me. I also felt very happy. All the time he had been courting me I had felt something gnawing at me, which I could never identify or make go away. That morning, it vanished . . . forever, and I felt alive in a very new way.

Was your sexual adjustment that easy?

How do you mean . . . sexually? Ah, no. At first, I did nothing. Alyosha, experienced at twenty-eight, performed orally on me. Only later, when I accepted that I loved him, could I do that for him. And with pleasure. But despite my loving him I could never be penetrated. So, we reversed roles and that was pleasurable for both of us. He was a most patient lover and understood that I needed time to make my sexual adjustment.

I never went through any feelings of guilt, however. Puzzlement? yes, but guilt, no. I did not understand what was wrong with me— and then, that is what I felt about men loving men, that something had to be "wrong." So, I began reading whatever psychology books Russian libraries permitted on their shelves that dealt with homosexuality plus whatever Alyosha's friends could smuggle from other sources. In my readings—Freud, Hirschfeld, Kinsey, but mainly Proust —I purged myself of all the clichés. I purged myself of the idea that homosexuality was a perversion.

Proust was truly the revelation of my life. He taught me that love is love and that if you feel it at all you are so much the fortunate one. And that was me. I was so much in love and therefore so much the fortunate one. Proust did more to help me understand my nature, and the nature of men loving men, than all the psychologists and their books put together. My affair with Alyosha lasted four years, although we did not live together. My schooling was in Moscow, while his portrait painting was anywhere a commission took him. But throughout our relationship, I never slept with other men. Only with women who continued to pursue me. I enjoyed that attention greatly. But in truth, in sex, I was always very passive with women. If they wanted it, fine. I never cared one way or the other.

What were the emotional differences you felt between sex with a man and sex with a women?

With women, sex, although pleasurable, was routine . . . mechanical. Not exciting. Never did it have the passion I came to know with Alyosha. In loving him, I suddenly found the male body erotic. Which is still so strange to me as I cannot recall experiencing any homosexual feelings prior to him. Sex with men is a very active endeavor on my part—very spirited and all-encompassing. When in love, as I was with Alyosha, it is also spiritual.

Could you have lived with Alyosha had you wished to? In other words, can two men live together as lovers in Russia?

Very rarely does that happen. It is much too dangerous. Too many people gossip. They would wonder why two men live together without women. Three men, or four, living together would cause no speculation, but two would make for nasty repercussions. You see, in Russia, privacy is not known. Everything is open for public inspection. Your life can be discussed at a committee meeting. And that can lead to arrest. Americans will find this hard to believe, but in Russia a woman can write to the committee to complain that her husband is not fulfilling his duties in bed and the committee will investigate. Americans have absolutely no concept of their own freedom. A week in Russia would teach them.

Of course there are men in Russia who do risk living together and everyone stares and gossips. Public intervention usually dooms the relationship. Truly, it is almost impossible for two men to love each other in Russia with any sense of completeness. Love is to be made where one can, when one can, and not always is it possible. Often, other than for such public and dangerous places as beaches and parks, there is no place to go.

Men do not have their own apartments in Russia?

The amount is so negligible that one can answer "no" to your question and not be incorrect.

What about hotels? Can't two men rent a room?

Hardly. It would not go unnoticed. Let me tell you about my youthful experience in a Moscow hotel. When I discovered Alyosha in bed with a "friend," I left him, and *all* men—or so I thought—forever. Within three months of this decision, I married. Nine months later, shortly after my son had been born, I began an avalanche of young men. One was a fairly famous French actor who had come to Russia on tour. I would spend day after day with him at his hotel. In a week, a chambermaid burst in upon us, found us in bed and threatened to call the police. Now, you may ask, how dare a chambermaid do such a thing? In Russia there is no privacy and a suspicious chambermaid has every right to enter without knocking.

When my French friend began to protest I quickly silenced him. Young as I was, I knew discovery could mean not only expulsion from the university but that my entire future career could be ruined. I phoned Alyosha, who came with 5,000 rubles—then worth about $600—he bribed everybody, promising to thrash me, his "younger brother," if they would just turn their backs this one time. They did. In truth, Alyosha saved my life.

To continue about hotel rooms, most cannot be locked from the inside. Just before leaving the Soviet Union I was enjoying a tryst with a delightful young tourist from Finland when again the chambermaid entered the room without knocking. This time there was nothing "indecent" but her presence. In other words, I was not in jeopardy. But I protested loudly at her rudeness. She became quite indignant and actually summoned the hotel manager who was equally indignant that I should think it necessary for her to knock before entering. Again, I risk repetition but I must reiterate: There is no concept of privacy in Russia. Secrets become known. One cannot hide.

During your marriage, were you able to keep your homosexuality private?

My wife knew nothing of my desire for men when we first married. In fact, she thought I hated homosexuals because I was so vocally against them when I spoke. It was a posture, a masquerade on my part to divert her from the truth. My wife, Vera, was actually quite naïve. She was a virgin when I met her and so ignorant of the facts of life that she became pregnant, which is why we married. Not that I was then reluctant to marry. At twenty-one I thought it might be . . . how you say . . . *settling* to be married and with child.

Vera knew nothing until our fourth year of marriage and then she received a phone call from a stranger informing her that when away on my various lecture tours I was dallying with young men. Which was true. As stated, shortly after Peter's birth, I became an almost voracious homosexual. And when I established rather quickly a reputation from my published works, I became much sought after by students and colleagues.

You cannot imagine the risks I took. Sex on beaches, in parks, in my own apartment when Vera was away. Soon enough word spreads via the . . . how you say . . . grapevine, yes? So I never knew who phoned Vera or why. I will never understand such a person's thinking. It put Vera through hell. It was a torture for her. She could not accept my homosexuality. You see, my wife loved me.

How did you feel during this time?

I led a typical double life and yet I never felt guilty. Should I have? Perhaps. Vera was a very good person. Our sex life was always pleasureable although never for me exciting. But then, excitement only comes with men so it was not Vera's lack. Prior to her discovery, we had sex four or five times a week. Afterwards, it varied. It truly depended on whether or not I had a lover. When I did, I could not, and did not, give her the attention she needed and deserved. And yet I was always a very responsible husband and father. I always supported them. Many times I felt I was depriving Vera of love she wanted and needed but I could not help her other than to offer sexual freedom. Initially she rejected this idea, but later she did take a lover. It was never a successful arrangement for her. Vera did not want another man any more than she wanted to share me with another. As I said, for Vera, my homosexuality was a source of constant torture. Particularly when people gossiped—and they did gossip. But, because I was married and the father of a child, I was beyond the reach of the gossips' claws. This is why gay men in Russia *do* marry. They must to survive—to avoid the gossip that can eventually lead to your destruction. There are very few single men in Russia because the bachelor is constantly harassed about his single status.

Did Vera ever ask for a divorce?

Initially, it looked like she might, although she did not want one. But she was quite inconsolable until her mother stepped in. She kept the marriage together by convincing Vera that "It is not the worst of events. He is not a thief or a murderer. He does respect you. And in his own way, he does love you." Which was true. I did love Vera as much as I was, and am, capable of loving a woman.

Vera eventually came to understand this. She also understood that to leave me would mean also leaving her position, which she liked. We moved in quite respected and social circles. My work gave me a status which Vera enjoyed. So, partly because her life would have been depleted without me and partly because she loved me, Vera stayed. In many ways, our life together was agony for her. She could never accept my sexual leanings. Often I offered her divorce, but as the years passed, she rejected that idea because she saw how attached Peter was to me.

It makes me very sad to speak of Vera today because I understand her pain. Also, I cannot tell you how good she was to me. Always, she protected me. No one ever knew of her unhappiness. She avoided gossip and scandal. Till the moment when divorce became mandatory because of my urgent need to leave Russia, she acted as my wife. She is a very good woman. She abided while the great love of my life took place during my marriage. It was with one of my students and despite his being straight, the relationship lasted for seven years.

> *How do you have a homosexual relationship with someone who is straight?*

Not very easily, I can assure you. It was months before he would let me embrace him. More than a year elapsed before he would come to bed with me. But he never really liked our sex. I had been his teacher. . . his spiritual leader at the university. He had idealized me into the perfect father even though I was but twenty-four myself at the time. Objectively, our sex life was terrible and yet, it was wonderful. Never have I known such love. He was not only beautiful physically but mentally he was most exciting. A brilliant boy! But he was always frightened and discomfited by our relationship. And I felt that as I also felt his love. That has always confused me. How can one love somebody—be that body man or woman—and not want to translate that love sexually? For me, when I love, that is such a necessary form of communication.

> *Why did the relationship end?*

During the fifth year we were together sex became so distasteful to him that I began looking for it elsewhere. As I did, he became more and more remote until he finally married and became, literally, a stranger to me. We would see one another and never speak. It was very hurtful.

Can a homosexual live in Russia without his homosexuality coming to the attention of the authorities?

I sincerely doubt if anything goes undetected by the authorities in Russia. I myself, I was to learn, was well known to the KGB and had two brushes with them. In 1965 the KGB tried to enlist me in their ranks by implying that I knew and trusted too many foreigners. They claimed the British Intelligence Service was interested in me, which, if true, was news to me. Then they suggested I keep records on a certain Italian student of mine. When I refused, the agent confronting me said, "You must understand. We do not wish to hurt your professional standing. We do not wish to *but* . . ." It was a very clear "but." Yet, I resisted. But, they persisted. Every six months to a year, they would ask me to attend certain lectures in Europe. What they really wanted was for me to spy on those in attendance. When I repeatedly refused, they used their trump card. "You know there are these rumors about you and certain young men . . ."

I instantly cut them off with "Ah, but that was years ago and I am happily married now." I refused to be threatened, which is most unusual behavior for a homosexual in Russia. Not that I am so brave, no . . . but, I knew, from having lived with the threats made to my father and mother, that one could survive the Russian tactics . . . the horror.

Of course, they could have had me jailed on some false charges, but as I said, that would have resulted in worldwide repercussions. Instead, they harassed me. They would not let me defend my doctoral dissertation and thus I was denied my Ph.D. Later, when they denied me visas to visit foreign countries where I would attend or give lectures, I knew it was time to leave Russia. Slowly, they were taking away whatever freedoms I had. And even as I applied for my papers, they tried to disconnect me. They spread the rumor in my circle that I was a KGB agent. Although very few believed them, enough were convinced to keep their distance for the good of their own being.

Of course, these events took place over a series of years. During that time I was pursued by a most beautiful young man who was quite articulate, educated and seemingly sensitive. We had a most impassioned affair for a week. And then, one night, in a drunken stupor, he confessed that he was a KGB agent who had been forced into service when his homosexuality had become known. In other words, he had been entrapped and now had become the entrapper. He was bitterly crying, resentful of his fate, but I could feel nothing but loathing for him.

"It is a filthy business," I said as I threw him out. "But how was I to know I would become involved with you?" he protested. "What am I to do? I have no recourse?"

And in truth, perhaps he did not, but I simply couldn't tolerate his being an informer. I could not sympathize. I was now in jeopardy yet I was not frightened. Again, not because I am brave, but I knew had he exposed me and my not very friendly attitudes toward Russia, I could have exposed him, for he verbally had shared many of my sentiments. It was a stalemate. He kept his mouth shut.

From what you say it would seem that to be homosexual in Russia is among the worst fates to befall a man.

Agreed! Yet, paradoxically, Russian homosexuals derive a certain benefit from their oppression. They have not internalized from childhood the assumption that they have two inalienable rights: privacy and independence. Therefore, they do not display the fear of intimacy and flight from responsibility which are so prominent in the West and virtually endemic to the gay scene here. To be responsible is a moral duty in Russia. To ruin a love affair because of a fear of intimacy or responsibility is virtually unheard of. There are enough external factors to ruin love affairs without the participants needing to add their neuroses to it.

You are now speaking of the fundamental differences between the Russian and American homosexual.

Correct. When I first arrived here a year ago, I had much casual sex. It is so available here. Then the novelty wore off and I was prepared to embark upon a more serious encounter. In San Francisco I become most infatuated with a handsome young intellectual. For a week we were inseparable. Then, without a word, he disappeared. He just broke it off. He felt our love was catastrophic. I was most hurt. It was then I realized Americans want intimacy but when it is offered they run. The fear of involvement is very widespread. Such a terror of getting close!

And Russians have no such terror?

In Russia, gay life is so difficult that if you are fortunate enough to meet someone you like, you treasure him and the relationship. You do everything you can to nurture it. Here, the more men have, the more they want. Yet, the less they have. Never before San Francisco have I seen such desperate men—men who search for love but who are unable to love. They do not trust. I ask myself, why? Is it they fear the pain that love can bring? But that cannot be, because to live life is to risk. Love is such a risk. But you do not fully live if you do not love.

That could be deemed a very romantic point of view.

Undoubtedly, but there is a great accent on love in Russia. Gay men trust one another there but, then, people in general are closer. Here, everyone has some forbidden ground upon which you have no right to intrude. Society here is more formal. In Russia, where privacy of any kind is unknown, there are less formalities. People, and in particular gays, need one another, and affection, to survive.

The world of feelings here seems untouchable. In Russia, because warmth is so desperately needed, any contact between people is seldom solely about sex. There, one must have support. Not to say that we do not have the quick and anonymous sex in Russia, because we do, but it is different. Always one receives a name. Always there is some communication. Here, so often, it is a "No names, please" situation. I recently met a young man in a known cruising area near Harvard. Being me, I made polite conversation, which he cut off with "I didn't come here to talk. Do you want to fuck or not."

In Russia, people also come to places to "fuck." But, always there is a meeting of another kind. There is more interest in another's needs . . . another's personhood. Here there is much callousness. People tend to . . . how you say . . . get their rocks off without much caring about their partner's rocks. For me, this is incomprehensible. Although I am not a particularly warm person, I am a man who is interested in my partner's *being*. Americans seem to resent that. They feel invaded by that kind of interest.

You are speaking of "Americans" and of "people." Are you therefore including women?

Yes. Although I am primarily homosexual, I am not exclusively so. I have numerous affairs with women, although I do not pretend that they have the same physical intensity as the affairs I have with men. The women I have known here have the exact same fear of closeness, of intimacy, that I described in gay men. There seems to be little difference.

Do Americans appear to be more promiscuous?

Very much so. Particularly homosexuals. That is one of the pitfalls of all this freedom gays enjoy here. There is an overabundance of *goods,* which has resulted in oversatiation. Except enough is never enough. One continues to dine at the banquet even though one is not hungry. Here, you can change your sexual partner every night if you wish. Sex in America is included in the consumer system. It is like breakfast or television—something taken for granted to have, to buy, to do. Something to consume. One pays, I fear, a great price for this kind of consumerism. One loses something from within. At first it is a hollowness, an unexplained frustration which accumulates. It is very strange and very deep. It seems to result in a pining for love but an avoidance of same.

But I must add, I do believe that if given the same freedom, Russian men and women would be no different. In other words: If the same opportunities for sex existed in Russia, the consequences of this enormous freedom I believe would be the same.

> *In America, a part of the homosexual population is very involved in "leather" and sado/masochism. Is that so in Russia?*

But of course. Except no one can afford leather, so you never see it. But we have as many people—men and women—involved in sado/masochism in Russia as you do here. I do not believe sex habits greatly differ anywhere in the world. But I have no understanding of this S&M phenomenon. And to me it is that . . . a phenomenon. True, intellectually I understand it, but emotionally, it is totally alien. I believe in "lovemaking" and not pain-giving. I believe in closeness, not distance. Here, people are so much less inhibited in their sexual behavior but so very guarded in their emotional giving. In Russia there is much more kindness and far less objectification. The person is appreciated and valued more. Here, much is about costume . . . the Western or leather look. Your Marlboro man. Only he does not exist.

> *After a year's residence in the United States, how do you view homosexual life?*

I am most disenchanted. I've stopped going to bars. At first they were exciting. So many men in one place. That is unheard of in Russia. But so few proved to be interesting. Today I much prefer the baths if it is sex that prompts my actions. They are quicker, more honest and less pretentious. But I do not go there to meet people because one generally can only meet a "body" at the baths. The same is true at the bars. The "people" stay home. It is the "bodies" that attend. And never have I seen such desperate faces as those of the men of forty-five and fifty-five in gay bars. The older the man, the greater his desperation, his terror. The loneliness is there, hardly hidden, in his eyes. It is very difficult here to be old and to be gay but then, other than Italy where the person is valued, that is true of everywhere. The accent is on physical beauty. Often I think gay life is only for the young. As you age, you find you have less and less to offer on the buying market.

Is this one of your fears?

Strangely enough, no. Age is not a bother. I am very clear with my-self as to what I can get and for how long. My head is not filled with fantasies. I understand the physical side of gay romance is very im-portant. And as you get older, you become more vulnerable because it becomes more and more difficult to be someone's physical ideal.

There is much cruelty in aging but one should never deny his age. I am aware and accepting that the beauty I once had is now lost to middle age. Not that I am unattractive but I am no longer a beautiful young man. But that does not make me sad. I face the future soberly. I will never be a sad old man, haunting bars, seeking any kind of companionship. I view old age as a time of great productivity, of great dignity and of friendship. I see it also as a time when one turns to help others reach their own pinnacle of productivity. So my friend, I may sleep alone one day but I will never be alone. My life *now* is very rich . . . very full. I do not feel lonely. So many wonderful new friends in America. Vital people live here. My work is beginning to . . . how you say . . . score points. It is a good life.

Do you feel any lack in your life?

I miss my son . . . very much. I also miss being in love. It is such a lovely time. But I am not upset by my not having a lover. I am still exploring my new "lover"—this country.

But indeed, I should like to love again, although I have hardly re-covered from that crushing disability of what happened in San Francisco.

Your wordage, "crushing disability," could you explain?

Well, I was such an assured person . . . had such self-confidence until this boy. He made me feel a hurt, a special pain that I had never known before. Nor do I know if I ever wish to feel such a pain again. I am terrified of such distress.

Ach! But I see! That is how it begins. Am I really now so different than the persons I have previously described? I see very clearly how one can become afraid of intimacy. So . . . I am not so different. But, I am not so young that I can stand the pain. It is easier to be young and rejected than be old and the same.

Do you always choose young men rather than peers for relationships?

Yes, I have very strong paternal instincts. Of course, I also have very strong attractions for the young, male body. But even when I was twenty-three and twenty-four I preferred the father role. Psychologically, men my own age do not satisfy me. I think I am born to be a father—to give other young men what I myself never received from my father: interest, acceptance, guidance. I love to teach. I love to help. I like to invest my energies in young minds. I have this intrinsic need to help young men. I receive emotional fulfillment from the role I play.

How to further explain. . . . I do not need anyone to take care of me but I do need to take care of someone. Basically, as a lover, I am the husband. I believe in psychological roles. I need to be the man in the house. It is my pleasure to be responsible for another person.

But doesn't an affair with a much younger person place you in a kind of jeopardy you might not experience with a peer?

Ah, but of course. The young tire of a lover very quickly. They are not ready to be settled, to think of permanency. The young are mercurial. The very fact that they are young makes them unafraid of the future. Also, one can be blinded by youth and its beauty. But most often, I am not. I know if I am to have a lasting relationship, I must find body and soul in the person. In Russia, that is much easier for a man like me who prefers the young. Here, the young men are much more independent. Very few need the "influence" and care of an older man. Thus, the chances narrow.

It is very interesting to me how, as I speak, I recognize a lack in my life, a feeling of incompleteness because I am not with a lover. Like now, there is a feeling that something is missing that can be found. I have not yet lost the hope to find somebody. It could happen tomorrow or happen never. I accept both possibilities.

Is it possible that a feeling of completeness might be attained through a relationship with a woman?

I think not. I know many homosexuals who have married as they have gotten older to avoid being alone. But that is not me. I cannot feel complete unless I feel excited about a person. Just being with *some-one* is not the answer. My true excitement is only with a man. Then only do I enjoy both a physical and emotional enjoinment . . . a totalness of pleasure.

I think what we are now discussing is an American malady . . . this fear of growing old and being alone. There is less family here, fewer ties with the state and the church. But I have yet to catch this malady. I do not fear being alone. Nor do I feel my life would be un-fulfilled if I do not meet The Great Passion. My life will always have great meaning and a great sense of fulfillment because of my work . . . my writing. I have great hopes for my future.

Do you have hopes to see your family again?

Ah, but that is painful. I do not care about my father. Once I disliked him but now I hate him. He fought my leaving Russia, delayed my departure by refusing to sign a form which declared he was not de-pendent upon me for his survival. Which he was not. My father is financially secure. Eventually, he signed but only with a stream of curses. He felt I had become anti-Russia. He was right.

My mother I miss. I do not think I shall see her again. We remain very close. She knows . . . understands. She is not like my father who is what we call a "Soviet square." She is not limited. She knows I am a homosexual and has never condemned me for it. But she has feared for me. She had a gay friend who was exterminated. She fully knows that to be gay in Russia is to carry a burden of double servitude. She understood that I had to leave. It was with her blessing. I want very much to see her again but I do not know if that will be possible.

Vera remains a wonderful friend. Truly, there is a great love be-tween us. Toward the end, she was very supportive. She saw that my leaving Russia was as necessary as drawing air to breathe. We speak on the phone frequently as I am in constant touch with Peter. I miss my son greatly.

How did you feel about leaving him in Russia?

Terrible. Very guilty. But, I had no choice. He could only have ac-companied me had Vera legally renounced her motherhood. Had she done so, she'd be considered a criminal. So, despite his attachment to me—and he was very attached—I left him. Even today, he under-stands. At fourteen, he already shares my political opinions. Just as Vera understood how I had to leave Russia, she knows that one day Peter, for his own life, must do the same.

When we speak on the telephone, I feel great sorrow. He was upset by my leaving and he is upset at my absence. We miss one another. We had a unique relationship. I was always available to him. Always we shared communication. I was often an absentee husband but I was never an absentee father. Thus, we have a mutual bond and I am sure he will come to the U.S. one day. Sure, I say. That is ironic. As though one can be sure of anything with Russia. Tomorrow, the curtain could fall again and that would be that.

How would you feel if Peter were to be homosexual?

But he will not be. He is, how you say here, very much all boy. But, to answer your question, I would not want him to be gay. It is too difficult. In Russia, it can mean incarceration. Here, it means rejection of a very poisonous nature. Despite all the freedom that exists here, the atmosphere regarding homosexuals is polluted. What father wants that for his son? Not me.

Will you tell him of your homosexuality?

Yes, when he is older. I do not want any secrets from him. This is a most intelligent and sophisticated boy. I believe he will be an even more intelligent and sophisticated young man. He will, I am certain, understand. I want and I pray for the day of his arrival in this country. His future will be very bright here.

Other than Peter, have you other regrets about leaving Russia?

Not a one. For so many years I suffered from cultural deprivation. No more. Life here is . . . how you say . . . swinging. There is so much thought . . . so many people active in their own pursuits. And that is such a gift! Here, I am allowed to fulfill myself. Here, I am allowed to make my life matter to *me*, first, *not* to the state. Which is wonderful because if my work is good, the state, society, will then benefit.

Truly, the question—regrets about leaving—is almost ludicrous. Yes, there are problems in America, deep-seated prejudices and prohibitions, but nonetheless, one is free. I can live here as a homosexual not necessarily with societal sanction but at least without fear of being sent into exile or imprisoned.

Regarding America: If I were condemned to work as a waiter for the rest of my life I would welcome that honorable position rather than return to Russia. Here, despite whatever the political, social and economic problems, one lives!

Richard Berger

A MILD-MANNERED Communications specialist by day, Richard Berger * becomes the mighty-man-of-financial-steel as he labors at night for the first literate-rather-than-lewd magazine for the homosexual population. At sixty-five, he doubles his pleasure and doubles his fun with his double life.

No miraculous change transforms the daytime Richard Berger into his evening counterpart. No matter what he wears, he continues to look like everyone's Uncle George or Harry. A medium-sized man of large cheer, he is more bald than not, myopic and considerably slow on the verbal draw. Thoughts are savored internally before they are shared.

Richard Berger makes no attempt to look younger than his years. His clothes are exactly what you would expect Uncle George or Harry to wear. Richard would be comfortable, even today, in the Brownsville section of Brooklyn where he was born but which he fled at sixteen to take his own apartment in Manhattan—a rather revolutionary act for a young man from a Russian/Jewish orthodox family in the 1920s.

I was always a rebel.

You say that proudly.

Yes, well, I made my own way . . . my own life, all my life. I hated my father and although I knew of no one who had left home at such an age, I did.

What were the problems between you and your father?

He was a cheap, miserly man. We lived without heat and electricity although we could well afford it. He treated my mother like a live-in domestic. The children, of which there were six, were raised to do his

* See Author's Note, page xii.

bidding. His dream was that we would one day support him as he desired. Happily, none of us did. He was a tyrant.

Where and how did you live at sixteen?

Quite nicely. I was running a debating society in Harlem and helping out at a children's center on the Upper West Side. They provided lodgings. Mornings I attended college. At seventeen, I was operating the West End Theatre, which then was like an off-Broadway house, and earning enough to get by. Summers I worked as a dramatics counselor at various summer camps. Believe me, I was much happier on my own.

Since you say you hated your father, was yours an unhappy childhood?

No, not in the large sense. I was very close to my mother, as I was in my early years to my brothers and sisters. Also, I was always very popular. People liked me and I liked them. Lots of friends, always. And I also was admired, as I was a very good student. I skipped half my grades in public school. So . . . although I never had a father, I had most everything else.

What were your interests in college?

English and speech. I thought then to be a playwright. I was always interested in theatre. From an early age, theatre has played a significant role in my life.

Why are you laughing?

My choice of words. When I was a kid, maybe twelve or so, each Saturday I'd go to a neighborhood movie and each Saturday I always managed to find a man to sit next to who I could fondle and who would fondle me.

Were there gay movie theatres in the 1920s?

If there were, they sure weren't in Brooklyn. No, I just had this sixth sense from a very early age as to which men would enjoy being with another male.

Then your homosexuality began early?

Yes, but I didn't know that's what it was. Looking back, I realize now I was always gay. My masturbatory fantasies were either about men or trips to Mars. You make the connection 'cause I can't. But although my feelings were homosexual, I never heard that word until my late teens.

Did your homosexual feelings bother you?

Not as a youth. That didn't occur until the war years and my experiences in the Army. Then the doubts began. Till then, I found it natural and enjoyable. My first affair occurred at summer camp. I knew at the first staff meeting that if I visited the athletics counselor later that night, something nice would happen. And it did. All summer long it did. I was fifteen and he was twenty-seven. When the season was over, so was the affair. I died, as the young do. But I recovered, as the young also do.

Incidentally, a pattern emerged with that relationship that has never altered. Oral sex was my thing. The Greek way, although tried, was never my way. Also, I've always been more interested in my partner's orgasm than in my own. I don't know why and it has never seemed important, as I have always enjoyed my sex thoroughly.

Another interesting fact. Up until that first affair, I had no idea what men did in bed. You hear a lot about "The Roaring Twenties" but they didn't roar that much if you were gay. Homosexuality simply wasn't discussed. Or seen. It was something clearly not acceptable. Actually, it required great ingenuity to have a sex life. Mine was about brief encounters—men met in subway trains and on the streets. If there was a gay society—and I think now there must have been—it was very well closeted. I probably would not have been involved even had I discovered its existence. Then, as now, I prefer mixed company.

Did you ever date women?

As a matter of fact, I did. But the dating ended when they wanted the sex to begin. And that never interested me. I have no regrets either. I figure if sex with a woman was something I really wanted to have, I'd have had it. But I always enjoyed the company of women and I even proposed to two. That happened after the Army when I started having serious doubts about whether the homosexual lifestyle could give me long-term happiness.

I assume your proposals were declined?

Happily, yes. I think I always unconsciously chose women who I was fairly certain would refuse me. I don't think I'm likely to propose again.

Since you came out quite young, were you able to deal with it?
Meaning: you were living on your own, supporting yourself,
attending college. How did it all mesh?

Although I was really a good-looking young man, I never got overwhelmed by sex. As you said, I was self-supporting. I had to finish
school. Sex was confined to hit-and-run affairs. I conserved my major
energies for my schooling and my work and I never felt deprived because I loved both. Even when I had spare time, I was more inclined
to spend it with my new family, the friends I had made on the job
and at school.

Your "new family." What happened to the old?

We drifted apart. Once I left, other members set off on their own.
For reasons I have never understood, the brothers and sisters became
distant, which was also rather new for the 1930s when "family" was
still the backbone of society.

How do you remember the thirties?

Happily I was young, because when the stock market crashed, everything tumbled with it. My theatre folded and I was faced with the
job of surviving. With the cheek only the young or foolish have, I
opened a publicity shop despite my having zero experience as a publi-
cist. Yet, I secured enough accounts to eat irregularly, but at least
to eat. In 1933, when the government funded the Federal Theater
Project, I was hired as an administrator. The theatre was located
where the Cherry Lane still stands. I moved to the Village and spent
wonderful years living and learning in that environment. When the
war broke out, the project was scrapped and I slowly starved until I
enlisted in the Army in 1942. There, at least, I knew I would be fed,
housed and clothed.

Anticipating your other question about the '30s, although there
was considerably more mention of homosexuality, it was still not
something one discussed casually or lightly. The concept of coming
out did not exist, as most homosexuals were rightfully very paranoid
about their sexuality. Even with one another. You seldom told your
last name or where you worked to a stranger you met. That was
taking too much of a risk. Then, discovery of your homosexuality
could mean a loss of your job and a loss of all respect.

I do not recall there being any gay bars then but there might have
been. I do recall a few speakeasy kind of places—private clubs where

men gathered quietly. Mainly, I recall salons where on Saturdays and Sundays homosexuals met to discuss the "lively arts"—among those arts . . . sex. I enjoyed the salons. Lots of interesting people frequented those private parties. I met partners there.

Could you describe the Village as it was in the thirties?

It was very bohemian, as opposed to gay. Lots of writers and artists, some of whom were homosexual, but that was not the common bond. It was a tight little community devoted to thought. There certainly was none of the open cruising you see today. Mainly you went to lectures and poetry meetings to meet people—men and women. And the theatre, too, was a place for contacts. "Respectable" best described the '30s. Like if there were orgies—and there must have been —they were unmentioned. People in those years didn't speak openly of their sex lives. But even if they had, orgies, had I been invited, would not have appealed to me. Sex has mainly been rewarding for me when there has been some kind of communication in addition to the sexual.

As a "really good-looking young man," what was your social and sexual experience in the thirties?

I was quite active, but mainly with a series of lovers. I have always preferred being with one man for however long a time to being with many. My love affairs, alas, never seemed to last. The sex would be good long after the communication was not. After X amount of months to a year—that was the longest—there would be nothing more to say and the relationship would slowly dissolve.

Was that then upsetting?

Not as much as it should have been. A pattern formed in those years that has remained. Always, I was more concerned with friends, with that sense of "family," than I was with a lover. It is as though unconsciously I felt one was permanent while the other was not. Then, too, I have always liked people—many people. I could never devote all my energies to one person. And I don't mean sexual energies. My intent from the beginning was to form lasting friendships. I believed in the long haul that would make for a much happier me.

Did it?

Yes, I believe so. Today, at near sixty-five, I have many friends and feel very much a part of many people's lives. I am not alone unless I choose to be. Let me make something clear. I always enjoyed sex and had a great deal of it. But it was never among the top three on my priorities list. Maybe fourth, however.

Earlier, you mentioned your doubts about the homosexual life-style emerged during your military service. Why did this happen?

I entered the Army expecting to have no sex at all. The first day at Fort Lewis in Washington where I was initially stationed, I had sex with a "straight" guy—one of my bunkmates. And that typified my one year in the service. I had one affair after another. And when I say affairs, I mean that. I didn't give blow jobs in the bushes but knew most of these men, played cards with them, joked with them and worried about the future with them. In other words, there was communication *always* with the sex. Except when women were around. Then, there would be communication and no sex.

Not that all my sex was with straight men. I met a number of attractive gays at Officers Candidate School, where I became a lieutenant. I took a lot of chances but when you are twenty-one, you do some foolish things. But I was never reckless. When I was stationed in Riverside, California, I took an apartment so that I would have a place for my affairs.

Were there gay bars in those years?

There were once I walked into them! Actually, the '40s gave birth to those mixed kind of places where straights and gays would congregate. You could always score if you had enough patience and seductive powers. I had both. There were always takers for what I had to offer.

Was most of your sex one-sided?

In the manner in which you are speaking, yes, but I never thought of it as such. You see, I was never the local "service station." I was usually friendly or friends with the men I made love to.

Was part of your attraction to these men the fact that they were straight?

I'm not certain. I have always been attracted to very masculine men. In those years, straight men seemed to have that quality more than gays. My lover of the past twenty years . . .

You never mentioned a lover.

Well, I'm mentioning him now. His name is Dan and he was straight when I met him. I was teaching a course in communications and he was one of my students. That first night of class I asked him to stay afterwards. He was young, married and a recent father of two. Within eight months, he was also my reciprocating lover.

Is he still married?

Oh yes. Very happily so. In fact, he is soon to be a grandfather.

How often do you see him?

Once a month at best.

Is that sufficient?

Only when I am with him. When we were younger, we were able to spend a few hours together each week. As he has aged, his sense of family responsibility prevents this.

How does this make you feel?

Relieved.

You're laughing again.

Yes, well, the truth is I don't think we'd have lasted twenty years had we seen each other more often than we do. We make much better lovers than we do friends. In other words, sexually it's terrific. Intellectually . . . not so good.

Is it then about sex or love?

Ninety-nine percent of it is sex, but each time I'm with him, I fall in love all over again. Obviously, ours is not the standard relationship. But perhaps it is really what I want. Perhaps it is all I am truly capable of.

Do you believe that?

I don't disbelieve it. I don't know. It is hard for me to know as I've never suffered because of his inaccessibility. It's allowed me freedom to pursue all my interests. I've never felt alone or abandoned, as I've always had friends with whom I could spend holidays and birthdays. Also, I am fortunate in that I am a very self-contained person. I can live alone and like it. I find there is too little time to do all I want to do. Now whether I set this up to avoid loneliness, what matter? I'm not lonely and that's what counts. I have many relationships instead of one. And these relationships have been the cornerstone, the foundation of my life. Like when I was placed under house arrest in the Army . . .

You've jumped . . . considerably. Why and how were you placed under house arrest?

Let me finish what I had started to tell you and I'll explain. Even when I was placed under house arrest, my fellow officers, the guys I went to school with, came by to offer emotional and professional, if possible, support. They knew where I was at but I was their friend first and whatever else came second. *That* got me through what was an awful time.

Now, to answer your question. One morning as I was returning from a week's leave, I phoned to ask about my assignment and was told to confine myself under house arrest. I was not told why. I was never told why. I never was confronted by an accuser either. I was simply offered a court martial and a dishonorable discharge or a quiet visit to a psychiatrist who would obtain for me a dishonorable discharge. I chose the psychiatrist. Wisely or unwisely, I decided not to fight. I wanted out. I was *that* hurt, that bewildered and *that* frightened. It wasn't getting thrown out of the Army that bothered me as much as that what-will-I-do-once-out. Particularly with a dishonorable discharge.

Do you know, it never occurred to me then to use my rights as a citizen and demand to know who my accusers were. I just knew there were "complaints" and that they were of a sexual nature. In the '50s, I finally got angry and I hired a lawyer. We reopened the case and I saw my file. There were five affidavits accusing me of homosexual activity. Four of the five were lies, trumped-up charges by men I hardly knew. The fifth was real . . . too real. It was by a "straight" man who had been a willing bed partner but who claimed in his affidavit that I had gotten him drunk and seduced him. In reading these falsified documents, something became quite clear. Someone wanted me *out*, but I never knew who. It no longer matters today, although the injustice does. But then there are so many injustices a homosexual faces in his lifetime. I never *abused* those men, as the affidavits read. Nor did they abuse or use me. We gave and took our mutual pleasure. But try to make the world understand that! We tried for two years and lost.

How did you manage once you were discharged?

That is exactly it—I managed just as I had from the age of sixteen. I fended for myself. I found someone who was able to secure honorable discharge papers for me and a "ruptured duck," which was a lapel pin the honorably discharged wore. I was also able to secure, illegally, veteran's financial aid, and I used the money to attend announcing school in Los Angeles. One week after graduation, I was giving the news and weather in San Diego. Six weeks later, I was the station's program manager. It was only after I was financially secure —knowing I could earn my keep—that the reactions to what had happened in the Army began to take place. It was then I began questioning my future as a homosexual. It was a questioning that was to go on for a decade. It was a torturous time. And an angry one. In San Diego, I found myself doing something I had never done before —picking up sailors and soldiers and *using* them like candy. For the first time, the person became unimportant. It was a revenge mechanism, although I didn't know it then. Happily, it didn't last long. But the brooding about my future went on and on. It was the kind of brooding many homosexuals then went through. In those years, a man who was gay had to hide it at all costs. Jobs were lost because of possible deviation from the norm. Then, too, a man without a "little woman" behind him had little chance of real advancement. He was passed by for promotions. Also worrying me was the transient life many homosexuals seemed to live. Shallow best describes it and them. Were either really shallow? I doubt it. More likely, fear kept people from revealing their real selves. So I worried about growing old and ugly and bitter and lonely and alone.

When did you begin to resolve some of these fears?

Ah, but that is the blessing of years, of learning as you age that nothing is as black or as white as you make it when you are young. As you turn gray, you can begin to see the grays. It's wonderful. Most of my fears proved groundless. I have had a long career in the communications industry and although I have never come out, I'm sure many of my employers suspected. In truth, some may even have cared but I think they cared more about my professional expertise. When I reached fifty, I suddenly realized, not overnight but gradually, that most of the fears that tortured me in my thirties belonged to those years. I was not alone or lonely. There were many consequential people who shared their lives, as I shared mine with them. What did prove to be true is . . . one can be alone at any age, regardless of sexual preference, and one can work or be unemployed at any age. Of course it is true that it becomes more difficult to find a good job past forty, but it is not impossible. I lost one four years ago and within weeks found another quite comparable in money and status.

In maturing but in not getting old—there is *that* difference—I found a very different life because gays, as a group, were experiencing a very different life-style. In the '30s and '40s we had no group identity. It was hard to be gay and have self-respect then. Today, in being around so many young people who are gay at the magazine, I see how the pendulum has shifted.

I've been rambling, I'm sure. But what I'm trying to say is . . . my fears resolved themselves. Aging makes you take yourself far less seriously. They say you get set in your ways as you get older but I have gotten more flexible. I've loosened up on me. I roll with things far more easily today. As I acquired an emotional and intellectual approach to life, all that soul-searching ended. I'm far less concerned with me today than I am concerned with the quality of life and what I can bring to it for others.

> *In looking back at your military experiences, the ones you have spoken of, what do you feel about them in retrospect?*

That no man who is straight has to worry about a dishonorable discharge because he is a heterosexual. That no man who is straight need hide the fact on his job. But who is "straight"? Is there such a person? And if there is, so what? Homosexuality actually began to creep from its closet during the war years. Men without women, when thrown together, are going to play. Unfortunately, some of these "players" are going to hate themselves the morning after, but instead of staying with their self-hatred, they turn it on the "fags." In other words, because they cannot deal with the desires that were turned on within them, they turn against the person who turned them on. They lie to themselves and believe me, they do lie. I was there. I know. I heard what many of these straight men yelled or groaned at point of orgasm.

> *Are you bitter about the dishonorable discharge and the fact that your accusers were never made known to you?*

I was but I'm not any more. You see, it has been, *and is*, a very good life despite what happened.

I caught the emphasis placed on "and is."

I want that made very clear. I am well aware I am your "older" or "old" man in your book. Neither term offends me, although I most certainly don't feel or think of myself as old. I feel I am first embarking on another life. And if I take after my mother, I will live till ninety. I hope and expect to be very productive—to actually experience a new career in publishing. I do not think of these as my twilight years. Hardly. They've never been brighter. Thus, if you are looking for the sad, old, lonely homosexual so popular in fiction, look some more. But, if you are looking to discover how one elderly man lives at sixty-five as a homosexual, I can help you.

Suppose you tell me about your life today and I'll ask questions as they come to mind.

Mainly, what I think will surprise many is that I feel this continuous excitement about life. The magazine has opened new vistas for me. Working with these young men and women has been an awakening . . . stimulating intellectually but far more so emotionally. The editor, Billy, is a remarkable, brilliant and forceful young man. He's also a beauty. The same could be said of many of the other editors. What makes them all to a person so beautiful is the openness. They are unafraid to be themselves . . . to be who and what they are. It is extraordinary to be around such people and to see such changes in one's lifetime. Years ago, we took such great pains to hide our homosexuality. Today, that is so much less true. Few men use "beards"—women who will act as your girlfriend—and equally few will dress according to a heterosexual norm. But these changes are minor in comparison to what I feel is the most significant difference between gays of today and yesterday. The young men and women I meet at or through the magazine have pride in themselves. They accept their sexuality and because they accept themselves, they accept others. Seldom do you see the paranoia I previously described. Today, last names are exchanged. Today, few are afraid to say . . . this is where I work . . . this is where I live. In more ways than most people, even gays, are aware, there has been a collective coming-out.

Could you explain that last statement?

Look at the scores of gay clubs that exist in New York. And they all do very well. In fact, the gay cabarets and discos have influenced the entire entertainment field today. But what gays seem to be saying by their mass support of these places is: Look how strong and united we are. I see solidarity within the gay community. Going to a gay bar today is almost like a mass rally. Years ago, to be gay was to feel on the outside of things. Today, the gay community is like an extended family; sometimes I think too much so.

Why do you say that?

Too many gays concentrate solely on being gay. I think those people experience only a quarter of what life can be. Many gay people live within the gay ghetto totally cut off from other relationships. That kind of defense—and that's what it is, a defense against rejection and humiliation—is detrimental to any minority group. You become frozen in one mode of thinking. You live encased, encapsulated, cut off from the mainstream. Your full potential goes untapped. As I said, I understand this defense but I can see the day when it will be unnecessary. Years ago, as I described, no one spoke of or knew of the gay community. Homosexuality was not discussed. But today, anyone of intelligence is aware that gay people exist. Both the press and television have given Americans a passing acquaintance with gay America. And this is good because from acquaintance comes knowledge and from knowledge, hopefully, comes a diminishing of prejudice and finally acceptance.

Have any of these changes you spoke of rubbed off on you?

Funny you should ask that. Just this week, Billy suggested that perhaps I was being too open with too many people after too many years of being closeted. In recent months, I have found myself coming out to friends of many years. I must admit I have been more than surprised that not a negative word or feeling came at me. But because I now work for a very conservative company, Billy feels it is best that I exercise considerable caution there.

From the way you speak of him, I assume Billy is a very significant person in your life.

He is that indeed. Our is a rather unorthodox coupling. Not too many sixty-five-year-old men live with a twenty-five-year-old. But it works for us and it is a strictly non-sexual relationship. We met two years ago when the magazine was still in its think-tank stage and we found many mutual interests. Eighteen months ago, we decided to take a two-bedroom apartment and to date, it has been a very satisfying arrangement.

Would you say that in some way you are feeding one another's respective emotional needs?

I believe so. Certainly, Billy feeds mine. Through him, because I was so much like him, I feel I am reliving my youth. Not that we cruise together, because we don't. That's not the kind of "reliving" I mean. It's the talking out of issues, working away at some kind of philosophy for living. I think I am giving him the kind of relationship I would have liked to have known when a young man. I give him as much emotional support as I can. He needs the stability of a good home. I am both father and mother to him at times. I enjoy that. I feel I can help him to succeed as an editor and writer. He is already a success as a person.

Yes, Billy is very important to me. He is the family, the son, I never had.

Since, as you say, he is attractive, does that ever produce conflict within you?

If you mean am I ever jealous, the answer is no. Sure many of his young boyfriends are very attractive, and yes I wouldn't mind a little dalliance with a few every now and then, but frankly, just every now and then. I wouldn't want his sex life at my age. Who has that kind of energy? When I was Billy's age, once a day was hardly enough. Now, once a week, if I'm lucky which I'm not, is more than sufficient. Sex is no longer a motivating factor in my life.

But when it is, where do you go to obtain it?

I don't. At my age, it isn't healthy, helpful, safe or desirable to put myself in any of the known cruising situations. A mature man is very realistic about what he can and cannot have sexually. I prefer young men. Yes, because they have beautiful bodies, but also because they have young minds. I am not yet a dirty old man but I haven't ruled out the possibility. But what I'm saying is even here, the motive is more emotional and intellectual than sexual. My attraction to the young is because usually they think young. They aren't boxed in as so many of my peers are. Most older men dry up, stop growing and stretching. They live out their lives rather than *live* them. I can't be around those kind of people. I have never tried to hold onto my youth physically but I do try to hold onto it intellectually and emotionally. I could see no purpose in living if I didn't.

But regarding my sex life, I put zero effort into the chase. I am not interested in pursuing paths that inevitably lead to rejection. And ninety-nine out of a hundred times, the older man is rejected sexually. Not only by the young but by the old. We are the discards, wanted by few and feared by many. Very few people can face the inevitable fact of their own aging.

How does that make you, as an older person, feel?

I'm not bitter about it. I understand. I also prepared for these years by thinking them through prior to their arrival. I knew as I aged, it would become progressively more difficult for me sexually and socially. I accepted that. The only time I get stuck in a self-pity rut is when I take a narrow view of me, which you can do at any age. The minute I attach more importance to sex than I should, I'm in trouble. Sex really is a much smaller part of life than most people, particularly the young, know.

But a man of sixty-five does require some sex, doesn't he?

Of course. We're not dead, you know, just older. But the truth is, at sixty-five, a good chess game becomes as important as a sex encounter and a lot easier to obtain. I don't expect you younger guys to understand how chess and sex can be equally enjoyable but I hope someday you will.

Do you rely mainly on masturbation for sex?

Yes and no. There are times when I meet a willing bed partner. Usually that occurs at a dinner party or some kind of social event where there is relating on a personal rather than a solely sexual level. That happens rarely, however. But then, so does masturbation. Somewhere between the need *arising,* so to speak, and my remembering what to do about it, the need disappears. As you can see, I don't take my sex life very seriously today. I am not one of those older men who wear hairpieces or corsets or makeup. I do not try to be young and groovy because I'm not. I feel sorry for those men of my age or thereabouts who try to be what they are not—who need sexual acceptance in order to feel good. I refuse to chase the butterfly. I have discovered as I have grown older that there are comparable stimulations and satisfactions in life.

Such as?

The young will scoff at this, but . . . such as the thrill of discovery, learning, of really being alive and absorbing all that sits there right under our noses day after day but which we don't see. If one wants to stay *in* life, one must grow, sharpen his senses to appreciate all there is. And believe me, there is so much more than a beautiful body to admire. How can I explain? . . . If you just open your eyes, older age can be wonderful. I do more today than I ever did. Of course I have more time in that I'm not out pursuing sex as I used to. Actually, the last time I bedded down with anyone was six weeks ago with my lover, Dan. So what? Sure I would like to have sex more often but I would also like to have a million dollars. I manage to live quite nicely without either.

Do you ever feel the need to be held . . . to be touched . . . kissed with tenderness?

Very often, yes, I do. And that is difficult. Years ago, I would have done anything to quiet that need. Today . . . no. I live with it. I will not let down one standard to obtain it. When those times occur, they are painful. I try then to be with friends who give me what they can although it is not the same.

Can you give nurturance to yourself?

Some, but the human need to be touched or held, I don't think one can give to oneself. But that can be a problem at any age. You can be twenty-five or thirty-five and if you are not in love and loved, no matter how much sex you have, that need to be touched remains unfulfilled.

Is your relationship with Billy about nurturance?

I never thought of it as such but, yes, it is. My love for him nurtures me. He really is my son. He so needs to be understood. He has a great deal of gay pride. Often, he is ready to do battle at the drop of a slur.

You know, had I been straight, I'd never have the kind of son Billy is to me today. As a surrogate father, I have no desire to confine or constrain him. My wish is to help him fly his own course in life. I do not treat him as many fathers treat their sons. No. I treat him as an equal. This is a very special young man. He is going to effect major changes for homosexuals in this country. He is devoted to that cause.

Does the possibility of his leaving to live on his own or with a lover ever enter your consciousness?

Of course. I would expect one or the other to happen as a natural course of development. It wouldn't shatter me. I have always, mainly, lived alone and I could live alone again. And not unhappily. The prospect is not frightening. Perhaps it would be if I were an isolate, without friends, but such is not the case.

What about as an older person living alone? Is there a fear of infirmity?

Yes. That and the fear of losing your job are probably the two worst fears an older person faces. But you can't let the worry consume you. You take care of those things that you can—like your health and your medical insurance premiums—and you get on with living.

Are you financially secure?

No. I must work to live. Social Security would not cover my expenses. Actually, I view this need to work as a positive rather than a negative. Because I *must* earn my keep, I remain vital. Retirement can often mean retiring from more than one's job. Financially I have far less security than I do emotionally. And I would choose that every time. I do not fear death but I do fear not living.

Many people as they age turn more toward religion and God. Is that applicable to you?

No, I have not "found God" in my old age. Religion to me is a business, a big business. God to me is a worthwhile concept that has been abused. I do not believe God is an all-powerful, judging, to-be-worshiped-and-obeyed deity. But I do believe there is some kind of life force, a creator, and a moral code by which people must live or else they find their own punishment. I very much believe in the do-unto-others kind of religion. I have always tried to do that.

One of the accusations often leveled against the homosexual lifestyle is that it is a selfish one . . . without contribution.

If you do unto others as you would have others do unto you, there can be no greater contribution. The most any one of us has to give is of ourselves. Today, I do that within my relationship to Billy. I also bring as much of me as possible to all the people with whom I work and socialize. I have been a stimulating or aggravating force in many people's lives. I have helped many to find and then make their *own* changes for their *own* betterment both professionally and personally.

The argument that heterosexuality is less selfish because of the "contribution" of children to society is a stupid one. My father was not atypical of many parents. His children were possessions. He contributed nothing to them. He wanted to take from them. He wanted them to be what *he* wanted them to be. If that is contribution, then I'm dealing from a different dictionary than most. Do you know, years ago, when I was thrashing out my own homosexual identity, I fell prey to that kind of stereotypical thinking. It was nonsense then and it is now. It was also nonsense to think one couldn't live a fulfilling life as an older homosexual. One can! One also can't. Meaning, it is up to the person. If one wants to "age well," one will. If I can climb up on a soapbox—and since I'm old I'll take advantage of my rights as a senior citizen and do that climbing—age is not to be feared. As I have been saying, life is not over because you are wrinkled, shriveled and bent. There are all kinds of outlets for gratification. It may take a new blueprint for living to find them but so what? Basically, what it's about is living in the present and not ruminating about what you might have missed in the past. It's the here-and-now, not even tomorrow, that matters.

If we could ruminate for a moment, what do you regret or feel that you missed?

I have very few regrets. Certainly I do not regret having been gay. Although that has its obvious minuses, it has its not so obvious pluses. A gay person because he is without family and without societal approval often learns to live with and by himself and by his wits. Because he is not tied by family obligations, he usually can remain more involved in life, more vital. A gay person, because he is accountable to no one but himself, has life as a perpetual banquet before him. What too many fail to see is that some of the more delectable morsels on life's plate are not genitals.

The obvious question is . . . have I missed not having had a long-lasting relationship. Not as much as I should. I do not suffer because I do not have it. Yet . . . I am not so old that I have given up hope. Love might be right around the corner and if I remember to wear my glasses, I might even recognize it. But I'm too busy to knock myself out looking for it. Yet I sure wouldn't run from it. And it could happen. Why not? I'm an oldie-but-goodie who is more than willing to act like a puppy again.

Andrew Allen

I̳ᴛ ɪꜱ ᴀɴ apartment of windows with no draperies, blinds or shades to shield its occupants from the life below and beyond. Andrew Allen,* a thirty-two-year-old analyst, shares this castle-in-air with Joe J., a writer and his lover of three years, and a dozen clients who visit for fifty minutes at a time.

Born and educated in Brooklyn, Andrew is currently a therapist and supervisor at a major mental institution, a position he has held for eight years. Previously, he was director of a major rehabilitation program for handicapped children in the Northwest. In his work today, Andrew supervises the staff therapists and their therapeutic group activities as well as running his own groups, one of which is exclusively for homosexuals. Andrew's private practice is composed mainly but not exclusively of homosexuals.

This year Andrew will finally complete his formal training in a new method of treatment that accepts much Freudian theory as a fundamental basis but focuses on problems rooted in pre-Oedipal periods. The four-year full-time program—Andrew took ten, part-time—requires the potential candidate to be in analysis while he is in training and afterward to retain some form of supervision in his treatment of clients.

Andrew most certainly does not fit the stereotypical picture of an analyst. With lots of shaggy curls framing a near-cherubic face, he resembles a hip teddy bear. He is a large man of quiet composure. His strength is something one feels rather than sees. His anger, however, is visible. Often it is about the treatment—professional and otherwise—that homosexuals receive in this country.

Andrew knew "at ten that I was a homosexual and that to be such a 'thing' was both aberrant and abhorrent. Society, in the spoken and unspoken word, made me feel that. I grew up hiding . . . in pain and unhappy."

His father was a baker who barely earned enough to support his family working for a baking company. Andrew remembers him as "a distant figure . . . a man guarded in his feelings . . . mild but

* See Author's Note, page xii.

with a potentially explosive temper." He recalls his father's love, never receiving it but loving him anyway.

He was his mother's "little genuis . . . toilet-trained at two weeks, talking at three, if one is to believe her." Before he was five years old he was studying both dance and the accordion. Throughout his schooling he had private tutors so that he could maintain his 95 percent scholastic average. "I was the 'perfect' son who needed to hide his imperfection—his homosexuality. I loved my mother but I felt her love was conditional, dependent upon my constant achievement."

Andrew claims to have "fooled them all" with his "fantastic social façade. I was charming, outwardly aggressive and inwardly . . . falling apart, a boy who had turned all his homosexual feeling against himself. I thought I was bad. I had to be. It was sex, wasn't it, and sex was never discussed. Not in our house. Sex was seemingly far too awful to allow into consciousness." He recalls masturbating regularly while fantasizing about boys, undressing and perhaps even touching them. In high school, although very popular, he did not date but was aware others did. By college, he was alienated, alone and frightened. "By then I knew sex was something nice people engaged in, but I was too frightened to be one of those people."

But that changed during his sophmore year. Women were the focus of his sexual attentions even though he continued to fantasize about men. His relations with women were always "satisfying," and one relationship that spanned two years "gave me my first recognizable feelings of romantic love." But because of his sexual conflicts —the fantasies he could not accept—Andrew began treatment with a psychologist in the hopes of working through his homosexual tendencies. At twenty-five, when his fantasies demanded a release, his therapist said, "Andrew, I'd hate to see you become one of *those* people."

"Within a week I terminated treatment with him. I sensed he had deep-seated sexual problems of his own just from that remark." Within another week, Andrew allowed himself to be seduced into his first homosexual experience, "with an extremely kind and sensitive man who sensed it was my first encounter. After we had made love, he gave me his phone number and said, 'If you become upset and need to talk about what just happened, call me.' Today, belatedly, I thank him for that. But I never called because I was far from being upset. Quite the contrary. I was ecstatic. All those years of self-hatred—all those negative judgments I had placed on myself for my homosexual feelings—eroded. You see . . . within that beautiful experience I saw clearly who and what I was and that both were good, not bad."

Over the next four years, as Andrew worked with a Freudian analyst, he explored his homosexuality both on the couch and "in the bars, streets and baths. I went through a period of great promiscuity —the proverbial kid let loose in the candy store. I indulged myself completely. It has only been in the last five years that I have stopped indiscriminately stuffing my face with the goodies."

Three years ago, in a Village bar, Andrew met Joe. He almost didn't talk to him because "he was dressed in black and I thought he might be one of those leather persons." But they did speak and they did make love that same night, "and since then, I have seen Joe every single day." But not without trial.

"Joe and I actually had a courtship period after that first night. We had to. In the past, sex always clouded the issue for me. I could never see the person clearly. This time, because I had very positive feelings for Joe, I asked if he would go through a period of sexual abstinence with me so that we might know one another on a different level. He agreed, and here we are three years later. I can assuredly tell you Joe is the best thing that has ever happened to me. He is a strong, secure person, a rarity in that he has access to his feelings. He is neither threatened by nor jealous of my work but understanding of the passion, and thus the hours, I bring to it. He has his own interests which he pursues and develops. We share a mutually healthy dependency while we each maintain our independence. Ours is a relationship of equals with no defined roles. We are whatever it is we wish to be on any given day. Although we are frequently together, we just as frequently are not. However, ours is a totally monogamous relationship."

Why have you chosen monogamy as opposed to an "open marriage"?

Not being monogamous makes it easy to fuck but it does nothing for developing or maintaining the relationship. Like most men, I can get turned on by almost any attractive person. Thank God! A great deal of my prior therapy was devoted to accepting that I do have lustful feelings and then to accepting that I need not act on those feelings if to do so is not in my best interests. Today, I make the choice *not* to act on the attraction. Today I know it would not be in my best interests to screw around. It would take me away from this relationship. You see, when you're involved in a non-monogamous relationship, you can always meet somebody "better" and then somebody even "better" than that "better" person. That way, you need never work at making "better" what you already have.

Then you believe in monogamy for all?

I would prefer to say I am in favor of putting a halt to other sexual activity if one truly wishes to allow what one has to develop and grow . . . to nurture it slowly.

Do you ever feel confined by the "bounds" in your relationship?

No. Actually, this relationship has been the most liberating experience of my life. Joe and I lead separate lives. We come together— figuratively and literally—when we wish. Previously, I used to think being part of a couple meant some form of symbiotic attachment— that everything had to be done together. Not so. I am free. Joe is free. We explore interests independent of one another. What we don't explore is other sexual interests. We have found this the key to maintaining our intimacy.

Your courtship period . . . would you advise it for others?

I not only would but I do. I believe in anything that will allow people *desirous of a relationship* to know one another out of bed. I'm all for dating and long engagements and cold showers. Sex should come last. Most people, and I'm speaking here of heterosexuals as well as homosexuals, have no idea of the *real* person in bed with them. I am beginning to believe we have an inborn resistance to knowing. We all have our panics but getting truly close to another person seems to be a universal one. And sex, which should be the ultimate in achieving intimacy, is now most often used as a barrier to the knowing, to the getting close.

It does not sound like you hold much respect for today's sexual liberation.

It's bullshit because it doesn't exist. In my work I encounter many people who can fuck and few who can have successful ongoing relationships. I fail to see how one can be sexually liberated if his or her feelings are bottled up. Most people are divorced from their feelings, so how can they be exercising their real choices—in bed or out. Nearly all of us brought up in this country are raised with far too many restrictions. We are not allowed to feel or express anger. We are not allowed to feel or express sexuality. We are not allowed to feel or express most of what we want. Early in life we become governed by psychological traps. Because we do not receive the proper nurturance, acceptance and love from our parents, we then seek it in our husbands, wives and lovers. They, of course, cannot fulfill these needs and thus, the relationship crumbles. That is what I meant when I said most of us have great resistances to knowing who that other person beside us in bed truly is. We prefer, often, to ascribe qualities to him or her that simply don't exist. Then, when disenchantment sets in, we set out . . . to fuck. That is easy, but to do it in a meaningful fashion is not.

Is this particularly true of homosexuals?

This is particularly true of all people. Part of the myth, legend, prejudice and just plain horseshit about homosexuals is that they do not fuck in a "meaningful" way. That's the kind of accusation that hangs heavy on homosexuals and is but one of the reasons why I choose to work primarily with gay men.

Could you explain that more fully?

There are many therapists who are not qualified to work with homosexuals because they have not adequately dealt with their own homosexuality, their training not requiring a personal analysis of their own. In many of these cases the homosexual feelings remain unexplored and repressed. Homosexuals frequently get raw deals in treatment because of these therapists, which is why I choose to be of service to this particular group of people.

Do you believe homosexuality is an illness?

Homosexuality *and* hetrosexuality are problems for those who, one, experience them as such and, two, enter into relationships based for the most part on the need to fulfill needs not met by a parent or parents. In other words, the man or woman looking to another man to be "daddy" will experience difficulties in the relationship.

Do you believe homosexuality can be cured?

The question is as infuriating as it is prejudicial. To speak of a cure is to consider homosexuality as aberrant behavior—as though there is something "sick" that needs remedy. From my understanding of all research done to date, there is absolutely no proof that homosexuality is an illness, and it offends me personally and professionally when people think otherwise.

What, then, of all the causes found to explain homosexuality?

You mean "causes" as one would find the "cause" of polio. There are none! Many have been put forth as possibilities but absolutely none have been proven. What interests me is . . . why has no one looked for "causes" to explain heterosexual behavior? That is automatically subsumed under "Normal Development." Who says? Why? How do we know? The theorists who develop these theories on homosexuality are, for the most part, heterosexual, heterosexuals who are investigating a minority group. They are not content, or able, to look at this group as different but must, for their own reasons, consider it different *and* aberrant. In fact, in developing their theories, these men look for evidence to support their theoretical contentions.

I, as an analyst and theorist, could proclaim that people who develop as homosexuals are really the healthy people and that it is the heterosexual who is aberrant. If I spent enough time developing this concept, I could probably produce a theory to support it. So what I am really saying is that there needs to be more impartial, scientific investigation before we can have any real understanding as to why one becomes hetero- or homosexual. I know of nothing so far to make me believe either is aberrant, but I see much to support my belief that *both* may be valid forms of sexual expression.

Would I be correct in assuming you are not that concerned with cause?

Yes. My concern is in helping the patient to reach, get in contact with, all his thoughts and feelings and to act on those he deems to be in his best interests. And if he decides to follow a homosexual lifestyle, then I would support that choice for him. But I, myself, as a therapist, have no "grand design" for my patients. My work is devoted to helping people become feeling people so that they can make their proper choices in *all* things. I am not interested in changing or converting a person's sexual orientation unless that person wants change or conversion.

In working with a large homosexual population, have you found a particular shared problem?

No. There are no problems indigenous to the homosexual. With one exception. No one straight has ever had to face their parents and say "Mom and Dad, I have something to tell you . . . I'm a heterosexual." *That* is often a problem indigenous to homosexuals.

What about paranoia?

Only in the sense of "discovery" is the homosexual more paranoid than the heterosexual. And for just reasons. No one penalizes the heterosexual when they "discover" he is straight. But the homosexual risks loss of security, status and love.

Basically, what you are expounding is that there are no problems central to homosexuals.

Correct! People—all people—have difficulty with their aggressive feelings. From birth, we are not taught how to deal with our aggression. Most mental illness is caused by the inability of people to deal with this aggression. And all people, consciously or unconsciously, have murderous, aggressive thoughts, usually repressed and denied. Yet, we come into this world angry, as well we should. We leave the warmth and safety of the womb only to be greeted by a slap on the ass. That begins the aggressive feelings. But never, not from that moment throughout childhood and adolescence, are we ever permitted to express what we feel. These negative feelings go inward and often we turn them against ourselves. Equally often, we grow up fantasizing our murderous thoughts into sexual acts or patterns of acts. The problem arises when one feels the need to act on the fantasy. Which is what sado/masochism is about—people's acting out of their aggressive fantasies. Which is a pity. Better it should remain as fantasy.

Why?

Because if one confines one's aggression to masturbatory fantasy— plays it out that way—it then leaves room, hopefully, for the warm, gentle feelings to emerge when with a partner.

Have you observed a rise in homosexual S&M activity?

There has been a rise in all S&M activity. Certainly S&M is not a homosexual phenomenon. Heterosexuals were involved in it long before it crossed the sexual fence. Neither personally nor professionally do I see S&M as positive behavior for anyone. We all have the tendencies—the murderous, aggressive feelings—but as stated, they are best left to fantasy. I believe we dehumanize ourselves when we dehumanize another. And, if we allow another to dehumanize us, then we are dehumanizing him in the process.

Do you see the baths or the sex bars as dehumanizing?

Just as I see the singles bars and the "Encounter Weekends" and the "Singles Cruises" as potentially dehumanizing. In sex bars, men reject the ritual—the drinking, talking, proposition and leaving for more "respectable places"—to get down to basics then and there. It may not be the best possible behavior but is it any less objectionable than going to a more "proper" bar where the means may differ but the end result does not. In other words, what I am suggesting is that if you are out for an evening's fuck—if that is your motivation—then there is little difference perhaps in the environments.

The baths are a multi-faced phenomenon, places to relieve horniness for some, and for others, places to reinforce guilt. For still others, they are places to escape—mainly from themselves. I'm all for getting laid and if people want to do it with ten people instead of one, fine! But, the danger in the baths is in *not* seeing them for what they are.

Which is?

Wonderful places to have multiple, anonymous sex . . . if that is what you want. And that, of course, is the problem. Is sex what really drives a man to the baths? I suggest that he should know before he goes. Because if he is looking for love or "deep relating," he is looking in the wrong place. The guidelines then become: What is it I want? Can I get it here? The baths are pure hell for lonely people. The anonymity of the sex reinforces their loneliness. Unfortunately, many people would rather experience the baths instead of the loneliness. They would rather have body contact with a stranger than emotional contact with themselves. They cannot *bear* to feel their loneliness. They cannot bear to feel their pain. The baths for many is like taking an aspirin . . . a temporary relief. If these people were in treatment with me, I would not seek to take that aspirin from them. To do so would be dangerous. A patient should be allowed his defenses until he is ready to give them up.

Are you then saying the baths are a defense?

For many, yes. They are a defense against feeling. For some of these men, to feel their own pain would result in psychosis, which is why, as I said, I allow my patients their resistances until they are ready to drop them.

But suppose one is not in therapy?

Then he may never drop his defenses. He may not even know he has them. He may run to the baths two or three times a week and think he is having a ball. His defenses prevent him from seeing himself and his true motivation for frequenting the baths.

Before, you labeled the baths as a homosexual phenomenon.

Because they are in that there is no *exact* heterosexual counterpart. As yet, there are no bathhouses men and women can frequent to get it on in multiple encounters. Yet, what do you think those well-advertised "Encounter Weekends" are about? Basically, they're group fucks. The Singles Cruises also evolve into "bedroom farce." Sex in multiples or sex used as a defense against feeling one's own true self is *not* a homosexual "thing" but a *human* condition. In other words, as I keep repeating, there is no sexual phenomenon that is the sole property of homosexuals. Watersports—golden showers —have long been a popular pastime with straights, as has been anal intercourse. I would wager more dildos are bought by heterosexuals than homosexuals and . . . they are used upon one another with equal verve. Really, we homosexuals are not very unique. The sole difference I see is in alienation. Since we know we are not, as homosexuals, going to be accepted no matter what we do, often we act outrageously in what we think are acts of freedom but which are actually acts of rebellion, and thus we become more unacceptable and thus, even more alienated.

An explanation, please.

It may start with simple hand-holding and end with public displays of fist-fucking. If hand-holding is going to cause rejection, why not really give them something to think about! Often, that is the misguided feeling—not conscious, but there nonetheless. In our quest for acceptance, which is constantly denied, we taunt our oppressors. Unfortunately, in the taunting, we do damage to ourselves. Instead of creating sympathy or understanding, we create hostility, and, as I said, further unacceptance.

Often, it would seem, homosexuals seem attracted to the "dangerous" in sex, often risking muggings, murder or arrest. Why is this?

Not just homosexuals. The character in *Looking for Mr. Goodbar* is not unlike many young women today who indiscriminately pick up men they do not know and take them home.

Straight or gay, there continue to be people who are attracted to danger, and for many reasons. None of which are good. Many seek to get caught—although they are unaware of that intention—because unconsciously they feel sex is bad and that they should be punished for their evil thoughts and actions. Deep within, because of parental attitudes imposed on the child, these people feel sex is dirty. And by the way, what better place to reduce sex to a dirty *and* dangerous experience than in a public john. For some of these people, the sex is secondary to the "thrill" of the threat of danger.

There is yet another motivation for some involved in public sex. It may be their seeking mastery over a particular situation. Meaning: these same people may have been caught masturbating as children and were punished or humiliated severely; now they attempt to overcome the impotence and rage they felt when caught and chastised.

And lastly, sex in public johns seems also to be associated with childhood attitudes toward bodily functions. As children, we cannot play with our shit, which most children want to do. Nor can we shit in our pants, although the *urge* may be there. Shitting can be a highly pleasurable sensation. Thus, it can be thought of as, and confused with, sex. What better place to play all this out than in a john?

But again, what seems like a homosexual phenomenon is not! I guarantee you that if there were co-ed johns the same thing would occur.

> *Then you do not believe this has anything to do with homosexual promiscuity?*

It is often maintained that homosexuals will have sex any place that two horny men can get it on. That's bullshit. It's part of the myth, legend and prejudice of which I spoke. Homosexuals are no more or less promiscuous than heterosexual men. Their opportunities for sex are just greater and thus it appears as if they are more promiscuous.

Till recently, not only was promiscuity the property of man but it was a not-so-secretly condoned and admired action. The macho heterosexual brags about his scoring. It was long thought man is more promiscuous by nature than woman. We are in the process now of finding out whether that is true. Till recently, women have not been as willing to hop into bed with the rapidity and frequency straight men would like. Thus, these men did not have sex as often as they desired. Had it been available, they would have been every bit as promiscuous as gay men who find one another willing partners. It is because of the availability that homosexuals appear to be more promiscuous.

Does this "available" promiscuity prevent relationships from lasting?

You are now speaking directly—and indirectly—of yet another myth: that the homosexual, because of his nature, is not capable of lasting love. That, too, is horseshit. My relationship is now better than three years old. I have every hope it will last, *in love,* for many more years. I know homosexual couples who are celebrating their twenty-sixth year together. I know others who are lucky to last twenty-six days. Homosexuals and heterosexuals share the same capabilities and, in some cases, limitations, for lasting love. It is, however, more difficult for homosexuals to have ongoing relationships because there are still no ground rules. We have no marriage certificate or social sanctions to bind us. No children hold us together, which, of course, is both a plus and a minus. It takes a tremendous amount of learning for two men to live together successfully, much more so than a man and a woman, as *all* men are trained from birth to be the bread- winner and the dominant factor in their homes. Thus, conflict can arise between two males who are lovers. It takes a great deal of winding down of roles for a relationship between two men to work.

You mention roles. In speaking strictly of those that are sexual, are there meanings to be found in preferences for the active or passive roles?

If you mean does the primarily passive personality in bed tend to be primarily passive out, the answer is yes. Generally, these people let others take over. Often, in treatment, just from the way someone describes his life, his position in it and attitude toward it, I can tell what his sexual preference will be. Interestingly, I have noticed that men who were married and then become homosexual tend to be passive in bed. It is as though they are saying, "Now it is my turn to be taken care of." There is also another type, one who aggressively attacks life professionally and socially, who then gives up the attack sexually in his need to be comforted . . . cared for.

But please, just a word of caution about labels. Often, being active or passive in bed can be forms of giving and taking. It can be a sign of strength and it can be a sign of weakness. *But,* the truly healthy personality needs to be both. He needs to give and to receive. He is that rare person who allows himself to feel all his feelings and can thus act in his own best interests.

In other words, no person feels the same from moment to moment. The healthy person pursues what he needs at a particular moment. If it is to be wildly aggressive one night, terrific! But if another night, it is to be a blob—and we all have those nights when all we wish to contribute is our presence—that's terrific too. Sexual health as I see it is being able to do whatever we wish and need to do to attain fulfillment. So many people are limited in their sexual expressions and responses because they either deny or are not in touch with their wants and needs.

Lastly, I tend to pity those who think they are more masculine because they are exclusively active in bed. I suspect they are denying one half of themselves. Also, the active/passive role-playing is not just a homosexual occurrence. Sorry, but as I keep saying, we are not unique. In heterosexual lovemaking, the roles may also switch from time to time.

But in homosexual relationships, doesn't the fantasy of the "stud"—the macho male—play a big part in the sexual acting out?

Yes, but the transference feelings for the all-powerful father are again not an exclusive homosexual phenomenon.

Could you explain?

Many women seek to marry the fathers they never had. They look for a certain strength or compassion they did not get from their fathers in their lovers and husbands. As previously stated, most people who become involved in a relationship seldom ever really see the other person for who he or she really is but ascribe assets and qualities to the partner that simply do not exist. Many men seek to marry their mamas, while many women seek to marry their papas. The "idealized significant other" is hardly again a homosexual phenomenon.

Is it also a myth that the homosexual has far more pain . . . is much unhappier, than the heterosexual?

Absolutely. Homosexuals, however, are frequently more vocal about their pain. Often, they are more in touch with their feelings than a heterosexual male.

Why would that be?

From childhood, men are raised to be strong. Unfortunately, strength, till recently, has been equated with showing no emotion . . . having no feelings. All men have feelings. But the homosexual, because he is societally considered to be something *less* than a man, allows himself the expression rather than the denial of feelings common to many heterosexual men. It is rather ironic that it is society's very oppression of homosexuals that *frees* us into being a generally more feeling person than a heterosexual male. The irony is twofold because the person who allows himself to feel and express his emotions is the healthier for it. But make no mistake. Scratch deeply and you will find the same amount of pain in a heterosexual as you will in a homosexual.

> *But doesn't the climate of opinion in this country create a pain within the homosexual that the heterosexual never has to deal with?*

Indeed. And it does present an obstacle to happiness and contentment. But to those homosexuals who wish to solely blame society for their unhappiness, I say bullshit! Depending on who you are and what you have going, you can deal or not deal with this climate of opinion. For some homosexuals, it is a lifetime of torture because they *need* societal approval. But these people would be tortured no matter what because they never had approval of any kind at any time in their lives.

I believe the child who is raised with the proper love and feelings of acceptance can come up against the brick wall that society erects and either chip away at it or walk around it. Each person reacts to that wall with however little or much he received as a child. The wall is not insurmountable. However, life would indeed be far less painful for the homosexual if the wall did not exist, but to say all ills are caused by this wall is irresponsible and untrue. The real ills begin in childhood and that is true for all "ills" and all people. In the groups I run at the hospital—one exclusively homosexual and the other not—the problems and issues discussed are the same. People, regardless of their sexual preference, are concerned about achieving intimacy, developing relationships, learning about their inner selves, removing blocks to learning and success. Invariably, in both groups and in all individual therapeutic hours, each person must come to grips with his or her sexual feelings . . . toward *both* sexes.

Then you believe man is potentially bisexual?

In his ability to feel his attraction to both sexes, yes. If I did not help a homosexual during treatment to feel his perhaps hidden attraction to women, I would feel remiss.

Why?

Because often this unaccepted sexual attraction, when denied—repressed—comes out as fear and/or hostility. Why should any homosexual feel uncomfortable in the presence of women? If he acknowledges his feelings, chances are he will not feel this discomfort. Similarly, when heterosexuals accept their homosexual leanings, they usually become far more comfortable in the presence of homosexuals.

But I want to make one thing very clear. As a therapist, I am not interested in people pursuing relationships with opposite or same sex members. I am *only* interested in their accepting *all* their feelings and then acting on those *they* feel to be in their best interests. Invariably, straight or gay, clients wish to move toward meaningful relationships. Straight or gay, they tend to set up structures in which they can live meaningfully. And if, as a therapist, or as a person, you come across a relationship that is working, how dare you, or anybody, say that it is wrong because it involves members of the same sex!

Why do you think society continues to say same-sex relationships are wrong?

Because their own homosexual feelings are so unacceptable to them that they must punish those who threaten their own safety. If you think about it, why should my relationship with Joe bother anyone? What skin are we off anyone's nose? The answer is none. But, because we stir up very repressed feelings—longings, in certain straights—we are objects of hatred and fear . . . fear of self-discovery, of the realization of their own homosexual tendencies.

Of course, some women experience another feeling. They become hostile to homosexual men because they are unavailable objects. They feel rejected.

Do women tend to accept homosexuality in their sons with greater ease than men?

There is no evidence to support that statement but from my experience I would say it is true. Actually, again, without evidence to support this statement, I would say, based on experience, women, in general, have an easier time accepting homosexuality, in themselves and others. They are not as threatened by the possibility.

Do most parents have a sense of a child's homosexuality?

Just as many do as don't. Frankly, I think there are more parents who *don't* want to know than there are gay children who want their parents to know. In my own case, my parents don't know. Yet, if they *really* don't know, I'll eat the chair I'm sitting in. My attitude today is to tell them as little as they want to know, which seems to be very little indeed. To tell them outright—to make a formal declaration —would be cruel. They really don't want to handle more than they do. If they did, they would ask me, who is that man who answers the phone in your apartment. But they never have asked. Nor, by their choice, have they visited my apartment in three years. We meet elsewhere for lunch or dinner. An old saw holds true here for *them* —ignorance is bliss.

What is the nature of your relationship with your parents today?

Comfortable. I no longer view them as All-Powerful People from whom all blessings flow. Therapy freed me from that childlike point of view. I deal with them today on an adult level. I have come to realize . . . painfully, that they can never give the child within me what he wants—unconditional love and acceptance. In realizing that, I have become free to accept whatever it is Joe is able to give me. And he gives me a lot. In his feelings toward me, there is a consistency I never knew as a child. His love is not contingent on my "continued success." I don't have to achieve anything to be loved. I don't always have to be "good."

How much do you credit therapy for the seeming success of your relationship with Joe?

Without therapy, there would be no relationship—not with Joe or anyone else. I would still be wrapped up in the negative feelings— the *only* feelings I had access to for the bulk of my life till midway through my therapy. I had no perspective other than the negative. Things weren't just bad—not in this neurotic's mind, oh no—things were terrible! But in the past five years I have come to enjoy good feelings, positive feelings, particularly about me. Therapy helped me to find the real person underneath all the garbage I, with the help of others, had heaped upon myself. Therapy freed the energy I used to spend in rumination and depression. I now use it to pursue life. I finally feel like a whole person and not like half a child. I seldom experience unhappy periods of any length any more. There is now direction and meaning to my life. There is also another person to whom I am deeply related. In short, besides freedom, what I have gained through therapy is everything!

Earlier, you had said you hoped your relationship would "last in love" for many years. Do you then think in terms of "forever"?

No, because the moment is more important. On those days when "forever" creeps into my thinking, I know I'm feeling insecure about something and want some kind of guarantee of permanence. There are things I plan for the future, but in itself, the future, with all its "somedays," plays very little role in my life. I would like to think, however, that it will be as lovely as today is. But I know if I neglect today, it won't be. Joe and I have thought about the future possibility of adopting children. He is currently more positive about it than I. A piece of me wants to and a piece thinks of the changes a child would make in my life. I would have to curtail the amount of hours I spend on work; the energies I now devote to my profession would have to be halved. A child deserves at least that and considerably more. Yet, I'd make a terrific father. I'd also make a terrific mother. As we now know, "mothering" is not solely a woman's function. Nor, as we now know, is it always a woman's instinct. Joe and I would make terrific parents because we like and respect children.

Then you do not believe that for a child to develop healthily, he needs both a masculine and feminine influence in his life?

The obvious retort is that Joe and I would be both a masculine and feminine influence, as all people have both qualities. But, you are referring to the notion that there should be both a *man* and a *woman* present for a child to develop "healthily." There is absolutely no evidence to support this. Most neurotics I treat had both parents present. Some had only one. It really seems to depend on what *each* child gets from a particular parent or parents that determines the health of the person.

Do you and Joe experience any societal difficulties as a homosexual couple?

None. But I continue to experience difficulties as a homosexual single. Professionally, to come out, to declare myself, would negatively affect my private practice. I would undoubtedly lose many patients for as many reasons. Some, because of their own unresolved homosexual feelings, would consider me "sick" and would terminate their therapy. Others would project their own homosexual feelings onto me and accuse me of seduction. Then, despite my working in a supposedly "enlightened" field, I would undoubtedly be denied my certificate from the institute where I am completing my studies. It is still largely dominated by the old guard—doctors in their sixties and seventies who continue to think of homosexuality as an illness. Terrible prejudices still exist within the profession. Recently, a psychology professor I know—a most respected name in his field—was bounced from his quite respectable teaching position because his colleagues discovered he was gay and had him purged. Even at the hospital, I initially had to deal with a kind of *liberalism* that is nothing more than a prejudicial put-down.

Because I worked with homosexuals and did very little to contradict the impression that I was one, I was immediately "typecast." Before I understood fully what was happening, women were talking to me about fashion and home decorating, men about hair stylists and clothing accessories. In other words, they were relating to me as the stereotypical homosexual. The fact that I know nothing about fashion or cooking never entered their minds. None of these people related to me as *me*, as a professional, which forced me to act as I really am not—as the ultraprofessional, the "doctor," the therapist. Eventually they related to me on those levels. But I was, and am, very resentful. I resent the heterosexual stereotypical view of homosexuals. I resent their thinking of us as limp-wrist faggots if we are men or truck-driver types if we are women. To be "lumped" is offensive. I am who I am and not someone's distorted view of what they think a homosexual is. It is time heterosexuals opened their eyes and realized we are all kinds of men and women who do all kinds of work and live all kinds of lives—often very similar to their own.

  You sound like a gay militant.

In certain respects I am. There is a gay community of which I am part, and of which I am very proud. This community includes some wonderfully brilliant and/or creative and/or sensitive and/or nice and/or healthy people. That is not to say that as a group we still haven't much to do because that would be untrue. But we have come very far very quickly. We have gotten self-protective. We have mobilized rapidly, particularly medically, where today a homosexual can get whatever medical attention he needs without embarrassment or harassment. We didn't have that before. Formerly, many straight doctors would condemn and belittle even as they treated. Today, we have a network of doctors who treat the homosexual patient with the respect he deserves. We also have a network of lawyers and politicians who actively and respectfully serve the homosexual community. And we have counselors and therapists for those homosexuals who feel the need to explore whatever problems they encounter in their lives. In truth, we have formed an incredible community to support us and our needs. We are no longer alone. We no longer sit back and wait for help. We help ourselves.

Is the gay community growing as a cohesive group?

Very definitely. Many young gays are unafraid to declare themselves. They are not trapped by the paranoia with which so many of the over-forties live. They do not feel their jobs, their lives, are in jeopardy. But times have changed—for the better—and there is less to lose today than there was twenty and thirty years ago when discovery could mean ruin. Still, conditions are not all that good, which is why many homosexuals continue to try and "pass." I do not blame them. As in my own case, one still risks in certain quarters a loss of job and/or home if one's homosexuality becomes known.

What are your feelings about "gay pride"?

For these young people—and some of their elders—it is good. It consolidates the group. But "gay pride" is not my ideal. "Person pride" is. Unfortunately, the former becomes immediately necessary if a certain minority group is to be allowed to breathe. For as long as gays are humiliated and denied their rights, "gay pride" and "gay is good" are as meaningful and necessary as slogans as was "black is beautiful." But, ultimately, what is important to all people is pride in themselves—the total self and not just the sexual preference or color.

Since you feel you cannot come out publicly, in what way do you envision making a contribution to the homosexual cause?

Through my teachings and writings. Eventually, I want to train analysts and I have every reason to believe that will be possible. Even today, in lecture classes I attend as a student, I am teaching other would-be analysts by questioning and contradicting lecturers who make bold but not very accurate statements about homosexuals. I always challenge my peers' thinking on the subject. In later years, as a trainer, I will be able, hopefully, to effect major changes in thought among those who will then go out to help others.

Additionally, I see my work as an analyst as one continuing contribution. To help people to help themselves to a richer, more fulfilling life . . . what could be more satisfying, more of a personal contribution and commitment?

And what is it that you wish for yourself, for your own life?

If I should die tomorrow, I would not feel I missed a thing except the accumulation of years. I've been very fortunate. I have secured the education and training I wanted and the work I needed to feel whole. Concurrently, I have obtained, and maintained, what can only be called a wonderful relationship . . . a love affair that has meant far more to me than I am capable of expressing verbally.

No, I would change nothing in my life. Even if Joe and I should end tomorrow, it would end with a huge thank you and an I love you. We have made ourselves, and one another, very happy.